THE Pioneer Woman Cooks
A YEAR OF HOLIDAYS

THE *Pioneer Woman Cooks*

A YEAR OF HOLIDAYS

140 STEP-BY-STEP RECIPES FOR SIMPLE, SCRUMPTIOUS CELEBRATIONS

REE DRUMMOND

WM

WILLIAM MORROW

An Imprint of HarperCollinsPublishers

Also by Ree Drummond

The Pioneer Woman Cooks: Recipes from an Accidental Country Girl
The Pioneer Woman Cooks: Food from My Frontier
The Pioneer Woman: Black Heels to Tractor Wheels—A Love Story
Charlie the Ranch Dog
Charlie and the Christmas Kitty
Charlie Goes to School

Recipes with this butterfly symbol 🦋 next to the recipe name have helpful how-to videos that you can access through a smartphone. Visit HC.com/PrintToLife to download information.

All photographs by Ree Drummond, except the title page, by Marlboro Man, and the vintage family photos, courtesy of Ree Drummond.

Designed by Kris Tobiassen / Matchbook Digital

Library of Congress Cataloging-in-Publication Data has been applied for.

ISBN 978-0-06-222522-1

13 14 15 16 17 ID/QG 10 9 8 7 6 5 4

To my mom and dad,
FOR A LIFETIME OF HOLIDAY MEMORIES.

To my husband and children,
FOR THE NEW ONES WE'RE MAKING TOGETHER.

CONTENTS

EASTER

CINCO DE MAYO

MOTHER'S DAY

FATHER'S DAY

FOURTH OF JULY

INTRODUCTION

There's nothing more delicious than a holiday.

Oh, is it ever true. Whenever a holiday approaches, memories rush to the surface, plans take shape, anticipation builds. And I don't care if it's a Hallmark holiday or one steeped in the traditions of the church—if a holiday is on the horizon, it makes me want to sing, dance, jump for joy . . . and hug everyone I see.

And one more thing: *It makes me want to cook!*

I've said it before and I'll say it again: Holidays really are just one enormous excuse to eat. Oh, don't get me wrong: I cherish the true meaning behind each holiday and carry its significance in my heart. But c'mon: What would Valentine's Day be without chocolate? What would Easter Sunday be without ham? What if Thanksgiving passed by without a big, succulent turkey?

And what would become of humankind if we couldn't celebrate Halloween by wolfing down a big ol' popcorn ball? I shudder to think.

If you're like me and attach so many of your holiday memories to food, I think you'll love this cookbook of mine. I share mouthwatering menus for all my favorite holidays throughout the year, from New Year's Day to New Year's Eve . . . and so many favorites in between. Easter, Thanksgiving, and Christmas play a significant role, but I also include scrumptious spreads for more casual, food-centric occasions such as Fourth of July, Valentine's Day, and (because Mexican food gives me reason to live) Cinco de Mayo.

Fourth of July at our house is all about the four F's: friends, fellowship, food . . . and fireworks!

*Fajitas for Cinco de Mayo.
Yes, please!*

*Glazed Easter ham.
Glorious!*

*Father's Day cake.
The key to any dad's heart.*

The book is organized by holiday, and I include plenty of cross references with each menu so you can borrow recipes from other holidays to construct your own unique spreads. I also give you ideas for stretching your holiday leftovers, with irresistible ways to use up your extra Easter ham and Thanksgiving turkey. In addition, because many of the recipes hold year-round appeal, a Recipes by Category index on page 378 will help you figure out which dishes to whip up on regular days throughout the year. So think of this as a holiday cookbook . . . that doubles as an everyday cookbook! There's food, glorious food in these here pages, and you shan't lack for things to make.

Finally, to ensure that you'll stay relaxed and giddy through each holiday, I came up with helpful do-ahead game plans for several of the major menus in the book. This way, you can knock out a lot of the prep and cooking ahead of time and not have to cram everything into one crazy, hectic, Calgon-take-me-away day. When it comes to holidays, life is way too short to try to be a superhero; planning ahead is the secret to making sure your holiday love continues to burn bright.

I hope you love this cookbook, my friends. I had so much fun putting it together. I hope it allows you to embrace the fun and meaning of every holiday in your house, so you can share even more love, good times, and great food with those around you.

That's really what holidays are all about.

Lots of Love,

Ree

The cattle and horses don't care
if it's a holiday; the ice on the
ponds still has to be chopped!

NEW YEAR'S DAY

Ahh, New Year's Day. There's nothing like it. It's a fresh start! A clean slate! A do-over to end all do-overs! The day I start exercising more, become more organized, become less forgetful, keep my junk drawers cleaned out, scrub my baseboards more, keep my truck clean, write more letters, read more books, watch less reality TV, compost, do all the dishes before I go to bed at night, and fit into my skinny jeans once and for all!

And then I wake up.

Okay, okay. New Year's Day *does* feel like a nice, fresh start and all. But I try not to put too much pressure on myself to suddenly transform into a whole new, physically active, more learned, organized, tidy, and engaged human who regularly throws her vegetable scraps into a bin outside in freezing temperatures just because it's January 1. Who needs that level of stress on New Year's Day? Not I, that's who.

So here's my trick, and feel absolutely free to borrow it: On New Year's Day, I actually resolve to *avoid stress* in the new year! And that totally means I need to avoid all other New Year's resolutions, because they are inherently stressful. So it all works out for me in the end!

Next year, I should probably resolve to stop rationalizing.

I'd better go write myself a note so I don't forget.

Just after I don't get off the treadmill that I'm not on.

Wait . . . what?

NEW YEAR'S DAY BRUNCH

I know, I know . . . last night was a rough one. Or, at the very least, a late one. Unless, of course, you decided to forgo all New Year's Eve festivities and crawl into bed at 8:30, in which case you're probably feeling better than I am this morning. How did you get to be so smart?

Anyway, whether you were wide awake or snoring when the clock struck midnight last night—I mean this morning; wait, I'm confused now—I say New Year's Day is a day for sleeping in! And later in the morning, after you've finally stumbled out of bed, splashed cold water on your face, brushed your teeth, walked the dog, jogged four miles, and taken a great big New Year's breath or two, try whipping up a scrumptious, satisfying brunch for friends and family. It's a great way to say, "Okay, guys—it's a brand-new year. Let's *do* this thing!"

(Just kidding on the "jogged four miles" part.)

OTHER RECIPES TO CONSIDER: Orange-Vanilla Fruit Salad (page 108); Eggs in Hash Brown Nests (page 102); Lemon-Rosemary Scones (page 168); Maple-Bacon Scones (page 171); Salmon Scrambled Eggs (page 172); Caramel Apple Sweet Rolls (page 321); Fried Quail (page 344) and Quail Gravy (page 348); Drop Biscuits (page 346)

RESOLUTION SMOOTHIES

MAKES 8 SERVINGS OF EACH VARIETY

Nothing kick-starts your New Year's Day quite like a bright, vibrant, creamy, delicious, flavorful, nutritious smoothie . . . or, in this case, *three* smoothies!

And okay. Maybe an aspirin or two. It all depends on how your New Year's Eve went. But that's outside the scope of this discussion.

There's no way to predict what's going to happen over the next 364½ days. So while you have some semblance of control over your brand new year, throw a bunch of healthy stuff in a blender and mix it up! Puree it with pride! Drink it with wild abandon!

Here are three luscious (and pretty) smoothies I just love.

GREEN SMOOTHIE

For this vividly verdant version (alliteration alert!), I throw a handful of green fruit into a blender with some yogurt and milk. But what catapults it into the Green Galaxy is a handful of ultranutritious kale. One sip and you can almost hear your body thanking you.

2 cups plain Greek yogurt
1 cup milk
2 cups pineapple chunks

1 cup green grapes
1 green apple, cut into chunks
1 green pear, cut into chunks

1 banana, peeled
½ bunch kale
¼ cup honey (optional)

1. Add the yogurt to the blender . . .

2. Along with the milk.

3. Add the pineapple, grapes, apple, pear, and banana . . .

4. Then top off the blender with ice.

5. Blend it until it's all combined . . .

6. Then throw in the kale!

8. Give it a taste, and if it needs a little sweetness, add the honey.

10. And serve it up!

7. Blend it until the kale is all mixed in and the smoothie is bright green.

9. Blend it again until it's smooth . . .

Variations

• *Add a handful of spinach leaves instead of (or in addition to) the kale.*

• *Substitute apple juice for the milk for a less creamy (and deeper green) smoothie.*

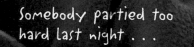

Somebody partied too hard last night . . .

ORANGE SMOOTHIE

If a Dreamsicle and an Orange Julius met, fell in love, and got hitched in a Las Vegas wedding chapel, this is what their babies would look like. A handful of carrots gives the orange color a beautiful boost.

    Warning: These are almost *too* good. It's hard to know when to stop sipping!

2 cups Greek yogurt

2 cups frozen mango chunks

2 cups frozen peach slices

1 cup pineapple chunks

1 cup miniature carrots or carrot chunks

1 banana, peeled

¼ cup honey

1 cup orange juice

1. Put all the ingredients in the blender . . .

(Get it? *Smoothie*? So clever!)

It's a new day . . . and a new year!

2. And blend it until everything's totally smooth.

See if you can drink just one.

PURPLE SMOOTHIE

In terms of sheer gorgeousness, it's pretty tough to beat this unabashedly purple smoothie. Frozen berries give it a sweet tartness, and a handful of red cabbage ensures two thumbs-up from your doc.

2 cups plain Greek yogurt

2 cups frozen blueberries

2 cups frozen mixed berries (or frozen strawberries)

1 banana, peeled

¼ head red cabbage

¼ cup honey

1 cup cranberry or grape juice (or any deep red/purple juice)

1. Add the yogurt, frozen berries, banana, cabbage, and honey to the blender.

2. Then pour in the juice . . .

3. And blend it . . .

4. Until it's smooth!

Luscious. Truly luscious.

What a great way to start the new year. I'll have one of each, please!

NOTE: *If you use fresh (not frozen) berries, just top off the blender with ice before blending.*

Variations

- *Blend 1 to 2 cups of granola into each smoothie variety for added texture.*

- *Add 1 teaspoon vanilla extract to each smoothie variety for added flavor.*

- *Other raw ingredients to mix and match: beets, cauliflower, flax seed, whole oats, apricots, honeydew melon, cantaloupe, and ice cream. (Just kidding on that last one.)*

BAKED FRENCH TOAST

MAKES 8 TO 12 SERVINGS

I have a love affair with baked French toast casseroles because they're a cinch to throw together and are best made the night before you need them, which means that in the morning you can just turn on the oven, grab the casserole dish from the fridge, and throw it in to bake whenever your hiney decides to get out of bed.

And hopefully you won't actually *throw* it in, as your dish will shatter and your French toast (and whole day, for that matter) will be ruined. Unless you use a metal baking pan, in which case it will not shatter. But your French toast will still probably be ruined. Or at least severely marred. And I'm sorry I brought your hiney into this.

So let me phrase this another way: You just get out of bed, turn on the oven, grab the casserole dish from the fridge, and very carefully and gingerly, and with a very happy disposition, place it on one of the oven racks before calmly and serenely closing the oven door.

I need to be more literal in my explanations from now on. I'll make that my New Year's resolution!

8 eggs

2 cups whole milk

½ cup heavy cream

½ cup sugar

2 tablespoons vanilla extract

1 large loaf artisan or crusty sourdough bread

Butter, for greasing the casserole

TOPPING

½ cup (1 stick) cold butter, cut into pieces

½ cup all-purpose flour

½ cup packed brown sugar

1 teaspoon ground cinnamon

¼ teaspoon ground nutmeg

¼ teaspoon salt

Softened butter, for serving

Warm maple or pancake syrup, for serving

1. In a large bowl, combine the eggs, milk, and cream.

3. And the vanilla . . .

2. Add the sugar . . .

4. And whisk them together until all combined.

5. Tear the loaf of bread into large chunks and place them into a well-buttered casserole dish . . .

6. Then pour the egg mixture all over the top.

7. To make the topping, add the cold butter and flour to a medium bowl.

8. Add the brown sugar . . .

9. The cinnamon, nutmeg, and salt.

10. Then use a pastry cutter to cut it all together until it's a chunky/crumbly mixture.

11. Sprinkle the butter-cinnamon topping all over the top, then cover the pan with foil and refrigerate several hours or overnight.

12. When you're ready to bake it in the morning, preheat the oven to 350°F and bake it for 45 minutes to 1 hour for a slightly softer, bread-pudding texture, or a little longer to make it more crisp.

13. Cool for 15 minutes before serving. Serve warm with a pat of butter and warm syrup. Positively scrumptious!

Variations

- *Stir ½ cup chopped pecans or walnuts into the topping before sprinkling it on top of the French toast.*

- *Sprinkle 1 cup blueberries over the bread just before pouring on the milk mixture.*

- *Sprinkle fresh blueberries over the baked French toast after removing it from the oven.*

COCONUT-GINGER BAKED FRENCH TOAST

MAKES 8 TO 12 SERVINGS

This crazy-delicious tropical variation on the baked French toast theme combines coconut and ginger to create probably one of the most delicious breakfast items I've ever eaten in all my days, and I've eaten a whole lotta breakfast items. It's so wonderfully tropical, in fact, that you'll wish you had one of those little paper umbrellas to stick right in the middle of your serving and you'll be struck with the sudden urge to rub zinc oxide all over your nose for fear you'll get a sunburn.

I really *feel* the food I eat, folks.

This breakfast delight is bursting with ginger and coconut flavors and while it does contain quite a few ingredients, it really is worth every step.

1. Tear the bread into large chunks and place them in a large buttered casserole dish.

2. Crack open a can of cream of coconut and give it a stir to make sure it's smooth. This stuff is dreamy!

3. Combine 1 cup with the milk and cream. Refrigerate the remaining cream of coconut for serving.

4. Add the ginger to the milk mixture and stir it together.

1 large artisan or crusty sourdough loaf

Butter, for greasing the casserole

One 15-ounce can cream of coconut (sold alongside drink mixers in stores)

1½ cups whole milk

½ cup heavy cream

2 tablespoons chopped fresh ginger

8 eggs

1 cup sugar

1 teaspoon vanilla extract

1 teaspoon coconut extract

½ cup unsweetened coconut flakes (not sweetened shredded coconut)

TOPPING

½ cup (1 stick) cold butter, cut into pieces

½ cup all-purpose flour

½ cup packed brown sugar

1 teaspoon ground ginger

¼ teaspoon salt

2 tablespoons finely minced candied ginger

½ cup unsweetened coconut flakes

Softened butter, for serving

Warm maple or pancake syrup, for serving

5. Pour the milk mixture into a bowl with the eggs, sugar, vanilla extract, and coconut extract. Whisk it together until smooth.

6. Stir in the coconut flakes . . .

7. Then pour the mixture all over the surface of the bread.

8. To make the topping, combine the butter, flour, brown sugar, ground ginger, and salt in a bowl and cut it together until it's crumbly and combined.

9. Slice the candied ginger into thin strips, then dice it finely . . .

10. And stir it into the topping mixture along with the coconut flakes.

11. Sprinkle the topping evenly on the bread, then cover the dish with foil and refrigerate it for several hours or overnight. The ginger and coconut flavors will marry and have many children. This is a very good thing.

12. When you're ready to bake the French toast, preheat the oven to 350°F. Bake it for 45 minutes to 1 hour for a softer casserole, or a little longer for a firmer French toast with a crisper topping. When the casserole is done, drizzle some of the remaining cream of coconut over the top. Cool for 15 minutes before serving.

13. Serve with softened butter and warm syrup . . .

And don't be afraid to drizzle on a little extra cream of coconut. It's a tropical paradise!

Variations

- Add ¼ to ½ cup Malibu rum to the milk-egg mixture. Naughty!
- Serve with a side of pineapple chunks for a true piña colada experience.
- Serve with a real piña colada if you want to be totally incorrigible.

BAGEL AND CREAM CHEESE BAKED FRENCH TOAST

MAKES 8 TO 12 SERVINGS

I based this pan of savory wonderfulness on an old casserole ladies in my hometown used to make for baby and wedding showers. But instead of the onion rolls the original recipe calls for, I chuck in big pieces of everything bagels. The flavor and texture are out of this world: Bagely, oniony . . . and oh, so lovely.

Perfect for a New Year's brunch crowd (otherwise known as NYBC).

6 everything bagels

Butter, for greasing the pan

One 8-ounce package cream cheese

2 cups grated Cheddar cheese

8 eggs

2 cups whole milk

½ cup heavy cream

1 tablespoon chopped chives, plus more for serving

1 teaspoon dry mustard

½ teaspoon cayenne pepper

½ teaspoon salt

1. Behold: Everything bagels! And they're called everything bagels because they're covered in . . . well, everything. Sesame seeds, onions, poppy seeds. You name it.

2. Just tear them into chunks . . .

3. And put them in a large buttered casserole dish.

4. Cut the cream cheese into chunks . . .

5. And distribute them all over the top of the bagels. Sprinkle on the grated cheese.

6. Combine the eggs, milk, cream, chives, dry mustard, cayenne, and salt in a bowl.

7. Whisk the mixture until combined . . .

8. And pour it all over the top. Cover the dish with foil and refrigerate for several hours or overnight.

9. When you're ready to bake the casserole, preheat the oven to 350°F and bake, covered, for 45 minutes. Remove the foil and continue baking for 15 to 20 minutes, or until the top is golden brown. Cool for 15 minutes before serving.

10. Sprinkle chives over each serving to make it extra pretty. And extra chivey.

You'll absolutely love this. So fabulously flavorful!

NEW YEAR'S DAY DINNER

So here's the deal with black-eyed peas, and I'm going to say it as calmly and coolly as possible because it's really not that big of a deal at all, so don't even give what I'm about to say much thought, okay? Here goes.

If you don't eat black-eyed peas on New Year's Day, your life will absolutely fall apart! I'm dead serious!

Okay, so maybe it's not quite that dire. But according to tradition, eating black-eyed peas on New Year's Day will in fact bring good luck and prosperity in the new year. Who in the world could argue with that?

So whether you whip up this casual New Year's Day meal for your family or invite your neighbors or friends over too, you're performing a valuable public service by providing other humans the opportunity to ingest at least one black-eyed pea on the first day of the new year.

Oh, what weighty work you do!

BLACK-EYED PEA SALSA

MAKES ABOUT 3 CUPS

You know what? I was interested to learn recently that eating black-eyed peas on New Year's Day in an effort to bring about happiness and prosperity is actually an old Jewish tradition that was introduced to the Southern states around the time of the Civil War! Isn't that just juicy and interesting? Yes, I'm a homeschooler. No piece of trivia is boring or insignificant to me.

Anyway, here's the real skinny about black-eyed peas: It isn't that *not* eating them will bring fire and brimstone upon your head. It's that *partaking* in the yummy little numbers at the start of the new year will reportedly bring about good luck. Now, whether that means you'll win the lottery tomorrow or you'll find a shiny penny on the sidewalk on your way to get the morning paper, I have no way of knowing. But luck is luck, man!

As for me, I eat black-eyed peas for an additional reason: they're absolutely delicious. New Year's Day just happens to be an annual reminder that it's been a while since I've eaten them. This super simple salsa is a yummy snack, and a really easy way to meet your quota.

Three 15-ounce cans black-eyed peas, drained and rinsed

3 celery stalks, finely diced

3 green onions, thinly sliced

1 red bell pepper, seeded and finely diced

1 cucumber, peeled, seeded, and finely diced

1 jalapeño, seeded and chopped

1 cup chopped cilantro

Salt to taste

Juice of 1 lime

Tortilla chips, for serving

1. Add the black-eyed peas to a mixing bowl . . .

3. Squeeze in the lime and stir it around until all combined. Cover and chill it until you're ready to serve it up!

2. Along with the celery, green onions, red bell pepper, cucumber, jalapeño, cilantro, and salt.

4. Pile it in a bowl with chips . . .

5. And dig right in!

Variations

- *Serve the salsa as a nice light salad.*

- *Spoon it on top of grilled chicken or fish. Makes a great relish!*

- *Pile it inside burritos or on tacos.*

Life is a highway . . .

HOPPIN' JOHN

MAKES 12 SERVINGS

Hoppin' John is, without hesitation, my very favorite thing about New Year's Day. It ranks right up there with getting to start a brand-new pug calendar!

Hoppin' John is basically a flavorful, hearty black-eyed pea stew, slow-cooked till the peas are soft and tender and the tastiness factor is through the roof. And speaking of hilariously particular holiday traditions: It is said that if you leave three (not four, not two) black-eyed peas on your plate after a feast of Hoppin' John, you'll enjoy even *more* love, happiness, prosperity, and luck than you would simply from eating the black-eyed peas in the first place.

Geez. Who comes up with these things?

And who knew all of life's challenges could be solved on the very first day of the year?

4 cups dried black-eyed peas

4 tablespoons (½ stick) butter

1 large onion, diced

4 garlic cloves, minced

1 green bell pepper, seeded and diced

1 red bell pepper, seeded and diced

1 orange or yellow bell pepper, seeded and diced

2 celery stalks, diced

Salt and pepper to taste

1 teaspoon cayenne pepper

5 cups low-sodium chicken broth, more as needed

1 or 2 ham hocks (or 2 cups diced ham)

2 tablespoons white vinegar

Cooked white or brown rice, for serving

1. Soak the black-eyed peas in cool water for 4 to 6 hours, then drain and rinse them.

2. In a large pot, melt the butter over medium-high heat, then add the onion, garlic, bell peppers, and celery.

Happy new year, Abigail!

3. Stir them around . . .

4. Next, pour in the black-eyed peas . . .

5. And the salt, pepper, cayenne, and chicken broth.

6. Then add the ham hocks (or ham), bring the mixture to a boil, cover the pot, reduce the heat to low, and simmer for 1 hour.

7. Check the consistency; if it's too soupy, cook for an additional 15 minutes with the lid off. If too much liquid has cooked off, add more chicken broth. With a few minutes of cooking time left, stir in the vinegar and taste for seasonings. Add a little more cayenne if it needs more spice!

8. When the beans are tender, remove the ham hock from the pot.

9. Serve the Hoppin' John over the cooked rice alongside cornbread and collards.

Best New Year's Day meal ever!

Variations

- *Use any color combination of bell pepper you'd like.*

- *Use ½ pound diced thick-cut bacon in place of ham hocks.*

- *Add ¼ cup jarred jalapeño slices to the pot for extra spice.*

- *Serve over a big square of Loaded Cornbread (page 20) instead of rice.*

LOADED CORNBREAD

MAKES 8 TO 12 SERVINGS

As long as I'm chopping bell peppers for Hoppin' John, I go ahead and do a few extras to bake inside this dense, delicious skillet cornbread, which goes just *poifectly* with the whole New Year's spread.

1 cup yellow cornmeal

½ cup all-purpose flour

1 teaspoon salt

1 tablespoon baking powder

½ teaspoon baking soda

1 cup buttermilk (see Note)

½ cup whole milk

1 egg

¼ cup shortening, melted and cooled slightly

2 tablespoons butter

1 yellow bell pepper, seeded and diced

1 green bell pepper, seeded and diced

1 red bell pepper, seeded and diced

3 garlic cloves, minced

1. Preheat the oven to 425°F.

2. Add the cornmeal to a large bowl . . .

4. Combine the buttermilk, milk, and egg in a separate bowl and whisk it until it's smooth.

6. And whisk to combine.

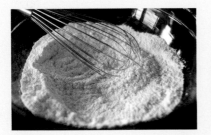

3. Along with the flour, salt, baking powder, and baking soda. Whisk to combine.

5. Then pour the mixture into the dry ingredients . . .

7. Finally, whisk in the melted shortening. Set the batter aside for a sec.

8. Melt the butter in a large skillet over medium heat . . .

9. And add the bell peppers and garlic, stirring to cook for 3 to 4 minutes or until the vegetables are soft.

10. With the veggies in a single layer, pour the batter all over the top.

11. Give it a gentle stir, then smooth out the surface of the batter . . .

12. And bake the cornbread for 20 to 25 minutes, or until nice and golden on top.

13. Cut it into wedges . . .

14. And serve it with Hoppin' John and collards!

NOTES

- *If you do not have buttermilk, measure just under 1 cup of whole milk and add 1 tablespoon of vinegar. Wait a few minutes, and you'll have buttermilk!*

- *You can bake the cornbread in a greased 9 x 13-inch baking dish instead; just spoon the cooked veggies on the bottom of the pan, top with the batter, and bake as directed.*

- *Use a muffin pan to make corn muffins! Spoon the veggies into well-greased muffin cups, then add ¼ cup batter to each cup. Bake for 15 to 18 minutes or until done.*

Variation

See page 268 for a purer, more unadulterated cornbread.

COLLARD GREENS

MAKES 6 SERVINGS

The New Year's Day significance of collard greens is this: They're the color of money, so eating them will supposedly bring the person eating them increased wealth.

Okay, um . . . what's with all this prosperity business? Why can't eating collard greens ensure a 24-inch waist? Why can't eating collard greens bring me the shimmering bronzed complexion I've always wanted? Why can't eating collard greens give me smooth, vein-free hands?

I'll never understand the injustices of this world.

The positive news, however, is that collards are delicious! Here's my favorite way to make 'em.

2 bunches (about 1 pound) collard greens, rinsed well

6 slices thick-cut bacon, cut into pieces

2 garlic cloves, minced

1 to 2 tablespoons apple cider vinegar

Salt and pepper to taste

1. Separate all the collard leaves . . .

3. Throw the bacon pieces into a large skillet and cook them over medium heat until the fat is rendered and the bacon is halfway cooked.

5. Then throw in all the greens!

2. And strip the leaves off the stalks. Discard the stalks.

4. Add the garlic to the pan and cook, stirring, for another minute . . .

6. Start tossing them gently with tongs (they'll start to wilt almost immediately) . . .

7. Then add the vinegar as you continue to toss them.

8. Season with salt and pepper and give them another quick toss . . .

9. And serve them when they're about halfway wilted.

Delicious and so, so good for your body and soul. (Even if they won't ever give you a shimmering bronzed complexion.)

Variations

- *Substitute kale leaves for the collards.*
- *Substitute spinach leaves for the collards.*
- *Do a mix of collards, kale, and spinach.*

BUILD IT IN A BOWL

Another way to serve it: Layer rice, collards, Hoppin' John, and crumbled cornbread all in the same bowl. Yum!

THE BIG GAME

If your house is like my house, where football is not just a sport, but also a religion, a way of life, and a reason to get out of bed in the morning, you'll understand how monumentally important it is to celebrate big rivalries in delicious style. Whether it's your alma mater's matchup against its archrival, the big National Championship game, the NFL playoffs, or the Super Bowl itself, I love whipping up a big spread of food to enjoy during the game.

As loud, raucous, and conflict-charged as it is, I always love having a bunch of football-crazed lunatics over to our house to watch football. And if they're all cheering for opposite teams, even better!

My estrogen and I just sit back, eat, and enjoy the show.

Don't mess with the bull . . .

FOOD AND FOOTBALL

What better way to celebrate the greatest game ever invented than with a big, beautiful smorgasbord of football-friendly grub? There's nothing like Buffalo chicken, mini burgers, and cupcakes to make this big game memorable!

(Have I mentioned football is important in our household?)

This spread is bountiful and bodacious, and is fit for *several* kings.

DO-AHEAD GAME PLAN

THE DAY BEFORE

• Cut the chicken into chunks for the Buffalo Chicken Bites.

• Make the Chipotle Chicken Chili.

• Grill the corn and slice off the kernels for the Grilled Corn Dip and Eight-Layer Dip.

• Grate the cheese and slice the green onions for the Classic Potato Skins and/or Southwestern Potato Skins.

• Grate the cheese and dice the pepperoni for the Pepperoni Pizza Potato Skins.

• Make the meat mixture and form the patties for the Spicy Whiskey BBQ Sliders.

• Dice the onions and jalapeños and grate the cheese for the Eight-Layer Dip.

• Make the cupcakes for the Dr Pepper Cupcakes.

THE DAY OF

• Assemble the Grilled Corn Dip.

• Prepare the potatoes for the Potato Skins.

• Make the icing for the Dr Pepper Cupcakes and ice the cupcakes.

• Prepare the rest of the food!

OTHER RECIPES TO CONSIDER: Blackberry Margaritas (page 128); Mango Pico de Gallo (page 132); Chipotle Salsa (page 138); Glorious Guacamole (page 136); Toasted Ravioli (page 180); Cocktail Wieners! (page 366); Dulce de Leche Brownies (page 156); Spreads (page 312)

BUFFALO CHICKEN BITES

MAKES 8 SERVINGS

These are the facts of the case and they are undisputed: During the course of my marriage to my football-loving husband, I have made approximately 9,332,453,293 Buffalo wings. That is because I love my beloved, and my beloved loves Buffalo wings. But that's not the only thing he loves!

He also loves football.

Ha.

Oh, don't get me wrong: I love Buffalo wings, too. They're tangy and spicy and wonderfully weird. But man, are they a royal mess to eat! Here's a poem I wrote about them.

BUFFALO WINGS

By Ree Drummond

Sauce on my fingers
Sauce on my nose
Sauce on my sweater
Sauce in my hair.

Pure art, I tell you. I don't blame you if you're a little choked up right now. I'll give you a minute to take it in.

Okay, back to wings: While nothing could ever replace the original, I've come up with this really cool small-bite version. They're perfect for a game-crazed crowd, and handy dandy toothpicks mean you'll stay nice and sauce free.

Except in your mouth, where it belongs.

Vegetable oil

BLUE CHEESE DIP

1 cup mayonnaise

½ cup sour cream

4 ounces crumbled blue cheese

3 to 4 dashes Worcestershire sauce

Salt and pepper to taste

½ cup buttermilk (see page 21), plus more as needed for thinning

CHICKEN BITES

1 cup all-purpose flour

1 tablespoon cornstarch

1 teaspoon salt

One 12-ounce bottle beer

2 pounds boneless, skinless chicken breasts

SAUCE

1 cup (2 sticks) butter

One 12-ounce bottle cayenne pepper sauce (such as Frank's or Louisiana)

3 to 4 dashes hot sauce

3 to 4 dashes Worcestershire sauce

1. Heat 3 or 4 inches of oil in a heavy pot over medium-high heat to 350°F. (I use a thermometer to make sure the temp stays consistent.) Preheat the oven to 325°F.

2. Next, make the blue cheese dip: Combine the mayonnaise, sour cream, blue cheese, Worcestershire, salt, pepper, and buttermilk in a bowl . . .

3. Then stir it all together until well combined. Add in a little more buttermilk to get it to the consistency you want, then cover the bowl and pop it in the fridge until you need it.

4. Now, on to the bites! Combine the flour, cornstarch, and salt in a medium bowl . . .

5. Then pour in the beer, whisking as you go.

6. Keep adding until the batter is somewhat thin but still thick enough to coat the chicken.

7. Cut up the chicken into 1-inch pieces.

8. Add a few pieces of chicken to the batter and toss them around . . .

"What time is kickoff?"

9. Then lift them out of the batter . . .

10. And carefully lower them into the hot oil.

11. Fry the chicken in batches until it's deep golden brown and cooked through, 3 to 4 minutes. Remove it to a paper towel–lined pan to drain.

"I'm rooting for the Philadelphia Beagles!"

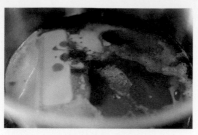

12. To make the sauce, combine the butter, cayenne pepper sauce, hot sauce, and Worcestershire in a medium saucepan over medium heat.

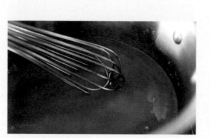

13. Melt it all together, whisking to combine.

14. Transfer the chicken to a large bowl and pour on the sauce, tossing the chicken to coat it well.

15. Remove the paper towel from the pan, pour on the chicken and sauce, and bake for 5 to 10 minutes to seal in the sauce.

16. Serve 'em with toothpicks on a platter next to the blue cheese dip.

Dig in!

Variation

For a kid-friendly snack, serve the chicken bites plain with a side of ketchup. (Omit the toothpicks!)

CHIPOTLE CHICKEN CHILI

MAKES 8 TO 12 SERVINGS

It takes a lot to get me excited about chili. I don't know why this is. It's just never been on my list of things I feel I must eat in the next five minutes or else I'll die. Now, coffee ice cream's definitely on the list. Sushi, absolutely. (This can be rather inconvenient when the craving hits me on our remote cattle ranch.)

The point is: chili? Not really. It just doesn't move me, Bob. (Wait. Who's Bob?)

Still, chili is undeniably the quintessential casual crowd pleaser, so I'm always looking for ways to keep it interesting. Compelling. Charming. Charismatic.

This chicken-chipotle pot of wonder totally fits the bill! It's delicious on its own or loaded up with all the fixins. Fitting for your food-centric football fiesta, Frank. (Wait. Who's Frank?)

2 tablespoons olive oil

1 large onion, diced

4 garlic cloves, minced

2 pounds boneless, skinless chicken breasts, cut into bite-size pieces

One 12-ounce bottle Mexican beer (or any beer)

One 14-ounce can diced tomatoes

3 chipotle peppers in adobo, minced

One 14-ounce can black beans, drained and rinsed

One 14-ounce can pinto beans, drained and rinsed

One 14-ounce can kidney beans, drained and rinsed

1 tablespoon chili powder

1 tablespoon ground cumin

2 teaspoons salt, more to taste

Heaping ¼ cup masa harina (corn flour)

Juice of 1 lime

Sour cream, for serving

Grated sharp Cheddar cheese, for serving

Chopped cilantro, for serving

1. Heat the olive oil in a large pot over medium-high heat, then add the onion and garlic. Stir them around and cook them for 2 to 3 minutes, until they start to soften.

2. Throw the chicken into the pot.

3. Stir the chicken around and cook 3 to 4 minutes, until lightly browned.

4. Pour in all but ¼ cup of the beer . . .

5. Then add the tomatoes . . .

6. The minced chipotles . . .

7. And all the beans!

8. Stir to combine, then add the chili powder . . .

9. The cumin . . .

10. And the salt.

11. Bring the chili to a boil, then reduce the heat to a simmer. Cover the pot and let it simmer for a good 45 minutes to 1 hour, until the sauce is slightly thicker and the flavors have had a chance to combine.

12. After that time, combine the masa harina with the remaining beer.

13. Whisk it with a fork until it's smooth . . .

14. Then pour it into the chili! This will thicken it up a little more and give it a really nice corn flavor.

15. Next, squeeze in the lime juice . . .

16. Then stir it around and let the chili simmer for another 10 minutes or so, until it's thick and luscious.

17. Lookie here! Now go ahead and taste a bite and make sure the seasonings are good. Add more of whatever it needs.

18. Serve it up with a dollop of sour cream, a sprinkling of Cheddar, and cilantro!

He loves football. (And his mama loves him!)

Variations

- Serve over baked potatoes.
- Serve inside Potato Skins (page 36), topped with Cheddar, sour cream, and cilantro.
- Use as a filling for crispy or soft tacos.

GRILLED CORN DIP

MAKES ABOUT 4 CUPS

Years and years ago, I tasted a cold corn dip at a party. It was served alongside a bowl of corn chips, and it was profoundly divine. I kept on tasting it and kept on tasting it (you see what's coming, don't you?) and before I knew it I was staring at an almost-empty bowl and looking around for a planter large enough for me to hide the evidence. Then, failing to find one, I decided to hide myself in the bathroom instead. My husband found me holding the bowl and sitting in the hostess's shower at the end of the evening.

It would be a long time before he'd take me to a party again.

Through the years, I've re-created different versions of that fatefully scrumptious corn dip, and this is the one I keep coming back to. The creamy-cheesy base is utter decadence, but it's the grilled corn that really makes the dip stand out.

4 ears of sweet corn, shucked

One 8-ounce package cream cheese, softened

1 cup sour cream

4 green onions, sliced

4 ounces sharp Cheddar cheese

4 ounces Monterey Jack cheese

4 ounces queso fresco, cotija, or similar Mexican cheese

1 teaspoon ground cumin

½ teaspoon paprika

¼ teaspoon cayenne pepper, more to taste

Salt and pepper to taste

Juice of 1 lime

Several dashes of hot sauce (I used Tabasco)

1. Holding the corn with tongs, carefully roast them over the burner on your stove (or you can grill them if it's not too cold outside!).

3. They land right in the pan. Such a cinch!

2. When the corn is cool enough to handle, slice the kernels off the cobs. Easy tip: Use a Bundt pan! Rest one end of the corn in the center hole and slice downward.

4. Add the cream cheese, sour cream, and green onions to the bowl of an electric mixer fitted with the paddle attachment . . .

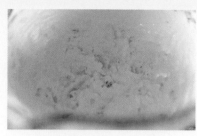

5. And whip it until it's totally combined.

6. Grate the Cheddar and Monterey Jack and crumble the queso fresco with a fork . . .

7. Then add them to the bowl with the other ingredients. Mix in the cheeses until they're totally combined.

8. Next, add the cumin, paprika, cayenne, salt, and pepper . . .

9. Along with the lime juice . . .

10. And the hot sauce. I go a little crazy with the hot sauce, but only because I love it when sweat pours out of my eyebrows. You can go a little lighter if you'd prefer.

11. Finally, throw in all that gorgeous corn!

12. Mix it until the corn is distributed. Cover and refrigerate the dip for at least 2 hours. It gets better as the flavors meld!

13. Serve in a bowl with tortilla chips, corn chips, crostini, or empty Potato Skins (page 36).

Variations

- Add ¼ cup chopped cilantro to the dip for a really fresh flavor.
- Add 1 seeded, diced jalapeño to the dip for a little more heat.
- Change up the cheese and use whatever combination you'd like!
- Use fresh raw corn if you don't want to go through the step of roasting it. It'll be crunchy but still delicious!
- Use cooked corn kernels if you want to be normal.
- Use the filling to make a quesadilla! Just spread some dip in between two flour tortillas, then grill in a skillet with a little butter until the tortillas are golden and the cheese is melted. Wow!

POTATO SKINS

MAKES 16 OF EACH POTATO SKIN VARIETY

I've adored and devoured potato skins since 1983.

Or was it 1982?

Or was it 1984?

Hmmm. Let me think for a minute. I was a young, freckle-faced teenager. I was at the mall with my BFF, Jenn. I was wearing gray acid-wash jeans that tapered at the ankle and were way too short. I had braces and a raging crush on both Adam Ant and Billy Idol. Jenn's mother had dropped us off and we had only two hours to ourselves. And instead of getting manicures and pedicures or trying on neon Cyndi Lauper–style plastic bangles at the accessory shop like the cool girls were doing, we decided . . . to go to one of those casual pub-style mall restaurants and pig out on potato skins.

We were probably the two coolest Valley Girls on the planet!

Except we were in northeastern Oklahoma.

What I'm trying to say here is that potato skins have stood the test of time for one important reason. They're awesome! They're delicious! And, you'll see in a minute, you can do absolutely anything with them.

This is party food at its most fun.

CLASSIC POTATO SKINS

8 small russet potatoes, scrubbed clean

4 tablespoons canola oil

Salt to taste

2 tablespoons butter, melted

1½ cups grated sharp Cheddar cheese

8 slices thick-cut bacon, fried and chopped

2 green onions, sliced

⅓ cup sour cream

1. Preheat the oven to 400°F.

2. Brush the potatoes with a good coating of canola oil.

3. Sprinkle them with salt . . .

4. And bake them for 35 to 45 minutes, until the potatoes are tender and the skin is starting to crisp.

5. Slice the potatoes in half lengthwise . . .

6. Then use a spoon to cut a rim around the edge of each half . . .

7. And scoop out the insides. (Store them in a plastic storage bag in the fridge for another use. Potato salad, anyone?)

8. Raise the oven temperature to 425°F.

9. Brush the skins on the inside with the melted butter, then put them back in the oven for 3 minutes. After that, use your tongs to turn the skins to the other side. Brush that side with more butter and return the skins to the oven until crisp, 3 to 4 minutes.

10. Remove them from the oven.

11. Fill the skins with a small amount of grated Cheddar . . .

12. And place them into the oven just long enough to melt the cheese.

13. Sprinkle on some of the chopped bacon . . .

14. Some of the sliced green onions . . .

15. And a little dollop of sour cream. Serve immediately!

PEPPERONI PIZZA POTATO SKINS

These tasty skins are positively pizzalicious, and you can add whatever ingredient combinations you can come up with. Have fun with them!

16 baked potato skins (Potato Skins [page 36] through step 10)

1 cup jarred pizza or marinara sauce

1 cup grated mozzarella cheese

½ cup diced pepperoni

1 tablespoon minced fresh parsley

1. Add a spoonful of sauce, some grated mozzarella, and some diced pepperoni to each potato skin.

2. Bake the skins for a few minutes, until the cheese is melted and bubbly, then sprinkle on some minced parsley.

3. Serve them immediately. Yum yum yum!

Variations

Instead of pepperoni, add cooked crumbled Italian sausage, cooked crumbled hamburger, diced Canadian bacon and pineapple, or any other pizza toppings.

CHILI POTATO SKINS

If you whipped up a pot of Chipotle Chicken Chili, these skins couldn't be easier. Dudes love 'em.
  (Dudettes love 'em, too.)

16 baked potato skins (Potato Skins [page 36] through step 10)

2 cups Chipotle Chicken Chili (page 31)

1½ cups grated sharp Cheddar cheese

¼ cup sour cream

½ chopped cilantro

1. Fill each potato skin with a small amount of chili, then top with cheese, a small dollop of sour cream, and a sprinkling of chopped cilantro.

Variation

Before adding the dip and cilantro, return the skins to the oven to melt the cheese over the chili. Add the dip and cilantro after removing the skins from the oven.

SOUTHWESTERN POTATO SKINS

This one's my favorite: Warm, crisp potato skins filled with cool, refreshing veggies and topped with creamy dressing. Think of it as a salad in a skin!

16 baked potato skins (Potato Skins [page 36] through step 10)

One 14-ounce can black beans, rinsed and drained

4 Roma tomatoes, diced

2 ears roasted corn (as prepared on page 34)

4 avocados, pitted, peeled, and diced

¼ cup bottled ranch dressing

2 green onions, sliced

1. Add some black beans to the inside of each skin . . .

3. Avocado . . .

2. Followed by diced tomato, corn . . .

4. A little drizzle of dressing . . .

5. And a sprinkling of green onions. Delightful!

SPICY WHISKEY BBQ SLIDERS

MAKES 12 SLIDERS

If you're hosting a crowd at your house for the Big Game, I strongly urge you to make these decadent, drippy, diminutive, dreamy, demonic, and divine little burgers. The juicy patties are covered in a spicy, smoky sauce and just one of them is guaranteed to send your taste buds into another stratosphere.

By the way . . . what's a stratosphere? I use that word all the time, and I pretty much have no idea what it means.

It sure is a good thing I homeschool my children.

2 pounds ground beef	**4 tablespoons (½ stick) butter**	**2 cups bottled barbecue sauce**
Salt and pepper to taste	**1 onion, diced**	**½ cup drained jarred jalapeño slices, more to taste**
5 or 6 dashes Worcestershire sauce	**½ cup whiskey**	**12 slider buns or dinner rolls, split**

1. Add the ground beef to a large bowl along with the salt, pepper, and Worcestershire.

3. Form the mixture into 12 small patties, then make a well in the center with your thumb. This'll keep the patties from plumping too much when they're cooked.

5. Remove the patties from the skillet and keep them on a plate, then throw the diced onion into the skillet . . .

2. Use your (very clean!) hands to smush and mix it all together.

4. Heat the butter in a large skillet over medium-high heat, then cook the patties on both sides until they're almost done in the middle.

6. And stir them around to cook, 2 to 3 minutes.

7. Next, pour in the whiskey! (If you're cooking over an open flame, turn off the burner long enough to pour in the whiskey, then turn it back on. And that's an order.)

9. Reduce the heat to low, then pour in the barbecue sauce.

11. Add the patties back into the skillet and use a large spoon to coat the top of the patties in the sauce. Let it simmer for 5 minutes, or until the sauce is bubbling and the patties are totally done in the middle.

8. Stir the whiskey and let it bubble up and reduce by half, 1 to 2 minutes. Your kitchen smells so good right about now!

10. Next, add the jalapeños to the skillet and stir them around. Splash in a little juice from the jalapeño jar for more heat and flavor.

12. Remove the patties and serve them on the rolls, spooning extra sauce over the top of the patties. So darn good.

Variations

• *Use ground turkey or even ground bison instead of beef. Just don't tell my cattle rancher of a husband I said that.*

• *Roll the meat mixture into smaller meatballs instead of sliders and serve on toothpicks right out of the skillet!*

• *You may omit the whiskey if you prefer. It's delicious either way!*

EIGHT-LAYER DIP

MAKES 12 TO 15 SERVINGS

This is exactly the same Seven-Layer Dip I ate growing up in the eighties, with the exception of the following modifications:

1. Mine is eight layers. Not seven. *Huge* difference there.
2. I season the refried beans. Revolutionary!
3. I use a platter, not a 9 x 13-inch pan like my mom did. There goes unpredictable Ree again!
4. I add kernels of roasted corn. Call me a wild and crazy gal.
5. I don't use that frozen guacamole product from the old country. Stings my tongue. (It's a citric acid thing.)
6. Instead of chopped tomatoes, I use homemade pico de gallo. I'm a rebel, that's all there is to it.
7. I wear larger jeans now.

Other than that, this dip is exactly the same!
Here's how to make the fun, flavorful classic.

6 Roma tomatoes, diced

½ large onion, diced

1 jalapeño, seeded and diced

Large handful cilantro, chopped

1½ limes

Salt to taste

2 avocados, pitted, peeled, and diced

One 16-ounce can refried beans

2 tablespoons taco seasoning

1 cup sour cream

¾ cup grated sharp Cheddar cheese

¾ cup grated Monterey Jack cheese

1 cup sliced black olives, drained

2 ears roasted corn kernels (as prepared on page 34)

1. First, make the pico de gallo: Throw the tomatoes, onion, jalapeño, and cilantro into a large bowl.

2. Squeeze in the juice of 1 lime . . .

3. Sprinkle in the salt . . .

4. And stir it all together till combined and set it aside. (Pssst: This is delicious with chips!)

5. Add the diced avocado to a separate bowl . . .

7. Add the refried beans to a medium bowl and sprinkle in the taco seasoning.

9. Spread the beans in a flat layer on a platter . . .

6. And stir in ½ cup of the pico de gallo. You just made chunky guacamole! Now set the bowl aside and try with all your might not to eat the whole thing with a fork. (I speak from experience here.)

8. Stir it around until the seasoning is totally mixed with the beans.

10. Add dollops of sour cream on top of the beans . . .

11. And carefully spread it in a thin layer.

14. The olives . . .

17. For a bit of freshness at the end, squeeze the juice of half a lime all over the top.

12. Sprinkle on the grated cheese . . .

15. The roasted corn . . .

13. Then spoon on the chunky guacamole . . .

16. And the pico de gallo!

18. Holy pile of tastiness, Batman! Serve this with a big bowl of chips . . . and a hearty, hearty appetite.

NOTE: *Because of the guacamole, the dip shouldn't be assembled more than an hour before serving.*

Variations

• *Use any combination of grated cheeses you want!*

• *Spread a layer of taco meat on top of the layer of refried beans.*

• *Neat trick: Make individual dips by layering all the ingredients in small, clear disposable glasses. Less mess.*

Perfect punt, Paige!

DR PEPPER CUPCAKES

MAKES 24 CUPCAKES

Oh, the lengths to which I'll go to work Dr Pepper into our lives. It's not enough that it's piped into the water supply in our area of the country; I've got to spike our cupcakes with it, too? It's a serious problem, I tell you.

Well . . . unless you love Dr Pepper.

These cupcakes are pretty much epic, and here's why: They're actually little deconstructed Dr Pepper cakes, containing many of the ingredients that make Dr Pepper . . . well, Dr Pepper. (And I'll bet you'll be a little surprised as you read the ingredient list.)

These really are delicious, and resemble more of a spice cake than anything else. They're a little bit mysterious, too; every bite is an experience!

CUPCAKES

½ cup prunes, roughly chopped

½ cup dried cherries, roughly chopped

1 cup Dr Pepper

1 cup (2 sticks) butter

¼ cup unsweetened cocoa powder

½ cup boiling water

½ cup buttermilk (see page 21)

3 eggs

1 teaspoon baking soda

1½ teaspoons vanilla extract

2 cups all-purpose flour

1⅓ cups sugar

½ teaspoon ground nutmeg

½ teaspoon anise seed

½ teaspoon ground ginger

½ teaspoon ground allspice

½ teaspoon ground cardamom

FROSTING

4 cups Dr Pepper

1½ cups (3 sticks) salted butter, softened

1 teaspoon ground ginger

2½ cups powdered sugar

1 tablespoon grated lemon zest

1 tablespoon grated orange zest

½ teaspoon vanilla extract

1. Preheat the oven to 325°F. Line two 12-cup muffin pans with paper cupcake liners.

2. Add the prunes and dried cherries to a medium saucepan.

3. Pour in 1 cup of Dr Pepper, then bring it to a slow boil over medium heat. Cook it for 5 minutes, then remove it from the heat and set it aside to cool, about 20 minutes.

4. In a separate saucepan, melt the butter over medium heat. Add the cocoa powder . . .

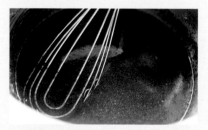

5. Then pour in the boiling water and whisk it together until smooth. Set this aside to cool.

6. In a small pitcher, combine the buttermilk, eggs, baking soda, and vanilla and whisk until combined.

7. In the bowl of an electric mixer fitted with the paddle attachment, add the flour, sugar, nutmeg, anise seed, ginger, allspice, and cardamom.

8. With the mixer on low, drizzle in the butter-cocoa mixture . . .

9. Then pour in the buttermilk mixture . . .

10. And the Dr Pepper–fruit mixture.

11. Mix until it's all combined. (Scrape the sides of the bowl once halfway through.)

12. Use an ice cream scoop or ¼ cup measure to fill the cups.

13. Bake the cupcakes for 18 minutes, until the cupcakes are done. Remove them from the pan and allow them to cool completely before frosting them.

14. To make the frosting, gently boil 4 cups of Dr Pepper in a small saucepan over medium heat until it has reduced to about ½ cup, 20 to 25 minutes. Set it aside to cool completely.

15. Add the butter to the bowl of an electric mixer fitted with the paddle attachment, then add the ginger, powdered sugar, zests, and vanilla.

16. Beat the heck out of it, scraping the sides of the bowl a couple of times, until the mixture is light and fluffy.

17. With the mixer on low, slowly drizzle in the Dr Pepper reduction until it's all been incorporated.

18. Continue beating and scraping until the frosting is smooth and perfect.

19. Then ice the cooled cupcakes.

20. Decorate them however your heart leads you, and serve 'em to the Big Game fanatics! They'll disappear very quickly.

Variations

• *Spread the Dr Pepper frosting on regular chocolate or vanilla cupcakes.*

• *Spread the batter into a 12 x 18-inch sheet pan and make a Dr Pepper sheet cake!*

• *Try substituting cola or root beer for the Dr Pepper. (Scandal!)*

Paige loves Walter!

VALENTINE'S DAY

The first Valentine's Day my strapping husband and I were married, I was pregnant due to an unforeseen circumstance that took place on our honeymoon the previous September. I won't go into any detail, except to say that come February, my belly was large . . . and getting larger by the minute.

Still, since it was our first Valentine's Day as husband and wife, I wanted to celebrate properly. Never mind that I could no longer button my jeans. The night before the big day, I made secret plans to get up early and make my man a romantic breakfast in bed. Oh, I had it all mapped out: sweet little heart-shaped pancakes, a side of Canadian bacon cut into the shape of a (you guessed it) heart, a glass of orange juice in a pretty red crystal wineglass his aunt had given us for a wedding gift. A weathered wooden tray. A lavender cloth napkin. A store-bought daisy in a bud vase. Perfect for his delicate sensibilities! Or not.

I was so excited about my love-filled breakfast scheme that I fell asleep the night of the thirteenth with visions of romance dancing in my head. I dreamed of Cupid and sweet nothings and chocolate hearts, and I dreamed of loving kisses with my new husband before an early morning Oklahoma sun. It was the best night of sleep I'd had in a long, long time.

It was so good, in fact, that the next thing I knew, it was 8:45 the next morning. I'd just woken up from a pregnancy coma. I had pillow indentations on my cheeks. My hair was gnarled and matted. And the very best part: My valentine had been gone working cattle for almost three hours. I hadn't even heard him leave. So much for romance!

Our baby was born the following June and we've since had three more babies, my sweetheart and me. And while Valentine's Day is traditionally a celebration of *romantic* love, I've found that once you become a parent, the lines become hilariously blurred. Now it's not the least bit unusual for me to ask one (or all!) of my kids if they'll be my Valentine as soon as they get out of bed that day. (Their dad totally understands.)

Forget tradition! Valentine's Day is the day to declare your love to everyone in your life—whether you married them, gave birth to them, or just love 'em to death.

(Pssst: Your favorite pooch definitely falls under that umbrella.)

VALENTINE'S BREAKFAST

Whether you're plotting a breakfast in bed for your love-muffin or a big breakfast at the table with all your kiddos, these sweet little breakfast ideas will get your day off to a lovely start.

OTHER RECIPES TO CONSIDER: Resolution Smoothies (page 3); Baked French Toast (page 8); Orange-Vanilla Fruit Salad (page 108); Lemon-Rosemary Scones (page 168); Perfect Cream Scones (page 166); Yogurt, Brown Sugar, and Berry Parfaits (page 174)

RED VELVET PANCAKES

MAKES 18 TO 20 PANCAKES

Before I begin, I need to apologize to all mankind for this recipe.

Mankind, I'm sorry. But these pancakes . . . they're just soooooo darn good.

Wait, was that an apology? I'm all confused now.

Anyway, if there was ever a day of the year when eating bright pink pancakes with a sweet, white icing was warranted, it's definitely February 14.

So enjoy, my love. Enjoy!

RED VELVET PANCAKES

Cooking spray

3 cups plus 2 tablespoons cake flour

3 tablespoons baking powder

2 tablespoons sugar

1 teaspoon salt

1½ teaspoons unsweetened cocoa powder

1½ cups milk

1 cup buttermilk (see page 21)

2 large eggs

3 teaspoons vanilla extract

2 teaspoons white vinegar

4 tablespoons (½ stick) butter, melted

2 to 4 teaspoons red food coloring (depending on how red you'd like the pancakes)

MAPLE BUTTERMILK ICING

2½ cups powdered sugar

Dash of salt

4 tablespoons (½ stick) butter, melted

¼ cup buttermilk

¼ cup whole milk

2 tablespoons maple syrup

1. Heat a skillet or griddle over medium-low heat. Spray the skillet with cooking spray.

2. Add the flour to a large bowl . . .

3. Along with the baking powder, sugar, and salt.

4. Add the cocoa powder . . .

5. And whisk to combine.

6. In a separate bowl, mix together the milk, buttermilk, eggs, vanilla, and vinegar . . .

7. And pour the mixture into the dry ingredients.

8. Whisk gently until the batter just comes together . . .

9. Then whisk in the melted butter until it's all combined.

10. Next, add 2 teaspoons of the food coloring . . .

11. And whisk it into the batter.

12. Check the color. If you'd like it to be a deeper red, add a little more food coloring.

13. Use a spoon or scoop to retrieve ¼-cup helpings of the batter . . .

14. And drop them on the skillet.

17. Add the buttermilk, milk . . .

21. And drizzle on the beautiful, luscious icing.

The sweetest start any Valentine's Day could possibly have!

15. Cook the pancakes very slowly until they're done, about 2 minutes per side. Watch to make sure they don't brown! You want them pure and pinkish red.

18. And maple syrup.

19. Whisk the mixture until it's nice and smooth.

Variations

• *Serve with softened butter and warm maple syrup instead of the icing.*

• *Serve as a special dessert after dinner!*

• *Make silver-dollar-size pancakes and serve the icing as a dipping sauce.*

16. Meanwhile, make the icing! Combine the powdered sugar, salt, and melted butter in a medium bowl.

20. Stack the pancakes on a plate . . .

HUEVO IN THE HEART

MAKES 1 SERVING

This is an adorably romantic (romantically adorable?) play on the beloved breakfast classic Egg-in-the-Hole, which is an absolute staple in our house. While the original bread-and-egg combination is impossible to beat, I actually love this slight Tex-Mex twist using tortillas and spicy salsa. It's a preciously perfect (perfectly precious?) thing to make your sweetie for breakfast.

Never mind that the salsa actually makes the heart look like it's kinda bleeding . . . which isn't really all that romantic when you think about it.

Oh well. At least it tastes real, real good!

2 tablespoons butter

2 corn, flour, whole wheat, or corn/wheat tortillas

1 medium egg

Salsa, for serving

1. Melt most of the butter in a large skillet over medium-low heat.

2. Use a heart-shaped cookie cutter . . .

3. And make a cut out of the center of both tortillas.

4. Place both tortillas (and the small hearts) in the skillet and lightly toast both sides, about 45 seconds per side.

5. Stack one of the tortillas on top of the other, then place a tiny bit of butter in the center hole.

6. Crack the egg into a small bowl . . .

7. Then slide it right into the cut-out heart. Cook it over low heat until the white is set and the yolk is slightly set.

8. Place the huevo-in-the-heart on a plate along with the toasted cut-out hearts.

9. Spoon a good amount of salsa over the top.

Simply delicious!

Variations

- Use any kind of sliced bread in place of the tortillas.

- Use a regular round cutter instead of a heart if you're not feelin' the love.

- If you prefer an over-easy or over-medium egg, use a large spatula to flip the tortilla and egg after they cook for 1½ minutes. Cook on the other side for 45 seconds to 1 minute.

- If not serving with salsa, sprinkle a little salt and pepper on the egg as it cooks.

He still sets my heart on fire.

CHOCOLATE-COVERED CHERRY SMOOTHIE

MAKES 6 TO 8 SERVINGS

This rich, fruity smoothie is a nod to that ol' clichéd box of chocolate-covered cherries boys have *supposedly* given girls on Valentine's Day since the beginning of time, even though no girl I know has ever received a box of chocolate-covered cherries from a boy.

Perfume? Yes.

Flowers? Yes.

A John Deere weed-eater? Yes. (Sorry. Didn't mean to bring my own marital issues into this.)

But chocolate-covered cherries? Balderdash!

You will fall madly in love with this treat. It's perfect for breakfast, lunch, or dinner!

1 (heaping) cup plain or vanilla Greek yogurt

1 cup milk

One 12-ounce bag frozen pitted cherries

¼ cup chocolate syrup

1 teaspoon vanilla extract

1 ounce semisweet chocolate

1. Add the yogurt to the blender . . .

2. Then pour in the milk.

3. Grab the cherries straight from the freezer and pour them into the blender.

4. Next, add the chocolate syrup . . .

5. And a splash of vanilla . . .

6. And pop on the lid!

7. Turn on the blender . . .

8. And mix until it's totally smooth. You can thin it with a little milk to get it to the consistency you want.

9. Pour each serving into a pretty glass . . .

10. Then shave the chocolate using a Microplane zester or grater.

11. Sprinkle the chocolate over the top!

Sweet and lovely. Just like you.

Variations

- *Substitute ⅓ cup semisweet chocolate chips for the chocolate syrup if you'd prefer little flecks of chocolate throughout.*

- *For even more of a treat, top with a spoonful of Sweetened Whipped Cream (page 369) before sprinkling on the shaved chocolate.*

TREATS FOR YOUR SWEETIE

I've always loved making and handing out Valentine's Day treats, and I've narrowed it down to two reasons. Okay, three. Okay, four. Okay, five. But definitely no more than five. I think.

First: chocolate. No explanation needed.

Second: red and pink. They're just so pretty together.

Third: passive aggression. Giving Valentine's treats is a really safe way to show your affection for someone without, like, *showing your affection for someone.* It's a way of being noticed by your love interest without, like, *being noticed.* It's a way to get attention from someone without, like, making him a huge poster board sign with red and pink glitter that reads *Happy Valentine's Day, Brad!!!* and leaving it by his locker with red and pink balloons attached so he and all his football friends will find it in between history class and gym.

Fourth: not that I would know anything about that.

Fifth: chocolate. Did I already say that?

Here are some of my favorite Valentine's Day treats; some of them have been on my roster since high school, when my V-Day gift giving really revved into overdrive. They can be delivered to your sweetie, but they're also perfect for your kids' classroom parties, office get-togethers, or just a gathering of friends.

OTHER RECIPES TO CONSIDER: Dulce de Leche Brownies (page 156); Easter Cookies with Buttercream and Sprinkles (but do heart shapes with pink and red sprinkles) (page 93); Chocolate Strawberry Cake (page 191); Eyeball Cake Balls (but dip in plain chocolate) (page 238); Marshmallow Pops (page 310); Spreads (page 312)

Pretty and yummy!
(And pretty yummy.)

HOMEMADE CHOCOLATE TRUFFLES

MAKES ABOUT 36 TRUFFLES

Homemade truffles are the very best kind of truffles, because they're not churned out on some nameless conveyor belt in some nameless chocolate factory on some nameless planet in some nameless universe . . . and they have a nice, homespun, rustic charm! You can change up the flavors you add to the chocolate filling, as well as the fun adornments you sprinkle on top of the finished truffles, and they make a great gift for your sweetie, teachers, preachers, or Orkin men.

8 ounces good semisweet chocolate chips

8 ounces good bittersweet chocolate chips

One 14-ounce can sweetened condensed milk

1 tablespoon vanilla extract

8 ounces chocolate almond bark, melted and cooled

8 ounces white almond bark, melted and cooled

Assorted pink and red sprinkles

1. Set a heatproof glass bowl over a saucepan of gently boiling water. Add the semisweet chocolate chips into the bowl . . .

2. Followed by the bittersweet chocolate chips.

3. Let the chips start to soften and melt . . .

4. Then pour in the sweetened condensed milk . . .

5. And the vanilla.

6. Stir until the mixture comes together, then remove the bowl from the pan, cover it with plastic wrap, and let it cool to room temperature. Refrigerate the chocolate mixture for 20 to 30 minutes if it seems too soft to roll.

7. When the chocolate mixture has cooled . . .

8. Scoop out a tablespoon or so . . .

9. Drop it in the palm of your hand . . .

10. And roll it into a neat, smooth ball. Place it on a parchment paper–lined baking sheet.

11. Or if you want to skip the rolling step and go for more of a rustic look, just scoop rough balls right onto the baking sheet.

12. Place the pan into the freezer for 20 to 30 minutes, until very firm.

13. One by one, drop the truffles into the almond bark.

14. Use a fork to cover with the chocolate . . .

15. Then lift out of the bowl, tapping the fork on the side to allow the chocolate to sheet over the sides of the truffle.

16. Do the same with the bowl of white almond bark.

17. As you remove the truffles from the melted chocolate, place them on another baking sheet lined with parchment paper. Use a toothpick to help slide the truffles off the fork if needed.

18. Before the chocolate has a chance to set, sprinkle the tops with edible sprinkles.

Pretty!

These are both darling . . .

And delicious!

Variations

- *Add ½ teaspoon peppermint extract in place of the vanilla extract for mint truffles.*

- *Coat truffles in high-quality dark, milk, or white chocolate instead of almond bark.*

- *Sprinkle a small amount of sea salt on top of the truffles before the chocolate sets. Sea salt truffles!*

- *Other sprinkle ideas: finely chopped nuts, finely chopped peppermint candies, different colors of sanding sugar, different colored sprinkles.*

CHOCOLATE VALENTINE COOKIES

MAKES 12 TO 18 COOKIES

My mom and I used to make these together every Valentine's Day, and the recipients ranged from cute little girlfriends in the early adolescent years to (much to my mom's consternation) polo shirt and Topsider–wearing boyfriends in the high school years. They're darling little chocolate heart cookies, personalized with stencils and sifted powdered sugar, which couldn't be an easier decorating method. I would have an absolute heyday with the things, spelling out conversation heart quotes like "Be Mine" and "Love You" and "You're Cute."

My mom nixed "Kiss Me," unfortunately. What a buzzkill she was!

1 cup (2 sticks) unsalted butter, softened

1 cup firmly packed brown sugar

1 egg

2 teaspoons vanilla extract

2¼ cups all-purpose flour

¼ cup unsweetened cocoa powder, plus more for sprinkling

1 teaspoon baking powder

¼ teaspoon salt

½ teaspoon ground cinnamon

Powdered sugar, for decorating

1. Combine the butter and brown sugar in the bowl of an electric mixer and beat them together until fluffy.

2. Crack in the egg . . .

3. Then add the vanilla . . .

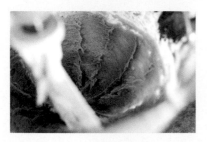

4. And mix until combined, scraping the bowl once with a rubber spatula to make sure it's all mixed together.

5. In a separate bowl, combine the flour, cocoa powder, baking powder, salt, and cinnamon . . .

6. And whisk them together.

7. Add the dry ingredients to the mixer bowl in batches, mixing gently after each addition.

8. Stop mixing when the dough just comes together.

9. Place the dough in a plastic bag and chill for at least 1 hour.

10. Preheat the oven to 350°F.

11. Roll out the chilled dough on a surface sprinkled lightly with cocoa to about ¼ inch thick.

12. Use a cutter to cut heart shapes all over the dough . . .

13. Then place them on a baking sheet lined with a baking mat or parchment paper and bake them for 9 to 11 minutes, or until just barely set. Remove the cookies to a rack and allow them to cool completely.

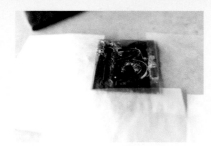

14. To decorate the cookies, spell out words by laying a stencil on each cookie. Use small squares of parchment to cover up any exposed areas of the cookie.

15. Then, using a sifter, sprinkle powdered sugar all over the stencil. Use tweezers to carefully remove the stencil, then gingerly slide off the parchment squares.

16. Keep going until you have all the letters you need!

Spell out things like this. (Hi, Mom!)

Or this.

Or this?

Just use the cookies to express your true feelings . . . whatever they may be.

HELPFUL HINT: *Make your own stencils on larger pieces of card stock to make covering the whole cookie easier.*

NOTE: *Powdered sugar will adhere to the baked cookies, but transport them with caution!*

Variations

- *Spread pink-tinted Buttercream Frosting (page 93) on the chocolate hearts instead of decorating them with powdered sugar.*

- *Spread them with plain buttercream frosting and decorate with different colors of sprinkles.*

SWOON.

CHOCOLATE-COVERED STRAWBERRIES

MAKES 12 TO 16 STRAWBERRIES

Chocolate-dipped strawberries are the new chocolate-covered cherries.

Wow. That was deep. And there's really no validity to my statement at all. I just wanted to say it to see how it sounded. And it sounded really dorky, so I think I'll move on to the recipe, which isn't really a recipe at all! These gorgeous, juicy little treats are too delightfully simple for that.

These are about the easiest Valentine's treats there are, and there are so many opportunities for changing them up and making them totally yours. Add sprinkles, use different colors of melted candies, and so on. Have a blast with them!

24 ounces good-quality semisweet chocolate chips

6 ounces white chocolate chips or white bar chocolate

12 to 16 large strawberries

1. Melt both chocolates in separate glass bowls set over saucepans of simmering water or in the microwave. Line a baking sheet with parchment paper.

3. Hold it by its leaves and twist it so that it's mostly coated with chocolate.

2. Grab a strawberry and gently lay it on its side in the bowl of semisweet chocolate.

4. Gently lay it on its side on a sheet of parchment . . .

5. Then repeat with the rest of the strawberries. Let them sit at room temperature for 30 minutes, to set slightly. (If you're in a hurry, you may place the strawberries in the fridge.)

6. Take the melted white chocolate, place it in a pastry bag or plastic storage bag with a small hole cut in the corner, and drizzle stripes all over the chocolate.

7. Decorate the rest of the strawberries (you can do any designs you like!), then store them in the fridge to set completely.

8. Serve them on a pretty cake stand . . . or pack them in small bags for delivery.

Variations

- *Use any colors of candy melts for the contrasting design.*
- *Dip the strawberries in white chocolate instead of semisweet chocolate.*
- *Dip the strawberries in milk chocolate instead of semisweet chocolate for a sweeter flavor.*
- *Instead of contrasting stripes, sprinkle on finely chopped nuts, mini chocolate chips, crushed chocolate cookies, or pink or red sprinkles.*

Toddie will always be my valentine.

JIGGLY HEARTS

MAKES 24 TO 30 SQUARES OR 18 TO 24 HEARTS

These cute little jiggly wonders are technically known as "finger Jell-O," and I don't think there's been a time I've made it when, halfway through the whole crazy saga, I didn't ask myself why in the heck I'd signed up for this. It's sheer torture, I tell you. Torture!

Now, before you run screaming from the room, let me clarify: It isn't complicated in the least. It requires only a little organization, time, and patience. It's a layered gelatin treat that you can customize depending on what colors and holidays are in the ether at the time, and though it seems to take forever, when you're finally finished, you'll have these cold, sweet, superfun treats that can become addictive if you're not careful. They're everything that's fabulous and familiar about Jell-O . . . but with a surprising creamy layer that adds a lovely richness.

Basically, it's like eating a cold, refreshing, creamy, happy gummy bear. What could be better than that?

The best advice I can give you is this: Keep a tea kettle boiling (you'll need hot water throughout the whole process) and have a couple of different mixing bowls and some small mixing spoons on hand. You'll want everything to be in grabbing distance!

Cooking spray

Nine ¼-ounce envelopes unflavored gelatin

Five 3-ounce boxes cherry, strawberry, or raspberry Jell-O

Two 14-ounce cans sweetened condensed milk

1. Spray a 9 x 13-inch glass baking pan with cooking spray, then give it a gentle wipe with a paper towel to remove the excess. You want every square inch of the pan to be thoroughly coated. Clear out space in your fridge to make sure there's room for the pan to sit level!

2. Light a candle and say a little prayer.

3. At the end of the (very long, harrowing, angst-filled) day, you'll have 5 red layers and 4 creamy layers. For the first red layer, grab 1 envelope of unflavored gelatin . . .

4. And sprinkle it into a glass bowl.

5. Add ¼ cup very cold water to the gelatin . . .

6. And stir it gently to combine. Let it sit for a minute.

7. Pour in 1 cup boiling water . . .

8. Then sprinkle in 1 package of flavored Jell-O.

9. Stir it gently to dissolve, being careful not to create bubbles.

10. Pour the mixture into the greased pan, then place the pan in the fridge until it's firm and set, about 30 minutes.

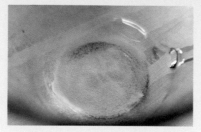

11. Meanwhile, mix up the first creamy layer by mixing 2 envelopes plain gelatin . . .

12. With ½ cup very cold water. Stir and let it sit for 1 minute.

13. In a separate container, combine 1 cup boiling water and 1 can of sweetened condensed milk.

14. Stir it together.

15. Pour into the gelatin mixture, then add ½ cup boiling water. Stir it gently and set it aside to cool for at least 10 minutes.

16. Pull the pan out of the fridge and pour about 1 cup of the creamy mixture all over the top. Note: Each batch of cream mixture is enough for 2 to 3 layers.

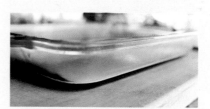

17. Tilt the pan carefully to get the cream mixture into an even layer (each layer will be very thin), then place the pan back into the fridge to chill and set for 20 to 30 minutes.

18. Continue this process, mixing a new colored layer as each cream layer is chilling . . .

19. And mixing another cream layer halfway through the whole process. (Note: You'll have a little extra creamy mixture left over. Pour into a separate bowl and chill, or discard.)

20. Keep going until you've built 9 layers, 5 red and 4 cream. Chill the whole thing in the fridge for 1 to 2 hours before serving.

21. To take the ultraeasy route, cut into squares . . .

22. Then cut the squares in half to make small rectangles.

23. Or if you want to take the fancy route, cut it into squares, then separate each square to make two shorter squares.

24. Apply gentle pressure with heart cutters of your desire to cut out the number of hearts you'd like. You can separate even more layers if you want tiny, 1-layer hearts. The layers come apart pretty easily!

Variations

Use any combination of flavors/colors of Jell-O to suit the occasion: green for St. Patrick's Day, red and green for Christmas, orange for Halloween, and so on.

HELPFUL HINTS (SOME OF THIS BEARS REPEATING!)

- *Thoroughly coat the glass dish with cooking spray.*
- *Allow each liquid mixture to cool for at least 10 minutes before pouring it into the pan.*
- *Have a teakettle going throughout the whole process so you'll have boiling water at the ready.*
- *Mix up each colorful layer as the top creamy layer is chilling.*
- *Each batch of cream mixture will cover 2 to 3 layers.*
- *Good luck! May the force be with you!*

CANDY-DIPPED S'MORES

MAKES 12 S'MORES

These spectacular little squares are almost exactly like classic French petits fours . . . except instead of using layers of fine cake, they use layers of graham crackers. And instead of filling the layers with a finely whipped buttercream, I use marshmallows. And instead of coating them with a perfectly smooth ganache, I use my grubby hands to dip them in candy melts I picked up for $4.99 at the craft shop in the next town over. And instead of adorning them with sugared flowers or 14k gold leaf, I riffle through my sprinkle drawer and grab whatever I can find.

But other than that, they're exactly like classic French petits fours!

One 12-ounce bag pink melting candies

One 12-ounce bag red melting candies

One 12-ounce bag white melting candies

½ cup chocolate-hazelnut spread (such as Nutella)

24 graham cracker squares (regular and/or chocolate)

12 large marshmallows

Assorted Valentine-themed sprinkles and decorations

1. Melt the candy discs in separate glass bowls by heating them in the microwave, stirring halfway through, or by placing the bowls over saucepans of simmering water. Set them aside until the candy is still melted but no longer hot.

3. Place the marshmallows on metal skewers or forks . . .

5. Place them, one by one, on 12 of the graham cracker squares.

2. Spread a very thin layer of chocolate hazelnut spread on the underside of the graham cracker squares, then place them, spread side up, on a baking sheet.

4. And toast them to your liking over the burner of your stove. (Be careful working with an open flame!) If you do not have a gas burner, place all the marshmallows on a cookie sheet and broil them on low until they soften and turn golden brown.

6. Immediately top with a second cracker, Nutella side down, pressing lightly to get the marshmallow to smush between the 2 crackers.

7. Set them aside as you build the rest of the sandwiches.

8. When you're ready to dip the s'mores, carefully lay each one into the candy color of your choice . . .

9. Then use a spatula to cover the top with candy.

10. Use your fingers to remove it from the candy, letting a little of the excess drip off . . .

11. Then place it on a baking sheet lined with parchment paper.

12. Let it sit for a couple of minutes, then sprinkle the top with your choice of decoration or sprinkle.

13. Repeat with the rest of the colors . . .

14. Using a variety of decorations.

15. For a fun decoration, place some of the melted candy in a squirt bottle or piping bag . . .

16. And make contrasting designs all over the surface.

Aw, so cute!

Look! A big scary-looking pink heart!

Hmmm. Wonder who this could be?

Have fun with these.

But most important . . .

Scarf them down. They're so unbelievably yummy.

NOTE: *S'mores will keep at room temperature, covered, for up to 3 days.*

CANDY-DIPPED GRAHAM CRACKERS

1. For a much simpler version, just dip the tops of the graham cracker squares in the different colors of candy melts and sprinkle on the different colors of decorations.

2. Let the candy set, then serve!

ROMANTIC DINNER FOR TWO

In the many blessed years my beloved and I have been married, we've had the chance to sit down and enjoy a Valentine's Day dinner for two approximately 2.7 times. The first time, my mother-in-law offered to keep our only child as a way of lending support to our romance, which I'm sure she feared was being muffled by the demands of both our new baby and our working cattle ranch.

And oh, man, did we make the most of that Valentine's Day we had alone. I made a romantic steak-and-potatoes dinner, then we both passed out on the couch in the middle of *When Harry Met Sally*. But at least we were in each other's arms! I think.

The second time, my mother-in-law offered to keep our *two* daughters as a way of lending support to our romance, for the same reasons mentioned above. (Romance/muffled/baby/ranch.) I made dinner, then we passed out on the couch in the middle of *My Best Friend's Wedding*. But at least we were in each other's arms! Actually, no we weren't.

The .7th time was when I made a Valentine's dinner for my husband after our four young children had gone to bed, and our baby woke up in the middle of dessert and I had to bring him to the table to nurse.

The moral of the story is, if you ever have the opportunity to make a romantic Valentine's Day dinner for your sugarplum sweetheart love-muffin honey-bear, this is pretty much the menu you need. It's hearty and yummy, but also simple and utterly doable, which will leave more time for more important things.

(Like passing out in each other's arms in the middle of your favorite romantic comedy . . .)

OTHER RECIPES TO CONSIDER: Rosemary-Garlic Roasted Potatoes (page 384); Burgundy Mushrooms (page 338); Caesar Salad (page 187); No-Knead Cloverleaf Rolls (page 278); Chocolate Strawberry Cake (page 191); Champagne Cocktails (page 354)

DO-AHEAD GAME PLAN

THE DAY BEFORE OR THE DAY OF

- Roast the garlic for the Roasted Garlic Mashed Potatoes.

- Assemble the Roasted Garlic Mashed Potatoes. Spread into a small baking dish, cover with foil, and store in the fridge.

- Make the dressing for the Cheddar-Bacon Wedge Salad, but do not add the bacon. Cover and store in the fridge.

- Grate the cheese for the Cheddar-Bacon Wedge Salad. Store in a small plastic zipper bag in the fridge.

- Make the Sticky Cherry Cake. Cover and set aside the cooled cake; cover and store the glaze in the fridge.

THE EVENING OF

- Reheat the Roasted Garlic Mashed Potatoes in a 350°F oven, covered, for 35 minutes before serving.

- Fry and chop the bacon and finish the dressing for the Cheddar-Bacon Wedge Salad.

- Reheat the glaze for the Sticky Cherry Cake and pour it onto the cake shortly before serving.

- Prepare the rest of the meal!

BACON-WRAPPED FILET

MAKES 2 SERVINGS

I think a good beef filet is pretty much the most romantic thing on earth. It's perfect for a dinner for two, because it's easy to eat, without any pesky bone to saw around and pick through, and the meat is so tender and divine that you can almost cut it with a fork. Also, it's not so huge that you'll be too stuffed to snuggle on the sofa after dinner and watch one of your favorite romantic movies, like *An Affair to Remember, Gone With the Wind,* or *The Godfather.*

   (*The Godfather* is totally romantic. You just have to keep an open mind.)

2 slices thick-cut bacon

Two 8-ounce beef tenderloin filet steaks

Salt and pepper to taste

2 tablespoons butter

1. Preheat the oven to 450°F.

2. Wrap 1 piece of bacon around each filet steak . . .

3. And secure the bacon with a toothpick.

4. Sprinkle both sides generously with salt and pepper.

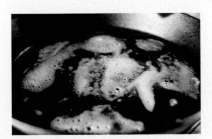

5. Melt the butter in a heavy ovenproof skillet over medium-high heat.

6. When the butter is melted and sizzling, place the steaks in the pan and sear them for about 30 seconds.

7. Use tongs to turn the filets over to the other side, then place the skillet in the oven for 3 minutes for medium-rare.

8. Remove the skillet from the oven, then transfer the steaks to a plate and let them rest for another 3 to 4 minutes. Remove the toothpicks.

9. Place the steaks on a plate with Roasted Garlic Mashed Potatoes (page 78) and Cheddar-Bacon Wedge Salad (page 80) and call your hot date to the table!

Mmmm . . . medium-rare steak. That's love right there.

Variation

Use a sirloin filet in place of tenderloin for a less pricey alternative.

Happy Valentine's Day, Deer! (Get it?)

ROASTED GARLIC MASHED POTATOES

MAKES 2 TO 4 SERVINGS

Two garlic breaths cancel each other out.
—Confucius

(At least I *think* Confucius said that. Or maybe it was Aristotle.)

Anyway, mashed potatoes on their own are the perfect pairing for a bacon-wrapped filet, of course—but take it one step further and stir in dark, delicious roasted garlic? The heavens up there high in the sky will open up and sing songs of glory and praise.

These aren't just perfect for Valentine's Day. They're a welcome star at any meal year-round. And they always, always, always disappear.

3 garlic bulbs

1 tablespoon olive oil

Salt and pepper to taste

2 pounds russet potatoes (5 or 6 potatoes), peeled and diced

4 tablespoons (½ stick) butter, softened

¼ cup heavy cream

4 ounces cream cheese, softened

1. Preheat the oven to 400°F.

2. Slice off the tops of the garlic to expose the cloves.

3. Place the garlic on a pie plate, drizzle the cut surfaces with a little olive oil, and sprinkle them with salt and pepper.

4. Seal the pan tightly in foil.

5. Roast the garlic in the oven for 1 hour, or until it is deep golden brown and totally soft. Set the bulbs aside.

6. Place the potatoes in a pot of water. Bring them to a boil over high heat and cook until the potatoes are fork-tender, about 25 minutes.

7. Drain the potatoes and place them in a large heatproof bowl. Add the butter along with some salt and pepper.

8. Next, add the cream . . .

9. And the cream cheese . . .

10. And mash the potatoes until they're totally smooth.

Bryce and Kitten-Kitten: Best buds forever!

11. Squeeze all the garlic cloves out of the roasted bulbs (reserve a few for garnish if you like) . . .

12. Then stir them in until the potatoes are smooth. Taste and adjust the seasonings as needed, then cover the bowl with aluminum foil and keep in a warm (250°F) oven until serving.

13. Serve them with a little extra roasted garlic on top!

CHEDDAR-BACON WEDGE SALAD

MAKES 2 TO 4 SERVINGS

There's no salad in existence that makes my husband swoon quite like a big ol' wedge of iceberg with some derivative of ranch dressing spooned over the top. And only 'cause it's Valentine's Day, just to send it over the top, I like to add a little bacon and grated Cheddar into the mix.

The things we do for love.

1 cup mayonnaise	½ teaspoon black pepper	4 slices thick-cut bacon, fried till slightly crisp
½ cup sour cream	⅛ teaspoon cayenne pepper	
½ cup buttermilk (see page 21)	½ teaspoon white vinegar	1 iceberg lettuce head
1 garlic clove, pressed	½ teaspoon Worcestershire sauce	½ cup grated sharp Cheddar or Cheddar-Jack cheese
¼ teaspoon salt		

1. In a large bowl, combine the mayonnaise, sour cream, buttermilk, and garlic.

3. And whisk until the mixture is totally smooth.

5. And whisk half into the dressing. Add more pepper if you'd like it to have more flecks.

2. Add the salt, pepper, cayenne, vinegar, and Worcestershire . . .

4. Chop up the bacon into pieces . . .

6. Cut the iceberg in half right through the middle . . .

7. Then cut the halves into wedges.

9. Then sprinkle on the cheese . . .

11. Then serve it up with the steak and a nice pile of potatoes.

8. Spoon a good amount of the dressing over each wedge so that it drips down the sides . . .

10. And the bacon.

Variations

- Add ⅓ cup crumbled blue cheese to the dressing for a nice tang.
- Use grated pepper Jack cheese instead of Cheddar for a little kick.
- Sprinkle 2 tablespoons finely diced red onion over the salad for added flavor.

Wishing they had a few studs to keep them warm . . .

"I'm ready for my close-up."

STICKY CHERRY CAKE

MAKES 8 SERVINGS

This vintage cake recipe is a sticky, gooey, sweet delight, and the perfect ending to what I'm 100 percent certain has been the most love-filled dinner you've ever enjoyed with your sugar.

(Did you kiss? Did you hold hands? Did you play footsie under the table? Did you feed each other bites while gazing longingly in each other's eyes? Details, please! I live for this stuff.)

This dessert is best served warm, and don't be the least bit concerned if the pieces are so sticky that they fall apart as you get them to the plates. That just means they're gonna be extra good.

CHERRY CAKE

One 15-ounce can cherries in syrup (not cherry pie filling)

1 cup sugar

2 tablespoons salted butter, softened, plus more for the pan

1 egg

1 cup all-purpose flour

1 teaspoon baking powder

½ teaspoon salt

½ cup whole milk

½ cup pecans, finely chopped

STICKY SYRUP

1 cup reserved juice from the cherries

1 cup sugar

1 tablespoon all-purpose flour

1 tablespoon butter

½ teaspoon vanilla extract

Unsweetened whipped cream, for serving

1. Preheat the oven to 325°F.

2. Start by draining the cherries, reserving the syrup for later. Set aside.

3. Add the sugar to the bowl of an electric mixer . . .

4. Along with the butter.

5. Cream together the sugar and butter, then beat in the egg.

6. In a separate bowl, sift together the flour, baking powder, and salt . . .

7. Then alternate adding the dry ingredients . . .

8. With the milk in three separate batches until the batter just comes together.

9. Add the drained cherries . . .

10. And the pecans . . .

11. And mix until the batter is just barely combined.

12. Generously butter an 8-inch square baking pan . . .

13. Then spread the batter in the dish. Bake it for 40 minutes, or until the cake is no longer jiggly like my bottom.

14. While the cake is baking, make the sticky syrup: Whisk 1 cup of the reserved syrup from the cherries with the sugar and flour.

15. Bring the mixture to a gentle boil and cook for 8 to 10 minutes, until the syrup is thick.

16. Remove the pan from the heat and use your very disturbing-looking hand to add 1 tablespoon of butter . . .

17. And the vanilla.

18. Remove the cake from the oven and immediately drizzle the sticky syrup all over the top. Make sure it evenly coats the center and the sides. Let the cake stand for at least 30 minutes to let the syrup seep into the cake.

19. While the cake is still warm, cut it into squares . . .

20. And serve it on a plate . . .

21. With a (great big!) dollop of unsweetened whipped cream.

Happy Valentine's Day!

forget sunsets . . . I think sunrises are pretty darn romantic.

Me, Easter 1975. I'd just eaten a chocolate bunny for breakfast. (Out of my brother's Easter basket . . .)

EASTER

I'm going to put this in the clearest, most simple terms so as to leave no ambiguity: *I love Easter.* It definitely ranks up there with my very favorite holidays, and if it weren't for that splashy, attention-grabbing, month-long celebration known as Christmas, Easter would definitely take the number one slot with me.

It's partly due to the time of year. After a long, brown, gnarly winter, the earth bursts forth with vibrant new life. The spring rains come, the grass grows, the tulips bloom, the bluebirds sing, and the Oklahoma redbuds dot the countryside with proud splashes of purple. And yes, the dang barn swallows start trying to build nests under our porch and I have to become a human scare-crow, checking several times a day and flapping my arms to get them to find another place to set up shop. Barn swallows are the one aspect of spring that threaten my inner peace. But since the rest of spring is so over-the-top glorious, I try not to let it kill my joy.

Easter is also the time I start planting my garden. The dead winter weeds come out, the new topsoil goes in, and lettuce, radish, and carrot seeds get sprinkled here and there. I get out my crazy gardening lady hat and dig out my crazy gardening lady gloves and go berserk, always ready, by the time spring arrives, to plant the biggest, most abundant garden in the county, completely forgetting that by the end of July I'll be cursing my horticultural ambition.

There's the fun of Easter, too: dyeing eggs, decorating treats, taking the kids to get new, clean (mud and manure free) outfits for church, and filling plastic Easter eggs with candy and coins for the big hunt at church.

But my favorite part of Easter is Easter itself. It's an emotional experience for me, reliving the death and resurrection of Jesus through scripture and liturgy and song. And this is not something that's happened since I became a sappy old woman after having four children and finding new significance in everyday things. And crying during insurance commercials, but that's another story for another time. I remember, as a child, having an unexplained lump in my throat during the choruses of "Christ the Lord Is Risen Today" and "Lift High the Cross" and not really understanding why. And don't even get me started on the Easter hymns we sing in our small-town church. ("Because He Lives," anyone? *Fugghetaboutit!*) What I'm saying is, it's not unusual for me to be a sobbing mess during the Easter service at church. That's normal, right? Okay, good. Explain that to my children, will you?

And so, in closing, to summarize, and to wrap things up, I love Easter because I *feel* it so intimately and acutely: The gorgeousness of the Earth, the family-centered traditions, and just the beautiful solemnity of the day.

I think I'll keep it.

EASTERTIME TREATS

Despite what you may have heard around town, Easter *isn't* just about the risen Lord. It's also about treats! And that may have been about as close to blasphemy as I've ever come in my life.

So let me rephrase: Easter treats are a lovely and delicious tradition, and the uses for them are endless! There are treats to deliver to friends on Good Friday. Treats to enjoy while decorating eggs. Treats for Sunday school parties. Treats for the Easter baskets. Treats to hide in a baggie in the middle drawer of your bedside table so your family won't find them.

(I'm troubled. Deeply troubled.)

Enjoy these sweet, meaningful Easter treats, my friends. They're meant to be shared!

Yay for Easter treats!

OTHER RECIPES TO CONSIDER: Candy-Dipped S'mores (coat in pastel colors of melting chocolate and use pastel sprinkles) (page 71); Jiggly Hearts (use different Easter colors; cut into egg shapes) (page 68); Homemade Chocolate Truffles (coat in white chocolate or white almond bark and add pastel sprinkles) (page 60); Marshmallow Pops (page 310)

HOT CROSS BUNS

MAKES ABOUT 24 BUNS

"Hot Cross Buns" was the first song I ever learned to play on the piano, and I played it so often, I drove my mom clinically berserk. It was followed closely by "Open Arms," and I played it so often, I drove my mom even *more* clinically berserk.

It's seriously amazing that she got through my adolescence with her sanity intact.

None of this has anything to do with actual hot cross buns, by the way. I just wanted to share one of my warmest childhood memories. Easter just brings it out in me.

But on the hot cross buns front, you'll love these delicious and meaningful treasures. Tradition says that if you deliver hot cross buns to others on Good Friday, you'll have blessings and friendships all year round. And while I haven't held scientific studies to prove this absolutely, I have a sneaking suspicion it's true.

BASIC DOUGH

4 cups whole milk

1 cup canola oil

1 cup sugar

9 cups all-purpose flour

2 packages (2¼ teaspoons each) active dry yeast

1 heaping teaspoon baking powder

1 scant teaspoon baking soda

1 tablespoon salt

SPICES AND FRUIT

½ cup sugar

1 teaspoon ground cinnamon

A pinch ground cardamom

A pinch ground nutmeg

A pinch ground allspice

½ cup raisins

GLAZE

2 egg whites

¼ cup whole milk

ICING

1 egg white

¼ cup whole milk

1 pound (about 4 cups) sifted powdered sugar

1. First, make the dough. Combine the milk and canola oil in a large pot.

2. Add the sugar . . .

3. And stir it around. Scald it (heat it to almost a boil), then turn off the heat. Let the mixture cool until it's warm . . . but not too warm!

4. Add 8 cups of the flour along with the yeast . . .

5. And stir it around until all combined. It'll be super sticky, but just have faith! (Get it?)

6. Cover the mixture with the lid of the pot or a dish towel and let it sit for an hour or so, until it's risen. (Get it?)

7. After it's had a chance to rise, sprinkle in the remaining cup of flour, the baking powder, the baking soda, and the salt . . .

8. And stir gently to combine. It takes a little while to get it stirred together!

9. For the spice–fruit mixture, combine the sugar, the cinnamon, cardamom, nutmeg, and allspice in a small bowl . . .

10. And stir them together to combine.

Charlie's Easter Sunday outfit. Too much?

11. Divide the dough in half and roll the first half into a rough rectangle. Sprinkle about 2 tablespoons of the cinnamon-sugar mixture all over the surface of the dough . . .

15. Sprinkle on more cinnamon, sugar, and raisins . . .

19. Place the balls of dough on a baking sheet lined with a baking mat or parchment paper, then repeat the whole process with the other half of the dough.

12. Followed by one-quarter of the raisins.

16. And fold the dough in on itself again. This process will just make sure the cinnamon-sugar and raisins are distributed all over the dough.

20. Cover the buns with a lightweight dish towel and let them rise in a warm place for 30 to 40 minutes, or until they're poufy and more uniformly round. (If they do not rise in that time, give them another 30 minutes.)

21. Preheat the oven to 400°F.

13. Fold the sides of the dough over so that the cinnamon/raisin filling is enclosed . . .

17. Pinch off a piece of dough and roll it into a ball with your hands.

14. Then roll the dough into another rectangle . . .

18. Then squeeze the bottom of the ball to force the sides to become smooth.

22. While the buns are rising, make the glaze: Mix together the egg whites and the milk.

23. Lightly brush the surface of the buns.

24. Bake the buns till they're nice and deep golden brown, about 20 minutes. Let them cool completely before icing.

25. While the buns are cooling, make the icing: Add the egg whites to the bowl of an electric mixer . . .

26. Then add the milk . . .

27. And the powdered sugar.

28. Then mix it all together until the icing is totally smooth and perfect. It needs to be thin enough to pipe easily onto the buns.

29. When the buns are cooled, place the icing in a piping bag or a plastic storage bag. Cut a tiny opening in the bag.

30. To pipe on the crosses, pipe a line going one direction . . .

31. And another line going across it.

So divine!

(Get it? *Divine*?)

(Sorry.)

NOTE: *The recipe can easily be halved.*

Variations

- *Use golden raisins, dried currants, or dried cherries instead of raisins.*
- *Use a simple Cream Cheese Frosting (page 110, omit the pecans) for a different, more decadent treat.*

EASTER COOKIES WITH BUTTERCREAM AND SPRINKLES

MAKES ABOUT 24 COOKIES

I have a handful of incredibly talented baker friends who approach decorating sugar cookies with the precision and artistry that Michelangelo applied to the ceiling of the Sistine Chapel . . . and I'm not even exaggerating. Their icing is smooth and beautiful, their piping techniques flawless. When I hold their cookies in my hands, I feel I'm in the presence of greatness.

My cookies . . . well, not so much.

I'm from the 1970s school of cookie decorating: Bake them. Slap some icing on them. Throw some sprinkles in their general direction and hope not too many wind up on the floor. Watch *The Brady Bunch* and *Gilligan's Island* while you eat them with a tall glass of whole milk, which was called "milk" back then, by the way. And fine. I still do this today.

The good news (get it?) about these cookies is that while they won't win any beauty pageants, they just might take home the "Most Delicious" award. Butter and sugar all over the place, and if you have a nice assortment of cookie cutters, you can wind up with a really nice variety.

1 batch My Favorite Sugar Cookie Dough (page 314, through step 6)

Flour, for rolling

BUTTERCREAM FROSTING

1 cup (2 sticks) butter, softened

4 cups powdered sugar

¼ cup heavy cream

Miscellaneous sprinkles and decorations

Gel food coloring (optional)

1. Preheat the oven to 375°F.

2. Remove the dough from the refrigerator and let it sit for 10 minutes to soften slightly.

3. Roll it on a floured surface to ¼ inch thick.

4. Use cutters to cut them into various Easter shapes: crosses, flowers, lambs, monkeys, and so on.

Just kidding on the monkey part.

5. Place the cookies on a baking sheet lined with a baking mat or parchment paper and bake them for 8 to 10 minutes, or until they're just barely done. You don't want them to start browning at all, so keep an eye on them!

6. In the bowl of an electric mixer, beat the butter, sugar, and cream until very light and fluffy. When the cookies are completely cooled, use a dinner knife to spread on the icing.

7. I like to use the knife to make little outlines and details in the cookies . . .

8. Then add sprinkles and other cookie decorations . . .

9. To make them really purty.

10. Cross cookies are always appropriate!

11. Candy dots are really fun, too.

12. You can mix up small amounts of the frosting in individual bowls with a drop or two of food coloring to make different colors of frosting. So bright and cheery.

13. The goal is to decorate each and every cookie differently.

Aw, sweet little lamb.

You can tell how much fun I have with these. You can have fun with 'em, too!

My four little lambs. They clean up nice!

KRISPY EGGS

MAKES 1 DOZEN EGGS

Imagine the Easter Bunny laying an egg.

Wait. That's not anatomically possible. And anyway, the Easter Bunny is a boy, right? It's even more impossible than I thought!

Okay, let's start this whole thing over. Imagine that the Easter Bunny's wife is a chicken, and imagine her laying an egg. These sweet, crispy eggs with a fun candy surprise inside would be what came out!

(Leave it to me to take something as innocent as an Easter treat and turn it into something disturbing. Please don't let me spoil this special time for you.)

Haunting visuals aside, these egg treats really are super fun and so easy to make. Change them up by altering the candy you plant in the center, and the decorations you sprinkle on at the end. They're the very definition of sweet.

4 tablespoons (½ stick) butter	**6 cups crispy rice cereal**	**12 small chocolate Easter eggs, jelly beans, or similar treats**
One 10-ounce package mini marshmallows	**Cooking spray**	**Assorted sprinkles in Easter colors**

1. Begin by placing the butter in a large saucepan or pot over medium heat.

3. And stir them around until the mixture is melted and smooth.

5. Gently stir the cereal to coat it evenly with marshmallow mixture.

2. Throw in the marshmallows . . .

4. Remove the pot from the heat and pour in the rice cereal.

6. Spray the inside of both halves of a plastic Easter egg with cooking spray.

7. Fill the bottom half with a small amount of the cereal mixture, then immediately press a chocolate egg into the center.

9. Immediately remove the egg from the plastic mold . . .

8. Fill the other half of the egg with more cereal mixture, then press the two halves together. You want the halves to be full enough that you meet with a little resistance when you close the egg. (It's okay to hear just a little bit of crunching!)

10. And place it in an egg crate while you mold the rest of the eggs. (Hint: Spray the plastic eggs each time!)

11. Add sprinkles to the individual eggs. Make each one of them different!

The perfect Eastertime treat.

Cows at the end of the rainbow.

EASTER BRUNCH

I love brunch on Easter Sunday, because everything is just so pretty. The flowers are pretty, the food is pretty, the plates are pretty, the clothes are pretty . . . and that $50 bill my mother-in-law hides in that one plastic egg among the other hundred plastic eggs containing mere dimes and quarters that she hides around her yard is pretty, too.

You know what? Family therapy time. To this day, I've never found that $50 egg. Not once. My husband has found it. I'm pretty sure each of my kids has found it at least once. My sister-in-law Missy has found it. *Twice!* But me? Nooooo. If it weren't Easter, I'd suspect a big fat conspiracy!

But seeing that it *is* Easter and all, I'll just settle in, let go of any and all plastic egg–related persecution complexes, and cherish this special time with the family. Here's a beautiful, timeless menu to adorn your Easter brunch table.

DO-AHEAD GAME PLAN

ANYTIME THE DAY BEFORE

• Make the Dr Pepper glaze for the Easter ham. Cool, then transfer to a bowl, cover, and store in the fridge.

• Bake the Hash Brown Nests through the first step. Cool in the muffin pans, then cover the pans with foil and set them in the fridge.

• Grate the cheese, chop the chives, and cut up the butter for the Cheddar-Chive Biscuits. Store in separate plastic zipper bags in the fridge.

• Combine the dry ingredients for the Cheddar-Chive Biscuits in a bowl. Cover with plastic wrap and set aside on the counter.

• Make the syrup for the Orange-Vanilla Fruit Salad. Cool, then transfer to a bowl, cover, and store in the fridge.

• Bake and ice Sigrid's Carrot Cake. Place it in the fridge to set the icing for 45 minutes, then carefully cover with plastic wrap or foil. Return to the fridge.

THE MORNING OF

- Remove the ham glaze from the fridge and bring to room temperature.

- Remove the Hash Brown Nests from the fridge and bring to room temperature.

- Remove Sigrid's Carrot Cake from the fridge to bring to room temperature for a softer cake and icing. (Note: The cake can also be served cold, straight from the fridge.)

- Make the rest of the food!

GLAZED EASTER HAM

SERVES AN ARMY

Easter is coming, the goose is getting fat!

Wait. That's Christmas.

And Christmas *isn't* coming. At least not for a long, long time.

Okay, now that I've both confused and depressed everyone: Here's my recipe for the yummy glazed ham I love to make for Easter brunch—that is, if the menfolk 'round here agree to forgo steaks for *one single solitary day*. (As in, "Can't you menfolk forgo steak for *one single solitary day*?" Holidays are such happy times around our house!)

This recipe is totally easy, exceedingly delicious, and results in a purty and glossy ham that'll make your guests say "Oooooooh!" with wide, expectant eyes and, hopefully, hugely hearty appetites.

This ham could seriously feed an army, man.

1 fully cooked bone-in ham (15 to 18 pounds)

40 to 50 whole cloves

3 cups lightly packed brown sugar

½ cup spicy brown mustard

3 tablespoons apple cider vinegar

One 12-ounce can Dr Pepper

1. Place the big ol' honkin' ham in a roasting pan with a rack.

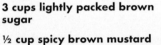

3. Then cut them at an angle in the other direction.

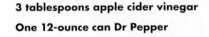

5. And keep going until the whole surface is dotted. I do this for appearance more than flavor: I just think it looks lovely and traditional when it's all done baking.

6. Cover the ham with foil, then put it into the oven to warm it up. I do 300°F to 325°F for at least 2 to 2½ hours, but you can just follow the instructions on the package. Some hams say to go 3 to 4 hours, some at a lower temperature. The whole goal here is just to heat the ham slowly . . . and it takes a while to do that.

2. Use a really sharp knife to score a diamond pattern all over the surface of the ham. First cut lines in one direction . . .

4. Poke the cloves into the center of the diamonds to make a nice pattern . . .

7. While the ham is in the oven, you can make the glaze: Throw the brown sugar into a saucepan . . .

8. Along with the spicy mustard for a nice tang . . .

9. The apple cider vinegar for a little bite . . .

10. And the star of the show: a whole can o' Dr Pepper! It's the right thing to do. Trust me. Just pour it on in.

11. Bring the mixture to a boil, then reduce the heat . . .

12. And simmer it for a good 15 to 20 minutes, until it's gotten darker and thicker.

13. After the ham has cooked for 2 hours, remove the foil and brush the surface with some of the glaze. Then pop it back into the oven, uncovered, for another 20 minutes.

14. Pull the ham out of the oven and brush on more glaze, then pop it back in for another 20 minutes.

15. After that time, pull it out and brush on more glaze! Are we seeing a pattern here? Just keep doing this until the layer of glaze is really gorgeous and glossy. (I usually brush on 3 layers of glaze.)

16. Serve the ham garnished with parsley and orange or apple slices if you want to be all fancy-like.

NOTE: *For ideas to use leftover ham, see the Easter Leftovers section (page 113).*

Variations

• *Substitute cola or root beer for the Dr Pepper, depending on your taste.*

• *Instead of brown sugar, add 1½ cups apple or plum jelly to the glaze.*

• *You may omit the cloves if you prefer! Just score the ham and leave it undecorated.*

EGGS IN HASH BROWN NESTS 🦋

MAKES 12 NESTS

These precious nests are the perfect little side dish for Easter brunch: Tender-but-crispy potato cups with a little baked egg in the middle. They go perfectly with Easter ham for your big after-church brunch . . . and they're great for a casual breakfast with a piece of bacon. Or two. Or three.

Or nineteen.

4 russet potatoes, scrubbed clean   **Salt and pepper to taste**   **Cooking spray**
12 large eggs

1. Preheat the oven to 400°F.

2. Bake the potatoes until they're baked but not quite tender enough to eat, about 25 minutes. This will make them easier to grate, and will also allow more room for baking later.

3. Let the potatoes cool completely, then peel them with a paring knife.

4. Grate all the potatoes, using the largest grating size. The potatoes should have just a tiny bit of "crunch" to them since they're not totally, totally cooked. Season the potatoes generously with salt and pepper: Just toss them around with your hands as you sprinkle.

5. Spray a muffin pan lightly with a little cooking spray to keep the potatoes from stickin'.

6. Drop a small amount (a little less than ¼ cup) of the potatoes into each muffin cup.

7. Use your fingers to lightly press the center so that the potatoes spill over the top a bit. (They'll shrink when they bake.)

8. Sprinkle on a tiny bit more salt and pepper . . .

9. Then give the tops just a very light spray again. I know this seems wacky and wild, but it helps the potatoes to sizzle a little bit as they cook.

10. Increase the oven temperature to 425°F.

11. Bake the nests for 20 to 25 minutes, until they're golden brown. Keep an eye on them so the ends of the potato shreds don't burn. Remember: The potatoes really shrink while they bake!

12. Let the nests cool a bit, then crack in the eggs.

13. Let the eggs bake for 10 to 15 minutes, until they get to the level of doneness you're looking for. (I like mine a little runny. But I'm weird.) Serve immediately.

NOTE: *Don't be concerned if the eggs all bake a little differently and don't all look exactly the same on top. Some whites will look perfect, some might look a little funky. Some whites will cover the yolk, some will gloriously reveal the yolk. But that's the beauty of these things! They're, like, totally rustic, dude.*

Variations

- *Add a few dashes of hot sauce to the top of each baked egg nest.*

- *Beat the eggs with ¼ cup half-and-half before pouring them into the nests to bake.*

- *Add diced ham, onions, and peppers to the beaten eggs before adding them to the nests. Yum!*

ASPARAGUS WITH DILL HOLLANDAISE

MAKES 12 SERVINGS

Who doesn't love a big bundle of fresh asparagus? Never not me, that's who!

Wait. Did that make any sense at all? I was trying to say that I don't not love asparagus. I've never not been able to not express a double negative correctly.

Wait. Can you express a double negative correctly? Are double negatives even correct in the first place?

These are the things that keep me up at night.

Anyway, asparagus. Yummy. Fresh. Good. But topped with a creamy hollandaise sauce seasoned with fresh dill?

Let's just say it'll definitely make your Easter brunch even more wonderful.

4 asparagus bundles, ends trimmed

1 cup (2 sticks) butter

4 egg yolks

Juice of 2 lemons

4 dill sprigs, minced, plus more whole sprigs

1 teaspoon salt

1. Steam the asparagus until bright green and just barely cooked.

2. Remove from the pot and set aside on a platter.

3. To make the hollandaise, melt the butter in a small saucepan until it's very hot and sizzling.

4. Add the egg yolks to the blender . . .

5. And squeeze in the lemon juice.

6. Then, with the blender on, slowly drizzle the hot butter into the blender with the yolks. It'll start to thicken right away.

7. After that, add the minced dill . . .

8. And the salt . . .

9. Then mix it again until it's all combined.

10. Drizzle it all over the top of the asparagus . . .

11. Then garnish the top with a little more dill, just to make it extra pretty.

Variations

- *Stir in the dill instead of blending it in if you'd like the dill leaves to be more visible in the hollandaise.*

- *Add a dash of cayenne pepper to the hollandaise for a little kick.*

- *Roast the asparagus instead of steaming them: Divide between two baking sheets, drizzle with olive oil, and roast at 425°F until they start to brown, 15 minutes.*

CHEDDAR-CHIVE BISCUITS

MAKES 30 BISCUITS

Drop biscuits are so easy and scrumptious, and they seem to insert themselves into many a holiday meal in my house. These are made extra delicious with white Cheddar and the sharpness of chives. Yum!

8 ounces white Cheddar cheese

⅓ cup chopped chives

6 cups all-purpose flour

¼ cup baking powder

1 teaspoon salt

1½ cups (3 sticks) cold butter, cut into small pieces, plus more for brushing (optional)

2½ cups buttermilk (see page 21)

1. Preheat the oven to 425°F.

2. Shred the cheese on the finest side of the grater . . .

3. Then slice up all the chives.

4. Add the flour, baking powder, salt, cheese, and most of the chives to the bowl of a food processor. You can also put it into a regular mixing bowl if you want to tackle all this by hand!

5. Pulse the ingredients until they're all combined. The chives and cheese pretty much become part of the dry ingredients! (Or, if you're using a regular bowl, just use a pastry cutter to cut the ingredients together.)

6. Throw in the cold butter . . .

7. Then pulse the mixture until it resembles coarse crumbs. (Or, again: Use a pastry cutter.)

8. Continue pulsing as you drizzle in the buttermilk. (Or stir it in.)

9. Stop pulsing just as it comes together. The dough smells delish!

10. Use a scoop to place small balls of dough on a baking sheet lined with a baking mat (or use a spoon to drop the dough onto the sheet as on page 347).

11. Bake the biscuits for 12 to 15 minutes, until they're nice and golden.

12. If you'd like a little extra decadence, melt some butter in a small saucepan . . .

13. And brush it on the tops of the biscuits right when they come out of the oven.

14. For a little extra green, sprinkle the rest of the chives on top.

Variations

- *Substitute 1 tablespoon ground black pepper for the chives and cheese for black pepper biscuits.*

- *Substitute 4 slices cooked, crumbled bacon and yellow Cheddar cheese for the chives and white cheese for bacon-Cheddar biscuits.*

ORANGE-VANILLA FRUIT SALAD

MAKES 12 SERVINGS

I predict you're going to absolutely love this fruit salad, which is drizzled with a lovely orange-vanilla syrup, which glosses it up and makes it visually irresistible, which makes you want to stand over the bowl and slurp up every single bite, which won't leave any for your brunch guests.

So logic would probably tell you not to make it.

But I think you should go ahead and take the chance! It's that good. Slightly citrusy, nice and sweet, with a little hint of vanilla lusciousness. And it's perfect not just for Easter brunch but also for baby or wedding showers, special luncheons . . . or just any meal that calls for a beautiful bowl of color.

1 cup sugar

Juice and zest of 1 orange

2 vanilla beans, or 2 teaspoons vanilla extract

4 pints strawberries, hulled and halved

2 pints blueberries

2 cups red grapes, halved

2 cups green grapes, halved

Mint leaves, for garnish

1. Add the sugar and 1 cup water to a small saucepan . . .

2. Then zest the orange and add the zest to the pan.

3. Cut the orange in half . . .

4. And squeeze the juice into the pan.

5. Slice the vanilla beans in half, scrape out the caviar, and add it to the pan.

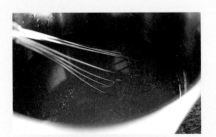

6. Stir it around and bring the mixture to a boil over medium-high heat, then reduce the heat to low and simmer the syrup for a good 15 to 20 minutes, until it's thickened a bit.

7. Chill the syrup in the fridge until you need it.

8. Pile all the prepared fruit into a big (and I mean big!) bowl.

9. Pour half the cold syrup over the top . . .

10. Then toss the fruit gently to coat it before drizzling in the rest.

11. Garnish with whole mint leaves. Sweet and stunning!

NOTE: *Make the syrup the night before you need it and chill it in the fridge to save time.*

Variations

- *Use lemon juice and lemon zest for a slightly different citrus flavor.*
- *Use any combination of fruit you'd like: melon chunks, orange pieces, apples, pears, berries, peaches . . . the works!*

There's nothing more handsome than a dude in his Sunday best.

SIGRID'S CARROT CAKE

MAKES 12 SERVINGS

I can't think of a more appropriate dessert for an Easter table than carrot cake, and my mom's longtime friend Sigrid has always made the best one in the Northern Hemisphere. (Southern, too.) It's chock-full of flavor, texture, and bright carrot color, and the cream cheese frosting is so over-the-top good, you'll want to give up all sweets for Lent just so this can be your first bite of bliss after the forty days are done.

Of course, what a person gives up for Lent is strictly his or her own decision and should not be influenced by anything a redheaded ranch wife in northeastern Oklahoma says.

(But next Ash Wednesday . . . think about it. Just think about it.)

CAKE

2 cups all-purpose flour

½ teaspoon salt

1 teaspoon baking powder

1 teaspoon baking soda

1 teaspoon ground cinnamon

2 cups sugar

1 cup vegetable oil

4 large eggs

4 to 6 large carrots, washed and peeled

CREAM CHEESE FROSTING

½ cup (1 stick) butter, softened

One 8-ounce package cream cheese, softened

1 pound powdered sugar

2 teaspoons vanilla extract

1 cup pecans, chopped fine, plus extra for garnish

1. Preheat the oven to 350°F.

2. Into a large bowl, sift together the flour, salt, baking powder, baking soda, and cinnamon. Set aside.

3. In the bowl of an electric mixer, combine the sugar and oil . . .

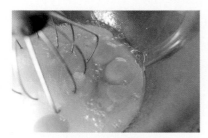

4. Then crack in the eggs . . .

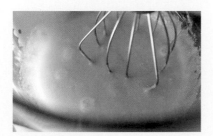

5. And mix until well combined.

6. Add the dry ingredients to the bowl . . .

7. And mix until smooth.

8. Grate the carrots (you should wind up with about 2 cups) . . .

9. Add the carrots to the mixing bowl . . .

10. And mix until they're completely incorporated into the batter, which, by the way, will look extremely weird at this stage.

11. Pour the batter into a well-greased Bundt pan.

12. Smooth out the surface of the batter with a spatula, then bake the cake for 40 to 45 minutes, until the cake is set.

13. Turn the cake out of the pan and allow it to cool completely before icing.

14. To make the icing, add the butter and cream cheese to the bowl of an electric mixer.

15. Then add the powdered sugar . . .

16. And the vanilla.

17. Mix it until the icing is light and fluffy and smooth. And sinful!

18. Add the pecans to the bowl . . .

19. And mix until they're all incorporated.

20. When the cake is fully cooled, spoon the icing all around the top . . .

21. And use a dinner knife to spread it evenly all over the surface of the cake.

22. Finally, sprinkle extra nuts all over the top of the cake.

23. Cut the cake into wedges and serve!

NOTE: *Refrigerate leftover cake.*

Variations

- *Make carrot cake muffins by filling a muffin pan with the batter and baking for 25 to 30 minutes.*

- *Make a carrot sheet cake by pouring the batter into a half sheet pan (13 x 18 inches) and baking for 30 to 35 minutes.*

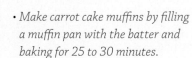

EASTER LEFTOVERS

Here's the thing about the day after Easter: You wake up feeling renewed and filled with all sorts of Easter joy . . . and then you realize you have all these hard-boiled eggs and cooked ham in your fridge with no hope that you'll ever be able to use them all.

So from perfect deviled eggs to a super-hearty scalloped potato dish, here are my very favorite ways to "resurrect" your Easter leftovers.

(Sorry about the whole "resurrect" thing. I just couldn't help myself.)

DEVILED EGGS

EACH VERSION MAKES 24 DEVILED EGGS

Fact: I once ate eleven deviled eggs at a picnic. This seems excessive in its own right, but when you consider the fact that I was six years old at the time, it might seem downright disturbing. But even though I had a three-day bellyache as a result of that little incident, it didn't affect my lifelong love of deviled eggs one bit.

I'd do it all again, is what I'm saying. Life is too short for deviled egg–related regrets!

Here are four of my favorite deviled egg variations, starting with the most basic version. Change them up, mix them up, add extra things, write a song about them. The world is your oyster, my friends.

BASIC DEVILED EGGS

These are basic, perfect, and incredible!

1 dozen hard-boiled eggs (see Note on page 116)

⅓ cup mayonnaise

1 tablespoon yellow mustard

Salt and pepper to taste

2 teaspoons chopped pickles or pickle relish

1 teaspoon white vinegar

1 teaspoon pickle juice

Paprika, for serving

1. Peel all the eggs. (Good news: Hard-boiled eggs are easier to peel the longer they sit in the fridge. They should be a cinch!)

3. Use your fingers to gently squeeze the yolks into a bowl; they should slide out easily. If they're stubborn, just use a spoon or small kitchen scoop to remove the yolks.

5. Until they're totally broken up.

2. Slice them in half lengthwise.

4. Mash the yolks with a fork . . .

6. Add the mayonnaise and mustard . . .

7. The salt and pepper . . .

8. And stir it all together until smooth.

9. Throw the pickles (or pickle relish) into the bowl . . .

10. And add the vinegar.

11. Optional: Splash in a little of the pickle juice from the jar. (I like to use sweet pickles so the juice adds a little sweetness.)

12. Then stir everything together until it's nice and smooth and wonderful. Give it a taste and add a little more of whatever it needs.

13. Use 2 small spoons (or a piping bag) to put large dollops of the egg yolk mixture into each egg half. (If you fill them really full, you might have a few leftover whites.)

14. Serve them on a bed of radicchio or red cabbage with a sprinkling of paprika. So pretty!

SRIRACHA DEVILED EGGS

I love these deviled eggs with a spicy Asian kick. What could be better, I ask you?

1 dozen hard-boiled eggs (see Note below), peeled, sliced open, and yolks removed

¼ cup mayonnaise

3 tablespoons Sriracha (a spicy Asian ketchup-like sauce)

1 teaspoon rice vinegar

Salt and pepper to taste

Black sesame seeds, for garnish

1. Mix the yolks with the mayonnaise and Sriracha . . .

3. Mash it and mix it together until the mixture is smooth. It will be a little on the thin side.

4. Spoon the filling into the egg halves . . .

5. Then sprinkle a few black sesame seeds on top (they look so pretty and dramatic) and serve them on a bed of chopped kale.

2. Then add the rice vinegar, salt, and pepper.

NOTES

• *To hard-boil eggs, fill a large pot halfway with water, then bring the water to a boil. Use a slotted spoon to gently lower eggs into the boiling water. Cover the pot, reduce the heat, and let the eggs simmer for 10 minutes. Remove the eggs from heat and run under cold water until completely cooled.*

• *Store deviled eggs in the fridge.*

DEVILED EGGS WITH SMOKED SALMON

Quite possibly my favorite deviled eggs ever. I blame the smoked salmon. Divine!

1 dozen hard-boiled eggs (see Note on page 116), peeled, sliced open, and yolks removed

2 tablespoons mayonnaise

3 dashes of Worcestershire sauce

2 tablespoons minced red onion

Salt and pepper to taste

1 tablespoon finely chopped capers, more for garnish

1 teaspoon caper juice

2 thin pieces (about 4 ounces) smoked salmon

1. Mix the egg yolks with the mayonnaise, Worcestershire sauce, and red onions.

2. Add the salt and pepper, chopped capers, and caper juice and mash it all together.

3. Cut a piece of smoked salmon in thin strips . . .

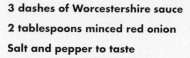

4. And roll each one into a small "rosebud" shape.

5. Fill the eggs with the egg mixture and top each one with a salmon rosebud. (You can also just chop the salmon and stir it into the egg mixture if you don't feel like being fancy.)

6. Add a couple of capers on top.

Splendidly scrumptious!

WHIPPED DEVILED EGGS WITH DILL

These are a little bit of an elegant spin on basic deviled eggs: The filling is whipped light and smooth and fresh dill makes 'em nice and zingy.

1 dozen hard-boiled eggs (see Note on page 116), peeled, sliced open, and yolks removed

6 tablespoons heavy cream

2 tablespoons Dijon mustard

1 teaspoon white vinegar

Salt and pepper to taste

1 tablespoon finely chopped dill, plus sprigs for serving

1. Add the yolks to the bowl of an electric mixer.

2. Then add the heavy cream . . .

3. The Dijon . . .

4. The vinegar, salt, and pepper. Whip the mixture together until light and fluffy, scraping the sides once halfway through.

5. Fold in the dill.

6. Add the mixture to a plastic bag or piping bag and snip off the corner . . .

7. Then pipe it right into each half.

Serve them on a bed of dill.

PERFECT EGG SALAD

MAKES 8 SERVINGS

I love egg salad. It's my life. At least, it's my life when I have a craving for egg salad. All other times, my life is whatever it is I'm craving during that particular two-minute period.

No, I'm not pregnant. I think.

Egg salad is the perfect thing to whip up the day after Easter, because you've got all those bright blue and orange and pink and purple Easter eggs sitting in the fridge longing for a new purpose now that the whole Easter egg hunt period of the eggs' lives has ended.

So in a way, it's really a ministry. You're giving these poor leftover Easter eggs renewed purpose!

Just before eating them for lunch.

1 dozen hard-boiled eggs (see Note on page 116), peeled

½ cup mayonnaise

1 to 2 tablespoons grainy mustard or country Dijon

1 teaspoon Worcestershire sauce

1 teaspoon white vinegar

Salt and pepper to taste

1. First of all, here's an awesome trick: Lay a cooling rack over a large bowl, then lay one of the peeled eggs on top.

2. Use your hand to squish the egg right through the rack!

3. Then just keep on going . . .

6. The mustard . . .

10. Serve a scoop of salad on a bed of greens . . .

4. Until you've got a big bowl of perfectly "chopped" eggs. So easy! (You can also just chop the eggs roughly with a knife if you'd rather.)

7. The Worcestershire . . .

8. And the vinegar, salt, and pepper.

11. Or with crackers and grapes for a nice snack. Delicious!

NOTE: *Make sure the hard-boiled eggs have spent sufficient time in the fridge (i.e., make sure they didn't sit outside in the yard all day!).*

5. To the bowl, add the mayonnaise . . .

9. Stir the mixture gently until it all comes together, then taste and adjust the ingredients to your taste.

Variations

- *Mix a mashed avocado in with the egg salad.*
- *Stir in 1 to 2 tablespoons Sriracha (or a few dashes of other hot sauce) for a spicier egg salad.*
- *Stir in ½ cup chopped green olives for a great flavor and texture.*

EASTER LEFTOVER SANDWICH

MAKES 1 SANDWICH

This absolutely enormous sandwich will go a long way toward finishing off your leftover Easter ham and eggs. If it weren't so delicious, it would be obscene.

1 kaiser roll or 2 slices bread of your choice

Dijon mustard to taste

Mayonnaise to taste

Salt and pepper to taste

1 slice Swiss cheese

2 or 3 thick slices leftover Glazed Easter Ham (page 100)

½ avocado, sliced

Thinly sliced red onion

1 Roma tomato, sliced

⅓ cup Perfect Egg Salad (page 119)

Lettuce

1. To build the sandwich, lay out the bread of your choice (I used a kaiser roll) and spread one half with Dijon and the other half with mayonnaise. Sprinkle with salt and pepper.

2. On the half with the Dijon, lay the Swiss cheese . . .

3. Then lay on the ham slices.

4. Meanwhile, on the mayo half, lay a bunch of luscious avocado pieces and the sliced red onion.

5. Lay on the tomato slices and top with the egg salad . . .

6. Then smush it down to flatten it a bit.

7. Finally, lay on the lettuce . . .

8. Then take a deep breath and put the two halves together.

9. Serve this sandwich with chips . . . and a very, very, very, very, very big appetite!

Variations

• *Add cooked bacon slices to the sandwich! (Sorry.)*

• *Use spinach, arugula, or any kind of greens you like.*

SCALLOPED POTATOES WITH HAM

MAKES 12 SERVINGS

My kids are madly in love with this dish to the point that I'm thinking of changing their names to Scalloped, Potatoes, With, and Ham. And I'm not even kidding.

Okay, so I might be kidding, but only about changing the kids' names. I meant every word I said about their love of this comfort casserole, which I always wind up making if I have leftover ham spilling out of my fridge.

Note: This feeds a big ol' crowd!

4 tablespoons (½ stick) butter, plus extra for greasing

½ yellow onion, diced

⅓ cup all-purpose flour

2 cups milk

1 cup half-and-half

1 teaspoon black pepper

2 pounds russet or Yukon gold potatoes, scrubbed clean

2 cups diced cooked ham

2 cups grated Monterey Jack cheese

Chopped parsley (optional)

1. Preheat the oven to 375°F.

2. Add the butter and onion to a large skillet over medium heat and sauté it until it's starting to soften, 3 to 4 minutes.

3. Sprinkle the flour over the onion and whisk them together . . .

4. Then continue cooking the onion/flour mixture for 2 minutes, or until golden brown.

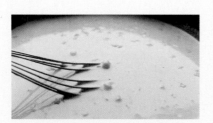

5. Stir in the milk and half-and-half and whisk the mixture around, allowing it to thicken. This'll take 3 to 4 minutes, give or take five years.

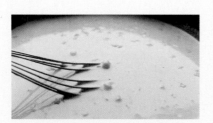

6. Add the pepper, then stir the sauce, reduce the heat, and keep it warm.

7. Slice the potatoes really thin using a mandoline (if you have one) or a really sharp knife. The thinner the better!

8. Generously butter a 2-quart baking dish . . .

9. Then add half the sliced potatoes and half the diced ham.

10. Sprinkle on half the cheese, then pour on half the sauce from the skillet.

11. Repeat with the rest of the ingredients. Sprinkle extra pepper on top.

12. Cover the dish with foil and bake it for 40 minutes, then remove the foil and bake it for an additional 15 to 20 minutes, until the cheese is golden brown and the sauce is bubbling.

13. Sprinkle with chopped parsley and serve it up!

CINCO DE MAYO

Cinco de Mayo is a holiday that's celebrated on—wait for it—the fifth of May! Aren't you glad I'm around so I can explain these things to you?

Okay, so you probably knew Cinco de Mayo was on May 5. But what you might not know is that Cinco de Mayo—in all its celebratory Mexican glory—is largely celebrated not in Mexico itself but *en los Estados Unidos.* And here's why.

(Warning: Homeschool history lesson ahead. I just can't help myself.)

In 1862, the Mexican army defeated French forces (whose numbers were double that of the Mexican troops) in a huge battle in a town called Puebla. It was an unexpected victory and was the source of much excitement and pride not only in Mexico, but also in many Mexican communities in the American West. When word of the May 5 victory reached mining communities in California, Mexican workers reportedly celebrated by firing rifles into the air and singing patriotic songs. That is said to be the very first Cinco de Mayo celebration . . . and they've increased in popularity ever since.

Now, Cinco de Mayo is not to be confused with Mexico's official Independence Day, which is celebrated across Mexico on September 16. But here in America, May 5 has become a day to embrace Mexican heritage and pride, and even if we're not from Mexico we Americans clearly have no qualms about taking part in the festivities year after year!

There are many reasons for this.

Guacamole, for one.

FIESTA!

There's something so fun (and slightly rebellious) about sandwiching a big, bold Cinco de Mayo party in between the more solemn, dignified holidays of Easter and Mother's Day. But it's May, baby! The earth is alive, the grass is turning green, and everyone's ready to party and have fun. And make no mistake about it: *Fun* is what Cinco de Mayo is all about!

(Well, and independence and freedom and all that jazz.)

Here are my very favorite recipes for one spectacularly delicious Cinco de Mayo spread.

(One fun piece of trivia: If you make every recipe on this Cinco de Mayo menu, you should expect to use approximately four million limes, give or take 3,999,975 or so. It's a lime-centric menu!)

OTHER RECIPES TO CONSIDER: Chipotle Chicken Chili (page 31); Southwestern Potato Skins (page 39); Eight-Layer Dip (page 42); Grilled Corn with Spicy Butter (page 206); Homemade Lemonade (page 198); Watermelon Sangria (page 200); Key Lime Pie (page 214)

DO-AHEAD GAME PLAN

THE DAY BEFORE

• Chop the onions and jalapeños for whichever pico de gallo varieties you're making.

• Make the Chipotle Salsa.

• Make the puree for the Blackberry Margaritas.

• Make the marinade for the Beef and Chicken Fajitas.

• Prepare the vegetables for the Beef and Chicken Fajitas.

• Make the Cinnamon Ice Cream so that it can freeze overnight.

• Make the Dulce de Leche Brownies.

THE MORNING OF

• Marinate the beef and chicken in separate plastic zipper bags. Store in the fridge until you grill.

• Make the Homemade Tortillas.

• Make the Cinnamon Crisps for the Cinnamon Ice Cream.

• Make the rest of the spread!

BLACKBERRY MARGARITAS

MAKES 8 TO 12 MARGARITAS

If you think you love margaritas now, wait till you take your first sip of this beautiful, vivid, refreshing (are you tired of adjectives yet?), tasty, and yummy blackberry version, which I find *muy* irresistible.

MARGARITAS

2 cups tequila

½ cup triple sec

Juice of 2 limes

¼ cup sugar

BLACKBERRY PUREE

4 cups fresh blackberries

½ cup sugar

Juice of 1 lime

LIME SUGAR

1 cup sugar

Zest of 3 limes

1 lime wedge

1. Place the tequila and triple sec in the freezer until they're very cold. (Because of the alcohol content, they will not freeze.)

2. To make the blackberry puree, add the blackberries to a medium saucepan . . .

3. Along with the sugar . . .

4. And the lime juice.

5. Bring them to a gentle boil over medium heat, stirring constantly. Then reduce the heat and let them cook for 20 to 25 minutes, until thick.

6. Place a fine-mesh strainer over a bowl and strain the berries, pressing to work as much liquid through as possible. All that should be left behind are seeds and pulp.

7. Cover the bowl with plastic wrap and refrigerate until the puree is completely cooled.

8. When it's margarita time, make the lime sugar: Place the sugar and lime zest on a plate . . .

9. And mix to combine.

10. Rub a lime wedge around the rims of the margarita glasses . . .

11. Then dip the rims into the lime sugar . . .

12. Until they're totally coated.

16. And the sugar.

19. Then get this party started!

Cheers!

13. To make the margaritas, fill a blender to the top with ice. Add the tequila . . .

17. Blend it until it's completely smooth. If you'd like a deeper purple color, blend in a little more of the blackberry puree. (Or save it for another batch of margaritas!)

NOTES

• *You can make the blackberry puree the day before the party. Just cover it tightly with plastic wrap and keep it in the fridge!*

• *Reserve half of the blackberry puree to make another batch of margaritas, or freeze it for up to 3 months.*

14. The triple sec . . .

15. About half the blackberry puree (see Note for freezing the remaining blackberry puree), the lime juice . . .

18. Fill the glasses . . .

STRAIGHT-UP PICO DE GALLO

MAKES 8 TO 12 SERVINGS

This is the original. The one and only. The big Mack Daddy. The pico that started it all.

This is a condiment in our house! For a snack or a relish or just a spoonful of freshness, there's nothing better in the world.

1 large onion, diced

12 Roma tomatoes, diced

½ bunch cilantro, chopped

2 jalapeños, seeded and diced

Juice of 1 lime

½ teaspoon salt

1. Combine all the ingredients in a large bowl . . .

2. And toss it all together to combine. Taste a little on a tortilla chip and add more of whatever it needs.

Pa-Pa loves pico de gallo more than life itself.

Pico de gallo for president!

MANGO PICO DE GALLO

MAKES 8 TO 12 SERVINGS

First of all, I realize most reasonable, sane people would call this mango *salsa*, not mango pico de gallo. But I cannot bring myself to call this luscious, beautiful, colorful side dish/appetizer/relish mango salsa. That is because when I think of salsa, I think of a pureed, pourable mixture—something you make in a blender or food processor. To me, big, fresh chunks of ingredients thrown together in a bowl and served with chips is pico de gallo every day of the week and twice on Sunday.

I mean on Cinco de Mayo.

I realize my logic is likely flawed.

I realize my brain doesn't work like most peoples'.

I realize that just because I give something a name doesn't mean that's its proper name.

I realize I'm taking up too much of your time and you'd like to move on to the recipe already.

So I'll just stop talking now if that's okay with you.

See? I stopped talking. I'm super duper good at stopping talking. I really am.

Aren't you glad I stopped talking?

8 ripe mangoes	**Juice of 1 lime**	**2 jalapeños, seeded and diced**
½ bunch cilantro, roughly chopped	**1 red onion, finely diced**	**Dash of salt**

1. Make sure your mangoes are nice and ripe, then cut off 2 thick slices on either side of the pit. (Snack on the area around the pit! Yum.)

2. In each section of mango, use a small knife to cut a diamond pattern all the way to the inside of the skin.

3. Use a spoon to scoop around the inside of the skin, allowing the chunks of mango to fall out.

Oh, what a beautiful day!

4. Pile the mango chunks in a bowl.

8. Stir it all around and give it a taste, adding a little more salt if needed.

9. Serve it with blue corn or regular tortilla chips.

5. Add the cilantro and lime juice . . .

6. The red onion . . .

7. The jalapeños and salt.

Variations

• *Serve over grilled chicken or fish.*

• *Serve on quesadillas as a garnish.*

• *Serve as a side salad for any number of dishes! Yum.*

WATERMELON PICO DE GALLO

MAKES 8 TO 12 SERVINGS

This spectacular pico de gallo definitely takes the prize for sheer color and beauty. Lovely chunks of fresh watermelon are front and center, and the way the sweetness of the melon mixes with the flavor of the bell peppers, the spiciness of the jalapeños, and the freshness of the cilantro is just not to be believed.

The really clever thing about this gorgeous bowl of wonder is that it can pass as a dip for chips, a garnish for grilled chicken or fish, or even a side salad alongside all the savory dishes on the menu.

One bite and you'll be addicted for life!

1 small seedless watermelon

½ red onion, finely diced

1 red bell pepper, seeded and finely diced

1 green bell pepper, seeded and finely diced

1 yellow bell pepper, seeded and finely diced

2 jalapeños, seeded and finely diced

1 bunch cilantro, chopped

Juice of 2 limes

½ teaspoon salt, more to taste

1. To dice the watermelon, lop off the top and bottom, then slice large pieces of rind off the sides.

2. Keep going . . .

3. Until all the rind is off.

4. Cut half the watermelon into slices, then wrap and save the other half for another use.

5. Stack a couple of the slices, then dice them up.

6. Repeat with the rest of the slices, then throw it all in a large bowl.

7. Then add the onion, bell peppers, and jalapeños.

8. Throw in the cilantro . . .

9. The lime juice and salt.

10. Toss the pico de gallo around gently and give it a taste. Add more of any ingredients you think it needs.

I'd walk a mile for Alex's smile.

11. Serve it both as a munchie before the meal and as a garnish for all the food. You'll love this!

NOTE: *Cut the unused half of the watermelon into chunks and serve it with the rest of the meal!*

GLORIOUS GUACAMOLE

MAKES ABOUT 3 CUPS

Before I begin, I would like to take this opportunity to very humbly, quietly, and calmly state something.

This is the best guacamole on the face of the gosh darn ding dang earth!

I feel cleansed. And I'm not being hyperbolic. Oh, I've been hyperbolic before, but this is definitely, 100 percent, beyond any doubt on the planet *not* one of those times.

The magical thing is, I created this version of "guac" (my nickname for guacamole; we're close like that) quite accidentally: After making three different varieties of pico de gallo one dark and stormy night (actually one bright and sunny evening), I decided to stir a little bit of each into the guacamole I was whipping up.

It was one of the most profound decisions of my entire life. Right up there with marrying my husband, having four of his children, and steering far away from turquoise eyeliner. I can't imagine if my life had gone a different way.

8 avocados

Juice of 1 lime

½ teaspoon salt

¼ cup Straight-Up Pico de Gallo (page 131)

¼ cup Mango Pico de Gallo (page 132)

¼ cup Watermelon Pico de Gallo (page 134)

1. Carefully slice the avocados in half, then use the knife to remove the pit.

2. Using a large tablespoon, scoop the avocados out of their shells . . .

3. And place them in a medium bowl.

4. Use a fork to mash the avocado until mostly smooth, with a few remaining chunks.

5. Squeeze in the lime juice . . .

6. Then stir in the salt.

7. Add the three varieties of pico de gallo . . .

8. And stir it until everything is combined. Give the guac a taste and add more of whatever variety of pico de gallo you'd like, or additional salt if it needs it.

9. Serve it with chips!

NOTE: *Serve guacamole within 1 hour of preparing.*

Variations

- *For a simpler, more basic guacamole, just use straight-up pico de gallo alone.*

- *You may also use ¾ cup of just one variety of pico de gallo, if you prefer.*

Pepper, Alex's faithful steed.

CHIPOTLE SALSA

MAKES ABOUT 5 CUPS

I'm addicted to this salsa. It's just like the restaurant-style salsa you find in . . . um, restaurants (clever, Ree!), but with the added smokiness and spice of chipotle peppers. And the best part about it is how easy it is to whip up. You'll want to make it by the gallon!

Two 15-ounce cans diced tomatoes

One 10- or 15-ounce can diced tomatoes with green chiles (such as Rotel)

1 medium onion, diced

1 to 3 (depending on your heat tolerance) chipotle peppers packed in adobo (sold in the Hispanic foods aisle)

1 teaspoon ground cumin

1 teaspoon salt

½ teaspoon ground pepper

1 teaspoon sugar

1 bunch cilantro, stems roughly removed

¼ cup lime juice

1. Into a blender or food processor, add the diced tomatoes . . .

2. The diced tomatoes with chiles . . .

3. And the onion.

4. Add the chipotles to the blender. One pepper will add a little bit of smoky flavor and a little spice, while three will add a stronger smoky flavor and a whole lotta spice!

5. Add the cumin . . .

6. The salt, pepper, and sugar . . .

7. And the cilantro and lime juice.

8. Blend it until it's totally combined.

It's really a shame Charlie doesn't get any attention around here.

9. Then give it a taste and add more of whatever seasonings it needs.

NOTES

- *Chipotle peppers are very, very spicy, so if you're not sure about it, start with 1 pepper and work your way up!*

- *Make the salsa several hours before serving, as it will give the flavors a chance to dance.*

- *The salsa will keep in the fridge, covered, for about 2 weeks. Not that it will last that long.*

BEEF AND CHICKEN FAJITAS

SERVES A CROWD!

I love serving fajitas (and all the marvelous fixins) to a Cinco de Mayo crowd because you're not *telling* your guests what to eat, which would be the case if you served something pre-assembled, such as enchiladas. Instead, you're merely providing a tableful (emphasis on *full*) of elements and letting folks put together their individual plates of deliciousness however their spirit leads them.

It's all about freedom, my friends!

3 pounds skirt steak

3 pounds boneless, skinless chicken breasts

MARINADE

½ cup olive oil

3 tablespoons Worcestershire sauce

3 garlic cloves, minced

1 tablespoon ground cumin

4 tablespoons chili powder

½ teaspoon red pepper flakes

1 teaspoon salt

½ teaspoon black pepper

1 tablespoon sugar

Juice of 3 limes

FAJITA VEGETABLES

2 tablespoons olive oil

2 tablespoons butter

2 medium onions, halved and sliced

1 red bell pepper, seeded and sliced into strips

1 orange bell pepper, seeded and sliced into strips

1 green bell pepper, seeded and sliced into strips

1 yellow bell pepper, seeded and sliced into strips

1 pound cremini or white button mushrooms, sliced thick

1. Place the beef and chicken in separate 2-quart baking dishes or large resealable plastic storage bags.

2. Make the marinade for the beef and chicken: In a blender, combine the olive oil, Worcestershire, garlic, cumin, chili powder, red pepper flakes, salt, pepper, sugar, and lime juice. Blend the marinade until it's totally combined and smooth.

3. Then pour half the marinade over the beef . . .

4. And the other half over the chicken.

5. Use your hands to work the marinade all over both sides of the beef . . .

6. Then do the same with the chicken. Give your hands a good wash, then cover the dishes with plastic wrap and let them marinate in the fridge for 4 to 6 hours. Wash the blender; you're gonna need it again!

7. About 30 minutes before you're ready to make the fajitas, remove the beef and chicken from the fridge. After 30 minutes, grill the beef over medium-high heat for about 2 minutes total for medium rare.

8. Rotate it 45 degrees on each side in order to get pretty grill marks.

9. Then remove it to a platter to rest for 5 to 10 minutes.

12. And sauté them until they're nice and deep golden brown.

15. And the chicken . . .

10. Grill the chicken on both sides until completely cooked through, about 4 minutes per side. Remove it to a platter to rest for 5 to 10 minutes.

13. Pile the veggies on a platter.

16. And pile all the slices onto a cutting board or platter.

17. Serve the beef and chicken with Chimichurri Shrimp and extra Chimichurri Sauce (page 146), Homemade Tortillas (page 143), the fajita veggies, Zesty Lime Rice (page 150), Fiesta Black Beans (148), Pico de Gallo (pages 131–135), Glorious Guacamole (page 136), and little dishes of salsa, grated cheese, and sour cream. It's fun to watch the different ways your guests pile up everything.

Happy Cinco de Mayo, *mis amigos*!

11. Meanwhile, heat the olive oil and butter in a large skillet over medium-high heat, then throw in the veggies . . .

14. With a sharp knife, slice the beef . . .

HOMEMADE TORTILLAS

MAKES 2 DOZEN TORTILLAS

There are few things better on this beautiful planet of ours than fresh homemade flour tortillas. The flavor, the texture, the color—absolutely nothing about them screams "store-bought." That's because you did not buy them at the store. You made them at home. Hence the name.

But seriously, my friends. I mean *en serio*. Homemade tortillas are the *bomb diggity dog diggity bibbity bobbity boo*. I just invented that phrase. And I did in order to demonstrate that these homemade tortillas are so good that you will lose your ability to speak coherently.

These are essentially flour tortillas, but I add a little butter to the shortening for flavor . . . as well as some masa to interject a bit of texture and yummy corn flavor. Once you try these once, you'll make 'em again and again!

One note about homemade tortillas: Generally speaking, they have a nice, rustic quality/texture and don't have the unnatural softness and pliability found in store-bought, mass-produced versions. But that's what makes them so great!

2 cups all-purpose flour

½ cup masa harina (corn flour, sold in the Hispanic foods aisle)

2½ teaspoons baking powder

1 teaspoon kosher salt

½ cup vegetable shortening

2 tablespoons salted butter

1 cup very hot water

1. Combine the flour, masa harina, baking powder, and salt in a medium bowl.

2. Stir the dry ingredients together, then add the shortening and the butter.

3. Use a pastry cutter to cut all the ingredients together. Keep going until the mixture resembles coarse crumbs.

4. Pour the hot water into the bowl, stirring constantly . . .

5. Until the dough just comes together. It should be very warm.

6. Turn the dough onto the countertop . . .

7. And knead it 30 to 40 times, about 1 minute.

8. Form the dough into a neat ball . . .

9. Then place it in a clean bowl, cover it with a dish towel, and set it aside to rest for 1 hour.

10. When you're ready to make the tortillas, place a heavy skillet over medium-high heat. Pinch off a walnut-size piece of dough and form it into a rough ball.

11. Place it in a tortilla press and flatten it completely, using flour to keep it from sticking. (Note: Tortilla presses can be found in cooking supply stores or in some supermarkets in the Hispanic foods aisle. Tortillas may also be rolled out with a rolling pin on a lightly floured surface!) Remove it from the press and place it on a lightly floured surface while you do the rest.

12. Keep going until they're all flattened.

13. One by one, place the tortillas in the hot skillet and let them cook for about 30 seconds . . .

14. Before flipping them to the other side for another 20 seconds or so.

15. Remove them to a flat surface and keep them lightly covered with a dish towel while you cook the rest!

Serve them while they're nice and warm!

HELPFUL HINTS

- *Make sure the water you pour in is very hot. I use a tea kettle!*

- *Allow the dough to rest the full hour after kneading. Use a rolling pin if you don't have a tortilla press; just be sure to roll them very thin on a lightly floured surface.*

- *Cook just long enough to lightly brown the tortilla in spots; don't cook so long that the tortillas crisp.*

- *Have fun! And enjoy them. They're absolutely scrumptious.*

NOTES

- *Tortillas can be made the day before you need them: Once they've cooled, just stack them and wrap together in aluminum foil. Then just warm them in a 300°F oven for 15 minutes before serving.*

- *Tortillas are delicious drizzled with honey for breakfast. Don't ask me how I know this.*

- *Use these tortillas to make the most delicious quesadillas you'll ever eat.*

He looks like he's almost ready for a siesta!

CHIMICHURRI SHRIMP

SERVES A CROWD!

Chimichurri, in its simplest definition, is a bright green sauce served over grilled meat. It comes all the way from Argentina (and boy are its arms tired!), and the basis of authentic chimichurri is a great big bunch of parsley. For my Cinco de Mayo spread, I actually prefer a cilantro-centric version to go with all the savory dishes. It's fresh, flavorful, and glorious!

In addition to using chimichurri as a sauce, I also like to use a little bit of the glorious green stuff to marinate shrimp. Incredibly tasty, baby!

CHIMICHURRI SAUCE

1 large bunch cilantro, stems removed

½ bunch flat-leaf parsley, stems removed

3 garlic cloves

Juice of 3 limes

1 teaspoon ground cumin

¼ teaspoon cayenne pepper

1 teaspoon salt

½ cup olive oil

SHRIMP

3 pounds raw jumbo shrimp, peeled and deveined, tails off

2 tablespoons olive oil

1. Fill a blender or food processor with the cilantro and parsley . . .

2. Then add the garlic . . .

3. Lime juice . . .

4. Cumin . . .

5. Cayenne . . .

6. And salt.

7. Place the lid on the blender, then remove the center piece. With the blender on low, drizzle in the olive oil . . .

8. And blend it until the chimichurri is totally pureed and somewhat smooth.

9. Place the shrimp in a 2-quart baking dish and drizzle in half the chimichurri.

10. Pour the other half into a small dish, cover it with plastic wrap, and put it in the fridge for serving later.

11. Toss the shrimp in the sauce, then cover it with plastic wrap and refrigerate it for at least 2 hours.

12. When you're ready to make the shrimp, heat the olive oil in a large skillet over medium-high heat. Throw in the shrimp . . .

13. And cook them, stirring them around, for 3 to 4 minutes, or until they're a nice pinky-gold.

14. Serve the shrimp with the remaining chimichurri sauce and the rest of the Cinco de Mayo spread!

FIESTA BLACK BEANS

MAKES 8 TO 12 SERVINGS

It's physically, psychologically, gastrointestinally, practically, and emotionally impossible for me to imagine a Cinco de Mayo spread without a big pot of beans coming into play somewhere. And the decision of whether to go with brown beans or black beans is always a weighty one. What will happen if I choose the wrong bean, I ask myself? What are the global and human consequences of going with the wrong choice? What will become of me if my bean choice is faulty? Will I wind up sad, friendless, and alone simply because of one errant bean decision?

Oh, the pressure.

Generally speaking, although I love regular pinto beans for everyday cooking around my house, I tend to reach for the pretty, shiny black variety whenever there's a fiesta going on. They always inject drama to the equation, and so far (I hope I don't jinx myself here) I haven't lost a single friend over them.

Plus, in case you might be wondering, they're delicious!

2 pounds dried black beans

2 green bell peppers, seeded and diced

2 orange bell peppers, seeded and diced

2 red bell peppers, seeded and diced

1 onion, diced

6 garlic cloves, minced

1 ham hock, or 6 slices thick-cut bacon, cut into pieces

1 teaspoon chili powder

1 teaspoon ground cumin

1 teaspoon salt

1 teaspoon black pepper

1. Place the beans in a large bowl and cover them with cold water. Set them aside and let them soak for 4 to 6 hours or overnight.

2. Drain and rinse the beans, then place them in a large pot.

3. Add the diced green, orange, and red bell peppers . . .

4. And the onion and garlic.

5. Cover them with water by about an inch . . .

6. Then add the ham hock or bacon . . .

7. The chili powder and cumin . . .

8. And the salt and pepper.

9. Stir to combine, then bring the mixture to a boil. Reduce the heat to low and simmer the beans for 2 hours.

10. After that time, check the beans. The beans should be tender and the cooking liquid should be nice and thick. (If it seems a little soupy, just drain off as much liquid as you like, then turn up the heat to medium-high and cook the beans for an additional 15 minutes.)

11. Serve the beans piping hot in a nice big bowl . . .

12. And spoon them over Zesty Lime Rice (page 150).

Charlie and Walter sittin' in a ford . . .
B-O-R-E-D, they're bored.

ZESTY LIME RICE

MAKES 8 TO 12 SERVINGS

"If you're serving beans at a Cinco de Mayo fiesta, you absolutely must serve rice alongside them."
      —Winston Churchill

Man, was Sir Winston right! And while you can take any number of approaches when it comes to the rice you make for your CdM party, I haven't found one I like better than this light, fresh version spiked with the zest and juice of lime. It has a nice tang and sharpness that really stand up to the rest of the flavors in this luscious spread . . . and the green flecks of lime zest are just so bright and pretty.

   ¡Olé!

(What does *¡olé!* mean? Thank you for your help in this matter.)

1 tablespoon olive oil

3 garlic cloves, minced

1 large onion, chopped

2 cups long-grain rice

4 cups low-sodium chicken or vegetable broth

1 teaspoon kosher salt

Juice and zest of 3 limes (about ¼ cup lime juice)

1. Heat the oil in a medium pan over medium-high heat . . .

3. Stir them around and cook them for 3 to 4 minutes, until the onion starts to soften.

5. Stir it around and let it cook for about 2 minutes. Don't let it burn!

2. And add the garlic and onion.

4. Reduce the heat to low and pour in the rice.

6. Stir in the broth and salt . . .

7. Then add the lime juice . . .

8. And half the lime zest.

9. Cover the pan and cook the rice for 20 to 25 minutes, until tender. Stir it once or twice during cooking to keep it from sticking to the pot.

10. Sprinkle on the rest of the lime zest . . .

11. And stir to combine.

¡Muy delicioso!

Variation

Sprinkle ½ cup chopped cilantro over the top of the rice just before serving.

CINNAMON ICE CREAM WITH CINNAMON CRISPS

MAKES 2 QUARTS ICE CREAM AND 15 TO 20 CRISPS

Warning: This cinnamony-sweet ice cream will rock your world, infiltrate your dreams, take over your thinking, and pretty much change everything you ever assumed about what flavor of ice cream was your favorite. It is nothing short of awesome.

Serve this to your Cinco de Mayo guests in small one-scoop bowls with a big ol' cinnamon crisp on the side.

Dessert doesn't get much better than this.

CINNAMON ICE CREAM

3 cups half-and-half

2 cups sugar

3 cinnamon sticks

1 vanilla bean, or 1 teaspoon vanilla extract

9 large egg yolks

3 cups heavy cream

1½ teaspoons ground cinnamon

CINNAMON CRISPS

⅓ cup sugar

1 tablespoon ground cinnamon

6 Homemade Tortillas (page 143) or flour tortillas

4 tablespoons (½ stick) butter, melted

1. In a medium saucepan over medium-low heat, combine the half-and-half . . .

5. And add it and the empty bean to the pan.

9. Remove and discard the cinnamon sticks . . .

2. And the sugar. Stir it around to combine.

6. Stir the mixture around and heat it up until it's hot but not boiling.

10. And the vanilla bean.

3. Next, add the cinnamon sticks . . .

7. Next, add the egg yolks to a medium bowl . . .

11. Then grab a ladle of the hot half-and-half mixture . . .

4. Then, using a small paring knife, split the vanilla bean down the middle. Scrape out the caviar inside . . .

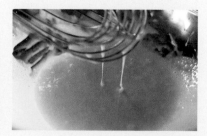

8. And whisk them vigorously for about 2 minutes, until the yolks are slightly lighter in color.

12. And drizzle it very slowly into the yolks, whisking constantly. This will temper the egg yolks so that they don't scramble when they're added to the pan.

13. Add another ladle of the hot liquid, and when it's mixed in . . .

14. Pour the egg mixture slowly into the pan with the half-and-half mixture, stirring with a spoon.

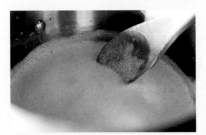

15. Stir and cook it for 2 minutes or so . . .

16. Until the mixture is thick and coating the spoon.

17. Set a fine-mesh strainer over a clean glass bowl and strain the custard. Don't worry if it looks a little lumpy! That just means you're perfectly imperfect.

18. Add the heavy cream to the bowl . . .

19. And stir to combine.

20. Finally, whisk in the ground cinnamon, then cover the bowl and refrigerate it until completely cool.

21. Once it's chilled, pour the mixture into the ice cream maker and process it according to your machine's instructions.

22. When it's finished churning, it will still be in the soft-serve stage . . .

23. So transfer it to a freezer container and place it in the freezer for several hours, or until it's frozen firm. (Overnight is best!)

24. Meanwhile, make the cinnamon crisps: Preheat the oven to 350°F. Combine the sugar and cinnamon in a small bowl.

27. And bake them for 15 to 20 minutes, or until very crisp. Allow them to cool to room temperature.

A fantastically delicious combo!

NOTE: *You can make the ice cream the day before you need it to save lots of time on party day! It needs the time to harden in the freezer, anyway.*

25. Place the tortillas on a baking sheet and brush both sides with the butter.

28. Break them into large pieces and set them aside.

Variations

- *Drizzle the ice cream with hot fudge sauce.*
- *Drizzle the ice cream with caramel sauce or warm dulce de leche.*
- *Sandwich a small scoop between 2 oatmeal cookies.*

26. Sprinkle both sides generously with the cinnamon-sugar mixture . . .

29. When the ice cream has frozen solid, serve a large scoop alongside a cinnamon crisp.

Just another family gathering.

DULCE DE LECHE BROWNIES

MAKES 16 BROWNIES

Dulce de leche literally translates to "candy of milk." In layman's terms, it's a caramel-like concoction made from boiling sweetened condensed milk until it becomes . . . well, pretty much an eighth deadly sin. What I love most about dulce de leche is that it has the beautiful color and deep flavor of caramel, but not the chewiness . . . so you don't have to expend needless energy flexing your jaw muscles.

I have a hard time controlling myself around a can of dulce de leche, and I've been known to spoon it into coffee, spread it on cookies, plop it onto ice cream, and yes, swirl it through big fudgy brownies like these.

These heavenly brownies are the perfect wrap-up to your Cinco de Mayo celebration.

Nonstick baking spray

Five 1-ounce squares unsweetened chocolate

1 cup (2 sticks) butter, softened

2 cups sugar

4 eggs

1¼ cups all-purpose flour

1 tablespoon vanilla extract

Half a 14-ounce can dulce de leche

1. Preheat the oven to 325°F. Generously spray an 8-inch square baking pan or an 8 x 10-inch baking pan with nonstick baking spray.

2. Place the chocolate in a microwave-safe bowl . . .

3. And nuke it in about 45-second intervals, stirring each time, until it's completely melted. Set it aside to cool for 20 minutes or so.

4. Add the butter and the sugar to the bowl of an electric mixer fitted with the paddle attachment . . .

5. And cream them together until they're light and fluffy.

6. Add the eggs, one at a time . . .

7. Beating well after each addition.

8. With the mixer on low, slowly drizzle in the chocolate . . .

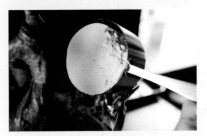

9. Until it's all combined.

10. Add the flour . . .

11. And the vanilla . . .

12. And mix it until it's all combined, scraping the sides of the bowl halfway through.

13. Spread the batter into the greased pan.

14. Next, crack open the can of dulce de leche . . .

15. And place half of it in a glass bowl. Warm it in the microwave for 30 to 45 seconds, just to make it a little more stirrable.

16. Drop large dollops of dulce de leche on the surface of the batter . . .

17. Then use a knife to slowly swirl it through the brownie batter. Don't drag the knife sideways through the batter; hold it so the thin side of the knife leads the way.

18. Bake the brownies for 45 to 50 minutes, or until the center is almost totally set.

19. Let the brownies cool in the pan for 15 minutes . . .

20. Then carefully turn them out of the pan and let them cool completely.

21. Use a very sharp serrated knife to cut the brownies into squares . . .

22. And place them on a pretty cake stand.

Come to Mama!

"I think I can . . . I think I can . . .
I think I can . . ."

Ga-Ga, my mom, and
my uncle John in 1942.

MOTHER'S DAY

I wound up with a pretty great mom. She was enthusiastic and involved (still is), cheerful and positive (still is), and had the patience of Job (still does).

My mom instilled in me a love of John Denver, the Carpenters, and Mozart, and she endured the many seasons of my redheaded, hysteria-laden, boy-crazy adolescence. And that time I bleached a white streak in my hair because I thought it would mean I was edgy, when in reality it just made me look like I'd bleached a white streak in my hair. It might have helped if I'd stopped wearing Izods.

My mom had a pretty great mother, too. Ga-Ga, my precious, beloved grandmother, was loving, peaceful, patient, kind, and good. She nurtured me, made me feel safe, and taught me the Serenity Prayer when I was three years old. If Ga-Ga only knew how many times I've closed my eyes and silently recited it through the years.

Above all else, both my mom and my grandmother taught me the value of joy. They were born to be mothers, it seemed; they did it with such cheer and effortless aplomb. And though they had both been schoolteachers, in my mind it was motherhood that defined them both.

Still, when I met my strapping cowboy of a husband—with his rippling muscles and just-snug-enough Wrangler jeans—I think I probably wanted one child. *Maybe* one and a half. Either way, I never would have described myself as a woman who knew without question that her destiny was to one day be a mother. My womb just didn't leap like that.

But before I knew it, I had a baby of my own. And the most hilarious thing happened: *My mind was completely blown.* I fell in love instantly. I was so smitten with this new baby, in fact, that as I was nursing her in those first weeks, I'd actually jot down numeric lists outlining all the things I loved about her. They went something like this.

> 1. *Her teeny tiny ears.*
> 2. *Her precious bubblegum lips.*
> 3. *The milky scent of her face.*

Yep. Total goner. And then I had three more babies and did exactly the same thing.

But that's motherhood for you. It changes you into this brand-new version of yourself—one that makes lists about bubblegum lips and would kill a dragon with your bare hands if it dared take one step toward your child.

Whether she's changing diapers, slaying dragons, or just fighting the good, daily fight of motherhood, moms are to be celebrated! Appreciated! *Cherished.* That's what Mother's Day is all about.

Mother's Day is also for mother figures in our lives! Reach out to the mentors, teachers, role models, guardians, protectors—any woman who's devoted her life to caring for children. (Remember, Mother Teresa had no biological children of her own!)

BREAKFAST IN BED FOR MOM

Here's a special breakfast/brunch menu that's pretty and perfect for mamas of any age. Invite Mom over to your house for breakfast at the kitchen table; or, if you still live with your mother, treat her to breakfast in bed served on a pretty tray with a handwritten note. It'll make her heart happy.

Dads of younger children: You can spearhead this operation if you like! Make it a family affair . . . but be sure to let the kiddos take all the credit. (I promise Mom will know the truth!)

DO-AHEAD GAME PLAN

THE DAY BEFORE

- Bake the scones (and glaze them if you're making Lemon-Rosemary or Maple-Bacon Scones). When the icing is set, cover them with a light dish towel and set them aside. The icing will keep them nice and fresh overnight.
- Make the Coffee Granita. Store in the freezer.
- Sieve and combine the egg mixture and chop the salmon for the Salmon Scrambled Eggs.
- Make Mom a homemade Mother's Day card! (Hide it so she won't see it!)

THE DAY OF

- Prepare the rest of the meal!

OTHER RECIPES TO CONSIDER: Resolution Smoothies (page 3); Baked French Toast (page 8); Red Velvet Pancakes with Maple Buttermilk Icing (page 51); Huevo in the Heart (page 54); Chocolate-Covered Cherry Smoothie (page 56); Orange-Vanilla Fruit Salad (page 108)

COFFEE GRANITA

MAKES 8 SERVINGS

I refer to granitas as glorified slushies . . . and that's exactly what they are. Cold and icy and yes, sometimes brain freeze–inducing. But in a really good way. If brain freezes can ever be considered good.

Typically, the granitas I make have a refreshing, fruity base, but this coffee-and-cream version is a total delight. Imagine a coffee slushie . . . with a sweet cream slushie on top. What a treat!

If your mom loves coffee, she'll delight at this one. (Trust me. I have firsthand experience with this.)

2 cups half-and-half

1 vanilla bean

¾ cup sugar

4 cups good strong coffee

1. First, add the half-and-half to a small saucepan over medium heat . . .

2. Then scrape out the caviar from the vanilla bean . . .

3. And add it to the pan along with ½ cup of the sugar. Let the mixture simmer for 5 minutes.

4. Then pour it into a 9 x 13-inch or 8-inch square glass baking pan.

5. Set it on a level surface in the freezer.

6. Meanwhile, add the remaining ¼ cup sugar to the coffee and stir it to dissolve.

7. Pour the coffee into a 9 x 13-inch baking pan and place it on a level surface in the freezer.

8. About 1½ hours later, check the 2 dishes. The top of the cream layer should be starting to freeze, so take a fork and gently scrape it to create a little "shaved" ice on top. When the fork starts hitting the softer and more liquid center, stop and place the pan back in the freezer for another 45 minutes.

9. Do the same with the coffee dish: Scrape off the top, more frozen layer, then place it back into the freezer for another 45 minutes.

10. Continue scraping at intervals of 45 minutes to 1 hour, leaving the shaved granita on top when you return it to the freezer. When all the ice is scraped, cover the pan with plastic wrap and store in the fridge until serving.

11. To serve it up, fill a glass three-quarters full with the coffee granita . . .

12. Followed by the creamy ice.

PERFECT CREAM SCONES

MAKES 24 SCONES

I've loved scones for hundreds of thousands of years, because they're sweet enough to eat on their own (unlike regular biscuits) and are equally delicious slathered with softened butter and jelly. They're also yummy dunked into a hot mug o' coffee, cappuccino, or even hot chocolate. Just ask my children.

I use this basic cream scone recipe for any variety of scones I get a hankerin' for. Add dried fruit, nuts, even chocolate to the dough, and drizzle on whatever flavor of glaze you crave. They're nice and thin and moist . . . and turn out perfect every time.

3 cups all-purpose flour	**¼ teaspoon salt**	**1 cup heavy cream**
⅔ cup sugar	**1 cup (2 sticks) cold unsalted butter, cut into pieces**	**1 egg**
4 teaspoons baking powder		

1. Preheat the oven to 350°F.

2. Place the flour, sugar, baking powder, and salt into a sifter or fine-mesh strainer . . .

4. Throw the butter pieces into the bowl . . .

6. Measure the cream, then crack in the egg . . .

3. Then sift it into a large bowl until it's all combined.

5. And use a pastry cutter to cut the butter into the dry ingredients.

7. And whisk until combined.

8. Drizzle the cream mixture into the dry ingredients, stirring gently with a fork until the dough barely comes together.

9. Use your hands to press the dough into a ball.

10. On a lightly floured surface, press the dough into a rough rectangle shape . . .

11. Then roll it to about ⅓ inch thick. Use your hands to shape it as you go, keeping it in a nice rectangle shape.

12. Use a pizza cutter or knife to cut the rectangle into 12 smaller rectangles . . .

13. Then cut each rectangle in half to get 24 smaller triangles.

14. Transfer the scones to 2 baking sheets lined with baking mats or parchment paper . . .

15. And bake them for 18 minutes, or until just barely golden brown.

16. Serve them with your favorite jelly, jam, or marmalade and a big cup of coffee.

Variations

- *Use this basic method to make Lemon-Rosemary Scones (page 168) and Maple-Bacon Scones (page 171).*
- *Add chopped almonds, pecans, or walnuts to the dry ingredients for a nice crunch.*
- *Add chopped dried cherries, cranberries, or raisins.*
- *Add miniature chocolate chips.*

LEMON-ROSEMARY SCONES

MAKES 24 SCONES

This scone variation is beautiful and herbaceous . . . just like your mother. Minus the herbaceous part. I don't think people can be referred to as herbaceous. Even though I think they should be. Especially moms! They work so hard, after all.

Never mind.

These beauties are made wonderful with the flavors of fresh citrus and rosemary both inside and out. I totally dunk the scones in the glaze to coat them completely, and this also serves to seal in the freshness of the scones and keep them perfectly delicious for days.

I absolutely love these things.

3 cups all-purpose flour

⅔ cup sugar

4 teaspoons baking powder

¼ teaspoon salt

1 cup (2 sticks) cold unsalted butter, cut into pieces

1 cup heavy cream

1 egg

2 lemons

Leaves from 2 rosemary sprigs

5 cups powdered sugar, sifted

½ cup whole milk, more if needed for thinning

1. Preheat the oven to 350°F.

2. Prepare the recipe for Perfect Cream Scones through step 5 (page 166).

3. Measure the cream in a pitcher and crack in the egg.

4. Zest 1 of the lemons and add the zest to the cream.

5. Finely mince the rosemary leaves . . .

6. And add half of the rosemary to the pitcher.

7. Whisk the cream mixture, then drizzle it into the flour-butter mixture, stirring gently with a fork.

8. When the dough is combined, roll it out and cut it as shown on page 167. Bake the scones for 18 minutes or so, until just barely golden brown, then allow to cool completely.

9. While the scones are cooling, make the glaze: Combine the powdered sugar and milk in a large bowl . . .

10. Then add the juice of the lemon you zested.

11. Whisk the mixture together, then zest the second lemon and add the zest to the bowl.

12. Add the rest of the rosemary . . .

13. And whisk it until it's all combined.

15. Flip them over to coat . . .

17. Allow the glaze to set completely before serving.

NOTE: *The scones will last several days in an airtight container.*

Variations

• *Substitute orange zest and juice for the lemon.*

• *Substitute fresh thyme leaves for the rosemary.*

• *Add the caviar of 1 vanilla bean to the cream mixture and the caviar of 1 vanilla bean to the glaze for vanilla bean scones.*

14. When the scones are completely cooled, drop them one by one into the glaze . . .

16. Then remove them to a cooling rack placed over a baking sheet to allow the excess to drip off.

My mother-in-law, Nan. She's hilarious, helpful, strong . . . and more fun than a mother-in-law should be.

MAPLE-BACON SCONES

MAKES 24 SCONES

If your mom is a lover of bacon, which my children's mother most definitely is, these scones are pretty much the cat's meow. What my children's mother loves most about this sinful variation is that the scone, while lovely and all, really only serves as a vessel for the sweet maple icing and salty bacon, which—did you know this?—is a combination so delicious that it causes grown-ups to get tears in their eyes.

I've seen it happen before. It isn't pretty.

1 recipe Perfect Cream Scones, page 166

5 cups powdered sugar, sifted

½ cup whole milk, more if needed for thinning

2 tablespoons maple extract

¼ teaspoon salt

8 thin slices bacon, fried crisp and chopped

1. Prepare the Perfect Cream Scones and allow them to cool completely.

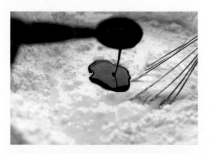

2. Make the maple glaze: Combine the powdered sugar, milk, maple extract, and salt.

3. Stir the mixture until it's smooth.

4. Drizzle 1 to 2 tablespoons maple glaze all over the cooled scones . . .

5. Then, before the glaze sets, sprinkle the tops with the chopped bacon.

Goodness gracious!

SALMON SCRAMBLED EGGS

MAKES 2 SERVINGS

I'm not the least bit picky about scrambled eggs. Nope, not me. Except I need for them to be soft but not too soft. I need for them to be salted but not too salted. I need for them to be whisked with just the precise amount of half-and-half, strained through a sieve to ensure absolute smoothness, and cooked with just the right amount of smoked salmon to add a natural saltiness without completely overpowering the eggs with salmon flavor.

See? I told you. Not picky at all.

Scrambled eggs are the perfect Mother's Day breakfast-in-bed, because kiddos can make them (with a little help from Dad or older sibs)—oh, and because most mamas just love them.

These are my favorite scrambled eggs on earth.

6 eggs

¼ cup half-and-half

¼ teaspoon salt

¼ teaspoon pepper

2 tablespoons butter

2 ounces smoked salmon

1 tablespoon finely chopped chives, for garnish

2. Use a spoon or ladle to force the eggs through.

4. And whisk gently to combine.

1. Crack the eggs into a fine-mesh strainer set over a bowl.

3. Add the half-and-half, salt, and pepper . . .

5. Melt the butter in a nonstick skillet over medium-low heat.

6. Pour the eggs into the skillet . . .

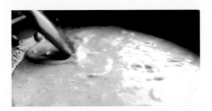

7. And as they cook, slowly and gently push the egg mixture around with a wooden spoon or rubber spatula.

8. Give the salmon a rough chop . . .

9. And when the eggs are halfway done . . .

10. Throw it into the skillet.

11. Stir the eggs around to cook them just a little more.

12. Sprinkle on the chives and serve the eggs while they're still soft and hot.

Variations

- *Add chopped shaved ham instead of the salmon.*
- *Add ¼ cup finely grated Swiss cheese to the eggs with the salmon or ham.*
- *Serve the eggs over a toasted bagel or English muffin.*

My mom was born to be a grandmother. Todd would definitely agree!

YOGURT, BROWN SUGAR, AND BERRY PARFAITS

MAKES 8 SERVINGS

Nothing looks prettier on a Mother's Day breakfast tray than this unbelievably, inconceivably, ridiculously, unapologetically scrumptious yogurt-and-berry piece of art.

And I would like to add that in no universe, as rich and decadent as it is, should this treat ever be considered breakfast. It has *dessert* stamped across its forehead plain as day!

But it's Mother's Day, you guys. She's totally worth it!

I apologize if that statement seems self-serving.

2 cups plain Greek yogurt
½ cup heavy cream
1 teaspoon vanilla extract
½ cup packed brown sugar
1 cup fresh blueberries
1 cup fresh raspberries

1. Add the yogurt to a medium bowl, then drizzle in the cream and vanilla.

2. Stir until the mixture is smooth.

3. Smooth out the surface into a flat layer . . .

4. Then sprinkle the brown sugar all over the top. Cover the bowl with plastic wrap . . .

5. And refrigerate it for 20 minutes, or until the brown sugar is halfway dissolved.

6. To build the parfait, layer the berries with the yogurt mixture into 8 small glasses or wine stems.

7. Be careful not to mix the yogurt too much; you want to see the streaks of brown sugar! Keep going with as many layers as you want.

Variation

Use any combination of fruit you'd like: blackberries, small melon chunks, kiwi dice, halved red or green grapes, and so on.

Oh, dear.

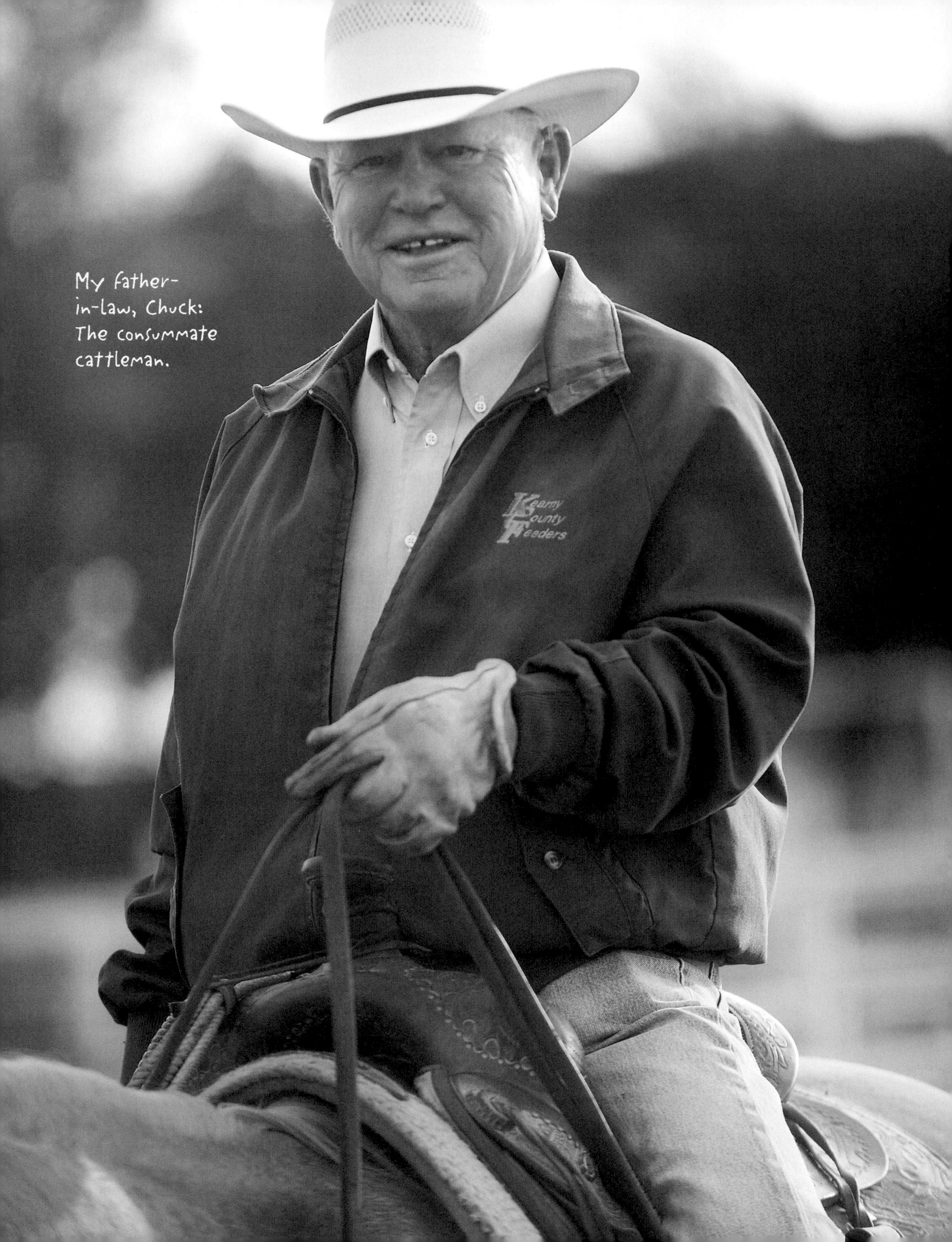

My father-
in-law, Chuck:
The consummate
cattleman.

FATHER'S DAY

My father-in-law, Chuck, has been ranching his whole life. He was born on a horse (not literally, thank goodness for his dear mother, Ruth) and has seen his share of both triumphs and tragedies in his seventy-plus years. He is happiest on his horse Old Yeller, where he surveys the ranch he put together and proudly looks on as his two sons teach his grandchildren the ins and outs of cattle ranching.

My own dad is a physician, and was away in Vietnam serving as a surgeon in an evacuation hospital for the first year of my life. His quiet, reserved nature has always been tempered by a dry, playful sense of humor that often only surfaces when he's around my sister and me. He's worked hard his whole adult life, spending his spare time pursuing passions for golf, ballroom dancing, then back to golf again.

On paper, Chuck and my dad couldn't be more different, whether in their choice of careers, their wardrobes (I'm not sure my dad owns a pair of jeans), or how they spend their days. But every day I realize more and more how strikingly similar their approaches to fatherhood are . . . and I understand more and more why I love them both so dearly.

The thread they share is self-sacrifice. They would do anything for their children. Absolutely anything. Take a bullet. Stand in front of a locomotive. Go hungry, give up all possessions, lose everything if it meant their children would have freedom and safety and choices in life.

They love their children, yes. But their primary role has always been Guardian. Protector. Provider. Defender. And through the years, I've watched as my own husband has fallen into the same role with our kids. It's a nice feeling, being surrounded by strong male figures in such a tangible way.

I love Father's Day because it gives us a chance to put our dads in the spotlight—a place they'd normally not choose to be. It's a day for us to say "We couldn't do it without you, Dad."

Because we couldn't.

My dad, Bill, at the 71st Evac Hospital in Pleiku, Vietnam, in 1969 . . . the year I was born.

DINNER FOR DEAR OL' DAD

"The way to a man's heart is through his stomach."

This is one of the deepest, most steadfast truths in the universe.

All the dads in my life—my own dad, my father-in-law, and my husband—love hearty, satisfying Italian food. Here's one of my favorite menus to serve them on Father's Day. Guaranteed to make any dad feel loved!

TOASTED RAVIOLI ☙

MAKES 24 RAVIOLI

Toasted ravioli is a St. Louis specialty; my husband and I first tried it when we visited St. Louis to attend my brother-in-law's wife's brother's wedding. At least I think that's whose wedding it was. It might have been my brother's wife's brother-in-law's wedding. Or it might have been my wife's brother-in-law's brother's wedding.

Don't pay any attention to me. I'll figure it out eventually.

Anyway, toasted ravioli, despite its moniker, is actually *fried* ravioli, and while it seems like it would be a complicated munchie to make, it really couldn't be easier. It's the perfect predinner bite for any Italian(ish) menu, and both my husband and my dad just love it.

Warning: Toasted ravioli are exceedingly addictive! Enter at your own risk.

4 cups vegetable or canola oil

6 eggs

½ cup half-and-half

2 cups all-purpose flour

2 cups seasoned breadcrumbs

12 frozen beef ravioli

12 frozen cheese ravioli

2 cups jarred marinara sauce, heated

¼ cup shredded Parmesan cheese

1 tablespoon minced fresh parsley

1. First, heat the oil in a medium pot over medium-high heat. Bring the temperature to 400°F. (The temperature will go down when the frozen ravioli are dropped in.)

2. Whisk together the eggs and half-and-half in a dish.

3. Next, place the flour in a separate shallow dish.

4. Then pour the breadcrumbs into a third dish. Dish, dish, dish!

5. Grab the ravioli (they should be frozen solid, not thawed) . . .

6. And one at a time, drop them into the egg mixture . . .

7. Then quickly dredge them in the flour.

8. Dunk them once again in the egg mixture . . .

9. Then coat them in the breadcrumbs.

10. Set aside on a plate . . .

11. Then repeat until they're all coated.

12. Three or four at a time, drop the breaded ravioli into the oil and fry them for 1½ to 2 minutes, until the surface is golden brown and the filling is hot. They brown pretty quickly, so stand watch the whole time!

13. Remove them with a spatula . . .

14. And drain them on a paper towel. The filling will continue to warm as they sit.

15. Transfer the ravioli to a serving platter with the marinara sauce, then sprinkle on the Parmesan and the parsley.

Dig in immediately!

NOTE: *The ravioli may be breaded, then transferred immediately to the freezer. Flash-freeze the breaded ravioli on a sheet pan for 30 minutes to set the breading, then transfer them to a plastic freezer bag for storing. When you're ready to fry them, just remove them from the freezer and begin with step 12.*

ARNOLD PALMERS

MAKES 8 TO 12 DRINKS

I always think of my dad whenever I think of Arnold Palmer, because my dad has been a lifelong golf enthusiast and I used to cut up his issues of *Golf Magazine* whenever I got a hankering to make a collage.

Do kids still make collages? I swear I made one at least once a week growing up. I guess I felt the need to express myself through the mediums of magazine photos and glue.

Anyway, Arnold Palmer, the man, was pretty much drilled into my head from a young age. So when I first heard of Arnold Palmers, the refreshing summer drink, I immediately assigned them to the category of Drinks My Dad Would Love.

Plus, they just seem a heckuva lot more manly than Shirley Temples.

LEMON ICE CUBES	ICED TEA CONCENTRATE	8 cups lemonade (store-bought is fine, or see the recipe on page 198)
1 cup fresh lemon juice	**4 family-size iced tea bags**	
½ cup sugar	**2 cups sugar**	
1 lemon		

1. To make the lemon ice cubes, pour the lemon juice into a small saucepan . . .

3. And the sugar. Stir the mixture and heat it over medium-low heat until the sugar is dissolved. Turn off the heat and let the liquid cool. Transfer the liquid into a pitcher.

5. And fill each well with the lemon syrup.

2. Along with 1 cup of water . . .

4. Cut the lemon into 6 slices, then cut each one in quarters. Place the wedges into two ice cube trays . . .

6. Freeze them until solid, at least 6 hours. Turn the ice cubes out of the trays, then store them in an airtight container in the freezer until you need them.

7. In the meantime, make the tea concentrate by dropping the tea bags into a pot containing 1 gallon of water.

8. Add the sugar . . .

9. Then turn the heat to low and let it steep for 25 to 30 minutes.

10. Turn off the heat and let the mixture cool . . .

11. Then transfer it to a pitcher and store it in the fridge until you need it. (Discard the tea bags.)

12. To make the Arnold Palmers, fill a large glass to the brim with ice. Fill it halfway with the tea concentrate . . .

13. Then fill the other half with lemonade.

14. Place 2 or 3 lemon ice cubes on top . . .

15. And serve it to dear ol' dad!

Variations

- *Add a shot of whiskey, dark rum, or tequila to each Arnold Palmer for a grown-up beverage.*

- *To save time, the lemon ice cubes may be omitted. Just throw a couple of lemon wedges on top of each glass instead!*

THREE-MEAT LASAGNA

MAKES 12 SERVINGS

Both my orthopedic surgeon pop and my cattle rancher father-in-law love a great big meaty lasagna (what carnivorous dude doesn't?), and this one pretty much takes the cake. It has a mega layer of a luscious ricotta mixture right smack dab in the middle, and the meaty sauce is made even richer and more delicious by adding big chunks of pepperoni. It's like eating a little slice of lasagna, pizza, and heaven all at the same time.

Beneficiaries of this lasagna will *not* go hungry!

2 tablespoons olive oil

1 large onion, diced

3 garlic cloves, minced

2 pounds ground beef

1 pound country/breakfast sausage

12 ounces pepperoni

One 28-ounce can whole tomatoes

One 12-ounce can tomato paste

¼ cup pesto, jarred or fresh

⅓ cup finely minced parsley

2 teaspoons salt

½ teaspoon red pepper flakes

1 teaspoon black pepper

30 ounces whole milk ricotta cheese

2 eggs

1 cup shredded Parmesan cheese

24 ounces fresh mozzarella cheese

12 lasagna noodles, cooked al dente

½ cup grated Parmesan cheese

1. Drizzle the olive oil into a large pot over medium-high heat . . .

3. Stir the meat around, breaking it up as it begins to cook. Cook the meat until brown, stirring occasionally.

5. Then throw them into the pot with the browned meat.

2. Then add the onion, garlic, ground beef, and sausage.

4. Cut the pepperoni into slices and the slices into quarters . . .

6. Continue cooking the meat mixture for another 3 minutes . . .

7. Then drain off the excess grease.

8. Add the tomatoes and tomato paste and stir them in completely.

9. Next, add the pesto . . .

10. Half the parsley . . .

11. One teaspoon of the salt, the red pepper flakes, and ½ teaspoon of the black pepper.

12. Stir, reduce the heat to low, and simmer for 25 to 30 minutes.

13. Meanwhile, make the cheese mixture: combine the ricotta and eggs in a large bowl.

14. Add the shredded Parmesan . . .

15. The rest of the parsley . . .

16. And the remaining 1 teaspoon salt and ½ teaspoon pepper.

17. Stir the mixture until totally combined, then set it aside.

18. Finally, cut the mozzarella into thin slices.

19. Preheat the oven to 350°F.

20. To assemble the lasagna, overlap 4 lasagna noodles in the bottom of a large rectangular baking dish.

21. Spoon two-thirds of the sauce over the noodles . . .

22. And smooth it out into a flat layer.

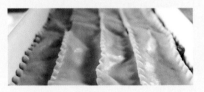

23. Lay on 4 more lasagna noodles . . .

24. Then spoon in all of the ricotta mixture . . .

25. And smooth it into a flat layer.

26. Lay the slices of mozzarella all over the ricotta layer . . .

27. Then add a final layer of noodles . . .

28. And the rest of the sauce.

29. Top it with the grated Parmesan.

30. Cover the lasagna with aluminum foil and bake it for 30 minutes, then remove the foil and bake it for 15 minutes or until hot and bubbly.

31. Remove the lasagna from the oven and let it sit for 10 to 15 minutes, then cut it into large squares.

32. Serve it with Caesar Salad (page 187).

Dad's gonna love it!

NOTES

• *Lasagna can be made up to 2 days ahead of time and stored in the fridge, unbaked.*

• *Lasagna can be frozen unbaked. Just thaw before you're ready to bake it.*

Variation

If you can't find sticks of pepperoni, just use the widely available pepperoni slices. Either cut them in half or throw them in whole!

CAESAR SALAD

MAKES 8 TO 12 SERVINGS

Few things go with a big honkin' piece of lasagna better than a big honkin' helping of this Caesar salad. My best friend, Hyacinth, and I perfected this dressing years and years ago, and we've been high-fiving each other, patting each other on the back, and crowning each other the Queen of Caesar Salad Land ever since. It's everything that's wonderful about Caesar salad dressing . . . but with a tad more wonderfulness added!

I like to make huge, crisp homemade croutons to throw into the salad for two reasons: One, I'll jump at any opportunity to eat bread. I think that's been well established. Two, having big croutons in the salad helps alleviate the temptation to make a big loaf of garlic cheese bread to go with the meal. So really, when you think about it, this salad facilitates healthy choices.

Let's go ahead and forget I ever said that, okay?

CROUTONS

½ cup (1 stick) butter, melted

½ cup olive oil

1 loaf French bread

1 tablespoon Italian seasoning

1 tablespoon kosher salt

1 tablespoon black pepper

2 teaspoons red pepper flakes

DRESSING

½ cup olive oil

2 garlic cloves, minced

4 whole anchovy fillets

2 tablespoons Dijon mustard

1 tablespoon balsamic or red wine vinegar (balsamic makes it nice and rich)

1 teaspoon Worcestershire sauce

Juice of ½ lemon

Dash of salt

Freshly ground black pepper

¼ cup freshly shredded Parmesan cheese

SALAD

2 Romaine lettuce heads

½ cup Parmesan shavings

1. First, make the croutons. Preheat the oven to 250°F. In a small saucepan over low heat, melt the butter in the olive oil.

2. Cut the bread into 1- to 1½-inch cubes, then throw them into a large bowl.

3. Drizzle in the butter/oil mixture . . .

4. And toss them until they're all coated.

5. Stir together the Italian seasoning, kosher salt, black pepper, and red pepper flakes . . .

6. And sprinkle the mixture all over the bread cubes.

7. Toss the bread around to coat . . .

8. Spread it out in a single layer on a baking sheet . . .

9. And bake for 45 minutes, tossing twice, until the croutons are crisp with just a small amount of chewiness. Set them aside to cool completely.

10. To make the Caesar dressing, add the olive oil and garlic to a blender.

11. Add the anchovies. Don't be grossed out! You won't even know they're there.

12. Next, add the Dijon, vinegar, Worcestershire, lemon juice, salt, and pepper.

13. Blend the dressing until totally smooth . . .

14. Then add the Parmesan and blend until smooth again.

15. Cut the lettuce into bite-size pieces and throw it into a large bowl.

16. Drizzle in three-quarters of the dressing, then toss it around.

18. Toss in the croutons (along with all the crispy bits from the baking pan).

17. Sprinkle on the Parmesan shavings, then toss it again.

19. Taste the salad to check the dressing amount; if you think it needs more, add it and toss the salad.

Best Caesar salad this side of the Rocky Mountains!

Part of fatherhood is teaching your children to take the reins.

There's nothin' more beautiful than a cowboy with a baby on his hip.

CHOCOLATE STRAWBERRY CAKE

MAKES 12 SERVINGS

My dad's weakness has always, *always* been chocolate. Always.

And I do mean always.

My husband's weakness has always, *always* been chocolate, steak, ice cream, mashed potatoes, and pie.

So what I'm saying is, chocolate is the common denominator.

And oh, boy. *This cake.* I made it on a whim once when I didn't have enough cream to make both the whipped cream layer and the ganache, which was my original plan for the chocolate layer. So in desperation, I reached for the half-eaten tub of Nutella I'd hidden on the top shelf of our pantry to keep my kids from finding it and wound up using it for the chocolate "icing."

I probably don't need to describe the bliss that ensued.

CAKE

1 cup (2 sticks) butter

4 heaping tablespoons unsweetened cocoa powder

2 cups all-purpose flour

2 cups sugar

¼ teaspoon salt

½ cup buttermilk (store-bought, or see page 21)

2 eggs

1 teaspoon vanilla extract

1 teaspoon baking soda

Nonstick baking spray

TOPPING

2 pints strawberries

¼ cup sugar

1 teaspoon vanilla extract

1 pint heavy whipping cream

½ cup powdered sugar

1½ cups chocolate-hazelnut spread (such as Nutella)

1. Preheat the oven to 350°F.

2. Melt the butter in a saucepan over medium heat.

3. Add the cocoa powder . . .

4. And stir until smooth.

5. Add 1 cup of boiling water.

6. Let it bubble up for 30 seconds or so, then remove the pan from the heat.

7. In a large bowl, combine the flour, sugar, and salt.

8. Pour in the chocolate mixture and stir it until it's about halfway combined.

9. In a separate bowl, combine the buttermilk, eggs, vanilla, and baking soda and stir until smooth . . .

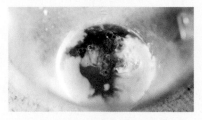

10. Then add the buttermilk mixture to the chocolate-flour mixture and stir until smooth.

11. Line two 9-inch round cake pans with parchment paper, then spray the parchment with nonstick baking spray.

12. Pour the batter evenly into the pans . . .

13. And bake 18 to 20 minutes, until no longer jiggly in the center. Remove them from the oven and let them cool for 15 minutes . . .

14. Then turn the cake layers out of the pans, carefully peel off the parchment, and set them aside to cool completely.

15. Meanwhile, prepare the toppings: Hull and slice the strawberries . . .

16. Then sprinkle on the sugar.

17. Add the vanilla . . .

18. And stir them around.

19. Let them sit and macerate for 15 minutes, then drain off the excess juices.

20. Whip the heavy cream with the powdered sugar until stiff. Now it's time to assemble the cake!

21. Place 1 cake layer upside down on a cake stand so that the top will be perfectly flat. Grab ¾ cup of Nutella . . .

22. And spread it on top.

23. Spread half the whipped cream over the top . . .

24. Then top with half the strawberries.

25. Place the other cake layer upside down on top of the berries . . .

26. And add the rest of the Nutella, whipped cream, and berries.

27. Use a serrated knife to cut slices and serve 'em up!

NOTE: *Assemble the cake no more than 2 hours before serving. Keep refrigerated.*

Variations

• *Halve all the quantities to make a 1-layer cake if you'd like something a little smaller.*

• *Double all the quantities to make a 4-layer cake if you'd like to make a big impression! (Just use five long skewers to secure the layers. I speak from experience here.)*

• *Substitute blueberries, blackberries, or raspberries (or a combination thereof) for the strawberries.*

Boom!

FOURTH OF JULY

Fourth of July is a total blast around our house.

I mean that quite literally!

(But I'll get back to that in a minute.)

Fourth of July is *our* holiday. We celebrate it every year with a big cookout at our house, and it's become a community tradition. Ladd and I started the whole thing over ten years ago when we invited a few people over to celebrate. We grilled and set out basic sides, our guests brought a few extras, and we had a wonderful time.

The next year we did it again, and a few more people showed up.

The next year, a few more people showed up.

The year after that, when the pastor asked if anyone had announcements during church the Sunday before the Fourth, I inexplicably raised my hand and invited the whole darn church over. I seriously don't know what came over me. It must have been the Holy Spirit. In any event, the entire church showed up on the Fourth, along with everyone else who'd ever shown up, along with some of their friends and family. At the end of the night, there wasn't a speck of food left. There wasn't a drop of lemonade. And it was one of the best nights ever.

To this day, the tradition continues, and we look forward to it every year. We never know how many people will show up, or what food anyone's going to bring, and that's part of the fun.

And then . . . there are the fireworks.

Basically, here's how it all plays out: My husband and his brother spend the week of July 4th driving around to area fireworks stands, completely cleaning them out of whichever of their fireworks selection are the biggest and baddest. They haul them home in horse trailers. The whole thing is just obscene, and I love every minute of it because it results in a fireworks show the likes of which no mortal has ever witnessed in person before.

I remind my husband every year (in vain, it turns out) that it might be nice to have a regular fireworks show, culminating in a great, explosive finale. This is how *normal, reasonable* people conduct their fireworks shows, I tell him. There's a little bit of a trickle, a boom, and a bang, then there's the finale. But my husband and brother-in-law prefer to have a 30- to 40-minute finale. Period. There's no easing everyone in. There's no teasing the crowd. It's just an all-in, testosterone-fueled igniting of the Oklahoma skies.

It really gets the patriotic juices flowing.

Food is a huge component of our Fourth of July gathering, and my approach has always been to make a good base of summer picnic staples, then let guests bring covered dishes as they see fit. Part of the fun and spontaneity of the event is that I never know who's bringing what, and I wouldn't even consider trying to orchestrate it. One year I wound up with seventeen desserts and two side dishes. Another year, we had four pans of barbecued ribs and no salads. Every year is an adventure!

Amazingly, while our Fourth of July feast is never the same two years in a row, it's always delicious and we always seem to have enough. It's like an Independence Day version of the loaves and fishes miracle! I love how beautifully organic the menu is. Everyone pitches in.

Here are some of my very favorite Fourth of July favorites, from homemade lemonade to the best strawberry ice cream in six states.

This menu will suit any summertime get-together, whether it's Independence Day, Memorial Day, Labor Day . . .

Or any day!

Happy Fourth, my friends!

OTHER RECIPES TO CONSIDER: Blackberry Margaritas (page 128); Grilled Corn Dip (page 34); Eight-Layer Dip (page 42); Glorious Guacamole (page 136); Dr Pepper Cupcakes (page 45); Caramel Apple Pie (page 279)

- Squeeze the lemon juice and make the syrup for the Homemade Lemonade.

- Make the caramelized onions and sautéed mushrooms for the Big Bad Burger Bar. Store in the fridge, then heat in the microwave just before serving.

- Make the butter mixture for the Grilled Corn with Spicy Butter.

- Dice the onions and peppers for the Baked Beans.

- Make the hard-boiled eggs for Perfect Potato Salad.

- Cook the pasta for My Favorite Pasta Salad. Drain and rinse with cold water, then toss with 2 tablespoons olive oil. Store in a large plastic storage bag in the fridge.

- Make the dressing and dice the cheese for My Favorite Pasta Salad.

- Make the Key Lime Pie.

- Make the Strawberry Ice Cream.

- Make the Watermelon Sangria. (Do not add sparkling wine until just before serving.)

- Make the meat mixture and form burger patties for Big Bad Burger Bar. Place in two layers between waxed paper on a baking sheet, then cover with aluminum foil, and keep in the fridge until grilling.

- Make the Perfect Potato Salad.

- Assemble My Favorite Pasta Salad.

- Make the Peach Cobbler.

HOMEMADE LEMONADE

MAKES 18 TO 20 SERVINGS

Making a big batch of lemonade on the Fourth of July is such a tradition for me, I'd feel seriously lost if something happened to the worldwide lemon crop one year and I wasn't able to make it. No mix or frozen concentrate can possibly impart the same fresh lemony flavor as the real stuff; plus, when you make your own, you can control the level of sweetness to suit your tastes.

And another plus: Your hands will smell like lemons for a week! *Mmmmm.*

4 cups sugar

2 dozen lemons

1. A few hours in advance, make a sugar syrup by combining 6 cups of water . . .

2. With the sugar in a large saucepan.

3. Heat it over medium heat until the sugar dissolves. Set the syrup aside and let it cool, or store it in the fridge, covered, until you're ready to make the lemonade.

4. Juice all the lemons into a pitcher . . .

5. Then pour the juice through a fine-mesh strainer to strain out all the pulp.

6. Pour the juice into a serving vat or tub . . .

7. Then pour in three-fourths of the syrup. Set the remaining syrup aside.

8. Just before serving the lemonade, fill the vat with ice . . .

9. Then pour in 8 cups of cold water.

10. Stir until the juice and water are well combined.

11. Give it a taste. If it seems overly tart, add the rest of the sugar syrup. If it seems too strong overall, add another 2 cups of water.

When it's totally perfect, serve it up!

NOTE: *Both the sugar syrup and the lemon juice can be prepared the day before, then stored in the fridge.*

Variations

- *Slice 3 lemons thinly and float the slices on top of the vat of lemonade.*

- *Do not strain the lemon juice if you want a more textured, tarter lemonade.*

- *Add 2 cups raspberries, blueberries, blackberries, or sliced strawberries to the lemonade for different flavors and some festive color.*

- *Make hard lemonade by adding 2 to 3 cups light rum or tequila. (Adults only!)*

- *Substitute lime juice for half the lemon juice for a lemon-limeade.*

WATERMELON SANGRIA

MAKES 18 TO 20 SERVINGS

Making sangria is a delicious part of my Fourth of July ritual, and any combination of wine and fruit will do just fine. While I love the versions that use mixed fruit (peaches, apples, oranges, grapes, and so on) and white wine, this preciously pink watermelon version is so cute and summery, it should be illegal. It's almost too adorable to eat. I mean drink. I mean *both*! (The little watermelon chunks, once soaked with wine, are delightfully naughty.)

In the good ol' summertime, I tend to like things light and fizzy, so pouring in a bottle of cold sparkling wine just before serving the sangria gives it a little extra personality and sends it way over the top.

I seriously can't be trusted around this stuff.

1 medium seedless watermelon

Six 750 ml bottles rosé wine, chilled

One 750 ml bottle sparkling wine, Champagne, or moscato, chilled

1. Several hours before serving, slice off a 2-inch-thick slice of rind.

2. Cut the rind into 2-inch strips . . .

3. And cut the strips in the other direction to make large chunks.

4. The rind should have a nice bit of color attached! That's what makes the sangria *¡muy bonita!*

5. Repeat with the rest of the rind . . .

6. And add the chunks to a large vat or tub.

7. Pour in the rosé wine, saving the sparkling wine for later.

10. Just before serving, pour in the sparkling wine and stir it gently.

Serve it to sangria-loving guests!

Variation

If you prefer a sweeter sangria, dissolve 1 cup of sugar in 2 cups of cold water and stir it into the mixture when you first combine the wine and fruit.

8. Glug glug glug!

9. Place the vat into the fridge and chill it for at least 6 hours to let the fruit soak up the wine and the watermelon flavor to permeate the wine.

"You woke me up way too early this morning."

BIG BAD BURGER BAR

MAKES 18 TO 24 SERVINGS

On some Fourth of Julys, the husband of my youth and I splurge and cook rib-eye steaks for everyone in attendance. They're delicious, crowd-pleasing, and steaky and all, but between all the side dishes I wind up making, not to mention all the scrumptious potluck dishes our friends wind up bringing, we often wonder the next day why we hadn't just stuck with good ol' reliable burgers.

These are the best burgers ever, not just because of the rich, flavorful meat mixture, but because of the fun bar of fixins that accompany them. And when it comes to building my burger, I go absolutely nuts: It isn't unusual for me to wind up with a thicker layer of fixins than the burger patty itself. I add a little bit of everything . . . a hundred times over.

Part of the fun of a burger bar is watching your guests build away. I've never seen two burgers exactly alike!

MEAT MIXTURE

5 pounds 80/20 ground beef (ask your butcher)

½ cup heavy cream

3 tablespoons Worcestershire sauce

Several dashes of hot sauce (such as Tabasco)

1 tablespoon salt

1 tablespoon black pepper

CARAMELIZED ONIONS

2 large yellow onions, peeled and sliced

4 tablespoons (½ stick) butter

SAUTÉED MUSHROOMS

16 ounces white mushrooms, sliced

4 tablespoons (½ stick) butter

OTHER FIXINS

Arugula

Bacon, sliced in half and fried till crisp

Tomato slices

Crumbled blue and feta cheese

Sliced Cheddar, Swiss, or pepper Jack cheese

Sliced red onions

Lettuce

Pickle slices

Avocado slices

18 to 24 burger buns

Hot dogs

Hot dog rolls

1. In a very large bowl, combine the ground beef and the cream.

2. Add the Worcestershire sauce . . .

3. The hot sauce . . .

4. And the salt and pepper.

5. Use your (very clean!) hands to mix it all together.

6. Form the mixture into ¼- to ⅓-pound patties . . .

7. Then layer them on baking sheets lined with parchment paper and store them in the fridge until you're ready to grill.

8. To make the caramelized onions, combine the onions and butter in a large skillet over medium heat.

9. Cook the onions, stirring occasionally, for 15 to 20 minutes, until they're golden brown.

10. Transfer them to a serving bowl for the fixins bar.

11. To make the sautéed mushrooms, add the sliced mushrooms and butter to the same skillet over medium heat . . .

12. Sauté them for 15 to 20 minutes, until dark brown and tender. Transfer them to a bowl and place them with the other fixins!

13. Then prepare all the other fixins: the arugula . . .

14. The bacon . . .

15. The tomatoes . . .

16. The blue cheese and feta . . .

17. The other cheeses, onions, lettuce, and pickles . . . and, well, any other ol' fixing you like!

18. Lay out the avocados at the very last minute. Squeeze a litle lemon or lime juice over them to avoid browning.

19. Fire up the grill and cook the burgers over medium-hot coals.

20. Flip them after they've cooked for 4 minutes, then cook them on the other side for 3 to 4 minutes, or until no longer pink in the middle.

21. (Psst. Grill up some hot dogs, too! The kiddos love 'em.)

22. Serve the burgers with the buns and all the fixins . . .

23. And let the guests build to their hearts' content!

There's nothing like a big, juicy burger before you watch the skies light up. Delicious!

NOTES

- The meat mixture quantities can easily be halved to serve fewer people.

- The hamburger patties can be made early in the day or the night before. Just keep them in the fridge until they're grilled!

- For a different burger flavor, substitute ground pork sausage for half the ground beef.

Variations

Other fixing ideas: Sliced brie, fresh mozzarella, basil leaves, Straight-Up Pico de Gallo (page 131), Glorious Guacamole (page 136), barbecue sauce, jarred sliced jalapeños, pickle relish

freedom is beautiful.

GRILLED CORN WITH SPICY BUTTER

MAKES 18 SERVINGS

We have a good family friend in Indiana (hi, Dave!) who keeps us supplied with the most succulent, delicious Indiana corn in the summertime. I always cross my fingers that he decides to visit our ranch before, and not after, the Fourth of July so I can share the bounty with our Independence Day guests.

Grilling corn couldn't be easier—it just requires a little advance prep—and the presentation is always dramatic and glorious. Just like the fireworks later in the evening!

18 ears of corn, still in the husks

1 cup (2 sticks) salted butter, softened

3 tablespoons Montreal seasoning (or seasoning mix of your choice)

¼ teaspoon cayenne pepper

1. Submerge the corn in cool water in a large pot.

2. Put the lid on the pot and soak the corn for at least 3 to 4 hours, or until the husks are totally saturated.

3. When you're ready to grill the corn, pour off the water . . .

4. And place the corn on the grill. Grill for 15 to 18 minutes, turning with tongs once or twice, until the husks are charred and the corn inside is hot.

5. To make the spicy butter, combine the butter with the Montreal seasoning and cayenne . . .

6. And stir it until it's all combined.

7. Peel the husks away from the corn, leaving them attached at the bottom. (Guests can remove and toss the corn silk.) Or you can remove the husk and silk before serving, if you prefer.

8. Smear half the butter all over the corn . . .

9. Then serve the rest on the side.

Watch it disappear!

BAKED BEANS

MAKES 18 SERVINGS

A big, whopping pan of slow-cooked, slightly caramelized baked beans is an absolute requirement of any Fourth of July spread, and this version is everything I've ever wanted in a dish of baked beans, and more!

Best part is, they're a cinch! The only thing you have to worry about is allowing plenty of time for them to sit in the oven and work their magic. You want 'em dark, rich, thick, and irresistible!

12 slices bacon

1 large onion, diced

1 red bell pepper, diced

1 green bell pepper, diced

1 yellow bell pepper, diced

1 orange bell pepper, diced

Four 28-ounce cans pork-and-beans, drained

½ cup barbecue sauce

1 cup packed brown sugar

¼ cup apple cider vinegar

½ teaspoon red pepper flakes, more to taste

2 tablespoons yellow mustard

1. Preheat the oven to 325°F.

2. Cut 6 slices of the bacon into small pieces. In a large pot over medium-high heat, cook the bacon pieces with the onion for 3 to 4 minutes, until the onion is translucent.

3. Add the bell peppers . . .

4. And stir them around to start cooking, about 2 minutes.

5. Add the beans . . .

6. And stir them around to combine.

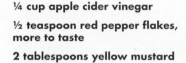

7. Add the barbecue sauce . . .

8. The brown sugar . . .

9. The vinegar . . .

10. The red pepper flakes . . .

11. And the mustard.

12. Stir and cook the mixture until totally hot and bubbly, then pour it into a large baking dish.

13. Lay the remaining bacon slices over the top . . .

14. Then bake the beans for 2 hours, until they're bubbly and thick.

15. Serve them to a (very) hungry crowd.

NOTES

· The beans can be made through step 13, then stored in the fridge up to 24 hours. Just bake them when you get closer to party time.

· The beans can be taken out of the oven up to 2 hours before serving. They're delicious when they're slightly warm.

The morning after our wild fireworks show. Does anyone have a broom I can borrow?

PERFECT POTATO SALAD

MAKES 12 TO 18 SERVINGS

There are as many potato salad recipes in the world as there are grains of sand in all the beaches in the world.

Okay, so maybe that's a tiny exaggeration. But there *are* a lot of different versions of potato salad. There are potato salads made with red potatoes, russet potatoes, or sweet potatoes. There are potato salads with a mustard base, a mayonnaise base, or an oil-and-vinegar base. There are potato salads with herbs, onions, water chestnuts, and bacon. The list goes on and on. And on and on and on!

This is potato salad the way I like it: Very smooth and creamy, with none of those annoying potato chunks to worry about, and with lots of crunch, flavor, and pizzazz. It's *ta die fer*, and the more it mixes with the beans and other stuff on your plate, the better!

8 medium russet potatoes,
scrubbed clean and cut into chunks

1½ cups mayonnaise

¼ cup yellow or Dijon mustard

5 green onions, white and light
green parts, sliced

1 teaspoon salt, more to taste

½ teaspoon black pepper

½ teaspoon paprika

10 small sweet or dill pickles

6 hard-boiled eggs
(see page 116), peeled

2 tablespoons pickle juice

1. Place the potatoes in a large pot of water. Bring them to a boil over high heat and cook them until fork-tender, about 25 minutes.

2. Drain the potatoes and process them through a food mill or potato ricer into a large bowl. Or if you prefer, simply mash the potatoes in a large bowl until mostly smooth.

3. Add the mayonnaise to the potatoes . . .

4. Along with the mustard . . .

5. The green onions, salt, and pepper . . .

6. And the paprika.

7. Slice the pickles . . .

8. And the hard-boiled eggs . . .

9. And add them to the bowl. (Reserve 1 sliced pickle and 1 sliced hard-boiled egg for garnish.)

10. Add the pickle juice . . .

11. Then stir it all together. Taste and adjust the seasonings, adding whatever the potato salad needs. I usually doctor it a couple of times before I decide it's finally perfect!

12. Transfer it to a serving bowl and garnish it with extra sliced eggs and pickles.

NOTE: *Potato salad can be made the day before serving and stored, covered, in the fridge.*

Variations

Stir in any of the following add-ons:

- *Sliced pimentos*
- *Chopped black or green olives*
- *Finely diced red onion*
- *1 tablespoon minced fresh dill*
- *2 tablespoons minced fresh parsley*
- *¼ teaspoon cayenne pepper, for heat*

J.B., Ladd's uncle. He comes to our celebration every year!

MY FAVORITE PASTA SALAD

MAKES 12 TO 18 SERVINGS

I am a lover, connoisseur, best buddy, constant companion, and loyal homegirl of pasta salad, and this is *absitively, posolutely* the best pasta salad in the world. The dressing is light and creamy, and the combination of tomatoes, basil, and—wait for it, my friends—smoked Gouda cheese seriously wins the prize. It's a nice, fresh complement to the burger and baked bean bonanza, and it gets better and better with each bite.

I used the letter *b* seven times in the preceding sentence. I just wanted you to know that.

16 ounces penne, mostaccioli, radiatore, or rotini

½ cup mayonnaise

¼ cup whole milk

2 to 3 tablespoons white vinegar

2 to 3 teaspoons adobo sauce (from canned chipotle peppers)

½ teaspoon salt, more to taste

Black pepper

3 cups red and/or yellow grape or cherry tomatoes, halved

1 pound smoked Gouda cheese

24 basil leaves, shredded

1. Cook the pasta according to the package directions. Drain it, rinse it with cool water, and set it aside in a large bowl.

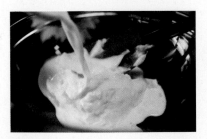

2. Combine the mayonnaise and milk in a medium bowl . . .

3. Then add 2 tablespoons of the vinegar and stir until smooth.

4. Add 2 tablespoons of the adobo sauce . . .

5. And the salt and pepper.

6. Stir the dressing until combined. Give it a taste and add more vinegar if you'd like it to have a little bite. Add more adobo sauce if you'd like it to have a little more heat.

7. Drizzle the dressing over the pasta.

8. Throw in the tomatoes . . .

9. Then cut the cheese into cubes . . .

10. And throw it into the bowl.

11. Stir the pasta salad around . . .

12. Then throw in the basil . . .

13. And stir it until it's all combined. Taste and adjust the seasonings as needed, then cover the bowl with plastic wrap and chill it in the fridge for at least 2 hours.

Totally glorious!

NOTE: *The pasta salad can be made earlier in the day and chilled.*

Variations

· *Substitute cubed mozzarella for the smoked Gouda.*

· *Add 2 diced cucumbers to the salad for a little crunch.*

My father-in-law loves the Fourth.

KEY LIME PIE

MAKES 8 TO 10 SERVINGS

Key lime pie purists: Please avert your eyes.

Everyone else: Please enjoy this yummy Key lime pie, which uses regular limes instead of Key limes! Because that's all I have available in my small town! And I don't live in Florida! So I can't grow my own!

I'm still calling it Key lime pie, though—no one can stop me. Not even you Key lime pie purists.

(Pssst. I love ya anyway.)

CRUST

15 whole graham crackers (the 4-section rectangles)

4 tablespoons (½ stick) butter, melted

¼ cup sugar

FILLING

One 14-ounce can sweetened condensed milk

2 egg yolks

1 tablespoon grated lime zest

½ cup lime juice

1. Preheat the oven to 350°F.

2. Break up the graham crackers and put them in the bowl of a food processor.

3. Pulse them until they're fine crumbs . . .

4. Then, while still pulsing, drizzle in the melted butter . . .

5. And pour in the sugar.

6. Pour the crumbs into a standard pie pan . . .

7. And press the crumbs into the pan to shape the crust. Bake the crust for 5 minutes, or until lightly crisp and set. Remove it from the oven and set it aside to cool. Leave the oven on.

8. While the crust is cooling, make the filling: Drizzle the sweetened condensed milk into the bowl of an electric mixer.

9. Add the egg yolks . . .

10. The lime zest . . .

11. And the lime juice.

12. Mix on high until the filling is smooth and thick, about 2 minutes.

13. Pour the filling into the cooled pie crust . . .

14. Smooth out the surface . . .

15. And bake the pie for 15 to 18 minutes, until set. Allow the pie to cool, then refrigerate for at least 2 hours, or until totally chilled.

16. Slice it into pieces and serve!

Variations

• Top with a dollop of whipped cream and a little lime zest for a pretty garnish.

• Use orange zest and orange juice instead of the lime for a different citrus twist!

• Use real Key lime juice and zest if you have them available. (Or don't.)

STRAWBERRY ICE CREAM

MAKES 2 QUARTS

Every time I make a different variety of homemade ice cream, I vehemently declare it to be my very favorite flavor in the whole entire galaxy universe world continent country state town.

But I really, really mean it this time. No, really!

Homemade strawberry ice cream is . . . well, it's just divine. And the funny thing is, I don't like strawberry ice cream unless it *is* homemade. I find it artificial, both in its pinkness and flavor. The same cannot be said, by the way, for chocolate, coffee, vanilla, and so on, which come in many deliciously acceptable store-bought versions. But strawberry . . . well, it has to be homemade or I want nothing whatsoever to do with it! If it's not homemade, it's dead to me! Hmmmph!

This beautiful frozen concoction starts with my basic ice cream base, then takes a beautifully fruity turn. It's definitely my very favorite homemade ice cream flavor!

Until the next flavor I make . . .

1 pound strawberries, hulled (reserve a few unhulled for garnish, if desired)

2 tablespoons sugar

1 recipe ice cream base (follow the recipe for Cinnamon Ice Cream on page 152—minus the cinnamon stick—through step 23), chilled

1. Place the strawberries in a blender or food processor.

2. Add the sugar . . .

3. And puree until smooth.

4. Pour the strawberry puree into the ice cream base . . .

5. And stir until totally combined.

6. Pour the mixture into an ice cream maker . . .

We try to instill a love of fireworks in our guests at a young age.

7. And freeze according to the manufacturer's instructions.

8. Transfer the ice cream to two 1-quart containers and freeze for several hours or overnight.

9. Serve when it's nice and firm!

10. Garnish with a sliced strawberry if you wanna be fancy.

Variations

- *Mash the strawberries with the sugar if you'd like larger chunks of strawberries in your ice cream. (Sometimes with this method, the larger chunks can become a little icy.)*

- *Add a drop or two of red food coloring if you'd like a pinker strawberry ice cream.*

- *Serve strawberry ice cream alongside a brownie. Yum!*

PEACH COBBLER

MAKES 12 SERVINGS

Cobbler is a *very* controversial subject. Were you aware of this?

No, really. It's true. People *feel* their preference of cobbler very deeply. Some believe strongly that fruit cobbler is simply fruit with a flat pie crust baked over the top. Others believe strongly that cobbler is fruit with a cake-like batter baked all around it. Still others believe strongly that a lumpy biscuit-like topping baked on a fruit base is the original, one true cobbler.

As for me, I have agonized and labored about this through the years, and I have finally made a firm decision regarding my cobbler beliefs. And here it is.

I don't care which cobbler is the correct version! I'll eat it however I can get it!

This peach cobbler is more in the lumpy biscuit-like camp, and I have to say that I do tend to believe this is closer to the original. Something about the cobblestone look of the crust makes me suspicious.

FRUIT

8 cups fresh sliced unpeeled peaches (about 10 peaches)

¼ cup sugar

2 tablespoons all-purpose flour

TOPPING

2 cups all-purpose flour

1 tablespoon baking powder

2 heaping tablespoons sugar, more for sprinkling

¼ teaspoon salt

½ cup (1 stick) cold butter, cut into pieces

½ cup milk

1 egg

1. Preheat the oven to 425°F.

2. Place the peaches in a large bowl and sprinkle in the sugar.

3. Add the flour . . .

4. And stir to combine.

5. To make the topping, in a separate bowl, combine the flour . . .

6. The baking powder, sugar, and salt.

7. Stir it around, then add the butter . . .

8. And use a pastry blender to cut the butter into the dry ingredients.

9. Whisk together the milk and egg . . .

10. Then drizzle it into the flour-butter mixture . . .

11. And stir until the dough just comes together. It should be lumpy and clumpy!

12. Pour the peaches into a 2-quart baking dish . . .

13. Then tear off pinches of the dough and dot them all over the top.

14. Sprinkle the top with extra sugar.

15. Cover lightly with foil and bake for 30 minutes, then remove the foil and bake for 15 minutes more, or until lightly browned.

16. Serve the cobbler warm or at room temperature . . .

17. With a big scoop of vanilla ice cream!

Variation

Substitute blackberries, blueberries, or rhubarb for the peaches.

HALLOWEEN

In the interest of full disclosure, I should tell you that Halloween is my mother's birthday.

I just want you to be fully aware of my lifelong bias toward the spookiest, most terrifying day of the year. Halloween always brings good feelings for me, not just because it really is the start of the fall and winter holiday season, but also because I remember celebrating my mom's birthday in the midst of all the trick-or-treat excitement, which, when you think about it, sort of defeats the purpose of Halloween, which is supposed to be a macabre, dark experience.

There goes my mom again. Ruining the true meaning of something as sacred as Halloween!

But it's okay. Because for all its roots in paganism and creepiness, Halloween really is all about the fun! Telling scary stories, watching horror movies, finding haunted houses to walk through, going trick-or-treating . . . it's all a celebration of just how thrilling it is for us human beings to feel spooked.

And then there are the costumes. I would now like to list a few of the Halloween costumes I've worn through the years. They're all burned into my October 31 memory, and I sincerely hope they don't change the way you feel about me.

Casper the Friendly Ghost. Fairy. Princess. Fairy princess. Fairy princess again. Dracula. Court jester. Shadow (I wore all black. Deep, man). Miss Piggy (blond wig and all). Luke Skywalker (I had a Dorothy Hamill haircut at the time, so it worked). Richard Nixon. (I had issues.) Cleopatra. Elvis. Witch. Nun. Cloud.

I glued 700 cotton balls to a white sweatshirt for that last one. Very efficient use of my time, and when I returned from trick-or-treating, the cotton had collected a whole bunch of animal hair and debris from the neighborhood. My mom was really grossed out, and I think that was the last costume I ever wore.

Happy Halloween!

TERRIFYING TREATS

One of the best parts of Halloween is the steady stream of fun and freaky treats, whether they're homemade delights you whip up for school or work . . . or the candy you embezzle from your children's trick-or-treat buckets.

You do that, too . . . right?

Right?

Oh, good.

Spooky!

PETRIFYING PUMPKIN PANCAKES

MAKES 12 TO 15 PANCAKES

Nothing starts off the scariest day of the year like these scrumptiously scary pumpkin pancakes.

Wait. Correction. Nothing starts off the *second* scariest day of the year like these scrumptiously scary pumpkin pancakes. The scariest day of the year is the day I decide to clean out the junk drawer in my kitchen.

Wait. Come to think of it, I never clean out the junk drawer in my kitchen.

So as I was saying, Halloween is definitely the scariest day of the year!

I'm so glad we had this talk.

3 cups cake flour

3 tablespoons sugar

2 tablespoons baking powder

1 teaspoon salt

2 cups canned pumpkin puree (not pumpkin pie filling)

2 eggs

3 teaspoons vanilla extract

¼ teaspoon pumpkin pie spice

2¾ cups milk, more if needed for thinning

¼ cup molasses

Black or dark brown food coloring

2 tablespoons butter

Warm maple or pancake syrup, for serving

1. Combine the cake flour, sugar, baking powder, and salt in a bowl and stir together.

2. In a separate bowl, combine the pumpkin puree, eggs . . .

3. Vanilla, pumpkin pie spice . . .

4. And milk.

5. Whisk until combined.

6. Pour the wet ingredients into the dry ingredients . . .

7. And stir until they just come together.

8. Remove 1 cup of the batter to a separate bowl . . .

9. Then add the molasses and food coloring. Stir until combined.

10. Heat a griddle or nonstick skillet over medium-low heat and melt 2 tablespoons of butter. Use a spoon or plastic squirt bottle to create the designs you want with the dark batter. (Psst. If you do any lettering, be sure to write backward!)

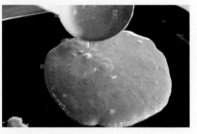

11. After about 30 seconds, carefully pour on enough of the regular batter to cover the design. Let the pancake cook for a good minute, or until bubbles start to form on the surface.

12. Carefully flip it over to the other side with a spatula and let it cook for 45 seconds to 1 minute, until it's done in the middle.

14. Then pour on the pancake batter!

13. To make a jack-o'-lantern, create the eyes and mouth . . .

Oooooh. Scary. So scary, in fact, I'm not sure I can eat it!

Serve with warm maple or pancake syrup.

"I really wanted to be a greyhound this year. Not an extinct lizard with horns."

BROCCOLI-CHEESE SOUP

MAKES 12 SERVINGS

Before you send your costume-clad children out into the neighborhood to scoop up as much candy as their trick-or-treating hands can grab, so you can then confiscate said candy and "put it in a safe place" under the guise of being a responsible parent, so you can then sneak into your closet with said candy to see just how many miniature candy bars you can polish off before your kids discover you . . . whip up a nice, hearty pot of soup to warm their bones!

Broccoli-cheese soup is a favorite of kiddos (and their mothers. And their fathers. And their aunts, uncles, grandmothers, friends, teachers, and pen pals), and this one is everything broccoli-cheese soup should be: creamy, thick, cheesy, and satisfying, which means the kids won't be quite as tempted to chow down on candy while they're out and about.

And that'll mean more candy for you later.

This is how my mind works. It's a little frightening, actually.

½ cup (1 stick) butter

1 large onion, diced

⅓ cup all-purpose flour

4 cups whole milk

2 cups half-and-half

Salt and pepper

½ teaspoon ground nutmeg

4 broccoli heads, cut into florets

½ cup chicken broth

3 cups shredded sharp Cheddar cheese, more for garnish

Small bread loaves for bowls (you can buy them in nice bakeries)

1. In a large pot over medium heat, melt the butter . . .

3. And stir it around to cook, 3 to 4 minutes.

5. And use a whisk to work in the flour. Once it's combined, cook the onion-flour mixture for 2 to 3 minutes . . .

2. Then add the onion . . .

4. Sprinkle the flour on top of the onion . . .

6. Then add the milk and half-and-half, whisking constantly until combined.

7. Sprinkle in the salt, pepper, and nutmeg . . .

8. Then add the broccoli florets . . .

9. And stir them into the soup. Cover the pot and reduce the heat to low, then simmer the soup until it's thickened and the broccoli is tender, 20 to 25 minutes.

10. Stir in the chicken broth and check the consistency. The soup should be thick, but if it still seems too thick, splash in a little more broth.

11. Then throw in the cheese!

12. Stir it in until it's melted, taste and adjust the seasonings . . . and get ready to serve it up.

13. At an angle, cut off the top third of the bread.

14. Remove the "lid" . . .

15. Then tear out chunks of bread, leaving a ½-inch rim around the crust. (Save the bread in a plastic storage bag for another use.)

16. Ladle in the thick, yummy soup and top it with more shredded cheese.

17. Serve it to trick-or-treaters before they head out to collect your . . . I mean *their* candy.

NOTES

• *For a smoother soup, use an immersion blender to puree the soup before adding the cheese.*

• *Substitute pepper Jack cheese for a slightly spicier soup.*

MUMMY DOGS

MAKES 16 DOGS

Mummy Dogs are a much-beloved Halloween treat, and are always a welcome switch from all the sweet, sticky, sugary craziness going on. Plus, they're totally adorable. (Well, as adorable as a mummified frankfurter can be.)

For my version of Mummy Dogs, I use the same trusty, no-fail dough I use for my trusty, no-fail cinnamon rolls, and it turns out perfectly golden and lovely (as lovely as mummified frankfurters can be) every time.

16 hot dogs
½ batch Basic Dough (page 89)
1 egg
Mustard, for serving

1. Preheat the oven to 375°F.

2. Unwrap the hot dogs and have them ready on a plate.

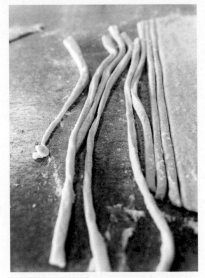

4. To cut skinny strips of dough.

6. Leave a little bit of open space around the "face" of the mummy . . .

3. Roll out the dough very thin, then use a pizza cutter or sharp knife . . .

5. Holding a hot dog in one hand, use your other hand to begin wrapping it in one of the strips of dough.

7. And, using a second strip, keep wrapping it in a crisscross pattern until it's almost totally covered. Tuck the end underneath the mummy dog.

8. Repeat with all the hot dogs and lay them on a baking sheet lined with a baking mat or parchment paper.

9. Make a glaze by cracking the egg into a small bowl . . .

10. And whisking it with 1 tablespoon of water.

11. Lightly brush the glaze all over the top of each mummy dog . . .

12. And bake them for 18 to 20 minutes, until the dough is nice and golden brown.

13. Before serving, dot the mummy dogs with little mustard "eyes." Freaky, man!

14. Serve them on a black platter or an iron griddle.

Variations

- *Use store-bought biscuit or pizza dough for a shortcut.*

- *Use cheese-stuffed dogs instead of regular hot dogs for extra yumminess.*

- *Serve with little dishes of ketchup and/or barbecue sauce.*

CARAMEL APPLES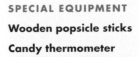

MAKES 10 TO 12 CARAMEL APPLES

Caramel apples always make me feel happy and warm inside, because to me they're the one treat that really signify the start of the fall/winter holiday season. You can add colorful and tasty sprinkles to make them crazy and fun, and you can wrap them in cellophane bags and hand them out to trick-or-treaters (assuming their parents trust you) . . . or just deliver them to people you love once the leaves start turning color. They proclaim with great deliciousness that fall has officially arrived.

While you could definitely take the easy road and coat the apples in melted store-bought caramels, I've found through the years that nothing can replace the deep, dark caramel you whip up yourself.

Make some caramel apples this year! They'll get you excited for the holidays, I promise.

10 to 12 medium apples

4 cups sugar

¼ cup corn syrup

½ cup (1 stick) plus 2 tablespoons butter, cut into pieces, softened

2 cups heavy cream, room temperature

SPECIAL EQUIPMENT

Wooden popsicle sticks

Candy thermometer

1. Start by skewering the apples so that the sticks are inserted about two-thirds of the way through the apples.

2. Then, in a medium saucepan over medium-high heat, combine the sugar and corn syrup . . .

3. And stir it together with a wooden spoon as it melts.

4. Within a few minutes, the sugars will start to caramelize and turn color.

5. When the sugar has dissolved completely and the mixture has turned a deep amber color, turn the heat to low and add the butter.

6. Finally, add the heavy cream . . .

7. And whisk the mixture until it's smooth and combined.

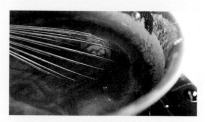

8. Turn up the heat to medium-high again. Cook the caramel until the thermometer gets to 245°F to 250°F, then remove the pan from the heat.

9. Let the caramel cool for 20 minutes, then dip an apple into the caramel, rolling it around to coat it completely.

10. Check the first apple. The caramel should coat it and begin to stick almost immediately. (If it does not, bring the caramel to a boil again and cook it for a few more minutes. Cool again before dipping.)

11. Repeat with the rest of the apples. Place them on a baking sheet lined with a baking mat or parchment paper and let the caramel cool and set completely.

12. Serve them to hungry witches, vampires, and zombies!

NOTES

- *It's better to undercook the caramel than to cook it too long. Stop just short of when you think it's ready; if it doesn't adhere to the first apple you dip, boil it for another 2 to 3 minutes and try again. (If the caramel cooks too long, it will be too hard to bite into.)*

- *Use caution when making caramel. Melted sugar is incredibly hot and can cause burns. Be sure to supervise kiddos!*

Variations

A couple of minutes after dipping the apples, sprinkle a variety of toppings all over the caramel, or carefully roll the dipped apple in the topping:

- *Crushed chocolate candies*
- *Colored or chocolate sprinkles*
- *Crushed chocolate sandwich cookies*
- *Chopped peanuts, walnuts, or almonds*
- *Chopped pretzels*
- *Miniature chocolate chips*
- *Miniature M&Ms*

POPCORN BALLS

MAKES 12 POPCORN BALLS

Popcorn balls are fun and Halloweenie and all (huh huh; I said weenie), but I'm often disappointed by the second bite or so. Either the flavor is bland and boring or they're so hard I break off all my teeth. And I don't look good toothless! Definitely makes me look ten years older.

A great tooth-saving solution is this combination popcorn ball–crispy treat, made sweet and sticky by marshmallows rather than a cooked syrup, which can have wildly varying (and I'll say it again—tooth-breaking) results.

These have definitely ruined me on all other popcorn balls for the rest of my life. Sweet and crispy and super duper delightful! No one can eat just one. Or two.

Or nine.

¼ cup peanut oil

6 tablespoons popcorn kernels

½ cup sugar

4 tablespoons (½ stick) butter

6 ounces mini marshmallows (about ⅔ of a package)

Orange food coloring (optional)

1 cup candy corn

½ cup shelled unsalted peanuts

Cooking spray

1. Add the oil to a medium saucepan (one that has a tight-fitting lid) over medium-high heat.

2. Add the popcorn and shake the pan gently to make sure the kernels are coated.

3. When the oil starts to sizzle, but before the corn starts popping, add the sugar to the pan.

4. Shake the pan again, and when the first couple of kernels pop . . .

5. Place the lid on the pan and shake the pan gently with the other hand while you hold the lid in place. Keep doing this as the popcorn pops, until the popping slows down. (Use caution while doing this, as the oil is hot!)

6. When almost all the kernels have popped . . .

7. Pour the popcorn onto a parchment paper–lined baking sheet, separating the kernels with a spatula or spoon.

8. Let the popcorn cool.

9. While the popcorn is cooling, melt the butter in a separate pot over low heat.

10. Add the marshmallows, stirring as they melt.

11. When the marshmallows are almost melted, add 2 or 3 drops of orange food coloring, if desired.

12. And stir to combine. Add more food coloring if you'd like it to have a deeper color.

13. Remove the pot from the heat and add the popcorn to the pot, immediately stirring to coat it as quickly as possible.

14. Right after stirring, add the candy corn . . .

15. And the peanuts . . .

17. Spray your hands lightly with cooking spray and form the popcorn mixture into individual balls 2 to 3 inches in diameter.

18. Set them aside and let them cool and set completely.

19. Serve them at room temperature.

And stir gently until the candy and nuts are totally worked into the popcorn.

Everybody—and I mean everybody, whether they're alive or dead—loves them!

Variations

• For a shortcut, use a bag of microwave popcorn instead of popping your own.

• Add different combinations of candies and nuts to the popcorn balls.

• Instead of adding candies and nuts to the popcorn mixture, make plain popcorn balls and add colorful sprinkles to the surface.

PLATTER OF DARKNESS

SERVES AS MANY AS YOU NEED!

This "recipe" for a fun and fear-inducing platter of grab-and-go treats isn't even a recipe at all, but adds so much fun and terrifying whimsy to any Halloween spread. Scale it up or down depending on the size of your crowd, and use your imagination and creativity to make it all yours.

1. To put together the platter, collect an assortment of black/dark candies and treats: licorice spirals, licorice ropes, black M&Ms, black jelly beans, chocolate sandwich cookies, even dried cherries, prunes, and/or blackberries are great! Any combination of dark goodies will do.

3. You want the overall visual effect to be "dark," so just be sure not to put any strawberries or pink bows in there. Cuteness has no place on this Platter of Darkness!

2. On top of a dark cutting board or platter, arrange the candies and cookies in a big bunch, with the different piles overlapping one another.

4. If you can get your hands on an enormous gummy rat, it would be a nice touch.

NOTE: *This is a really fun thing for kids to help arrange. Just give them all the elements and tell them to go for it!*

Variation

For more of a "graveyard" look, spread chocolate cookie crumbs all over a rimmed baking sheet to give a "dirt" appearance. Arrange the candies all over the crumbs.

CHEESE BALL OF DEATH

MAKES 12 SERVINGS

Okay, so I'm having a little too much fun with these macabre recipe titles. But don't let them deter you! There's nothing inherently scary or dangerous about this creamy, savory, scrumptious cheese ball. *Au contraire*, my little monsters. It's one of the yummiest Halloween snacks in Transylvania!

One 8-ounce package cream cheese

Two 6-ounce packages goat cheese

½ teaspoon salt

1 tablespoon black pepper

2 tablespoons chopped parsley

2 tablespoons chopped chives

¼ cup black sesame seeds

Dark crackers, for serving

1 large gummy tarantula (optional)

1. Add the cream cheese and goat cheese to the bowl of an electric mixer fitted with the whisk attachment.

2. Add the salt . . .

3. The pepper . . .

4. And the chopped herbs.

5. Whip it until the mixture is light and fluffy, scraping the bowl halfway through to make sure it's all combined.

6. Turn out the mixture onto a large piece of plastic wrap . . .

7. Then gather up the sides of the plastic wrap and twist the excess, forcing the cheese mixture into a ball. Place the ball, seam side down, in the freezer to firm up, 45 minutes to 1 hour.

8. When firm, remove the plastic wrap . . .

9. And press sesame seeds all over the surface, covering it completely.

10. Serve it with dark crackers and a gummy tarantula on top, if you have one available.

Variations

- *Add grated cheese of your choice for more of a textured cheese mixture.*
- *Make a cream cheese–only ball (omit the herbs, salt, pepper, and goat cheese) and coat it in crushed Oreos. Serve with pretzels!*

Who are these masked children?

EYEBALL CAKE BALLS

MAKES ABOUT 24 CAKE BALLS

Cake balls are always a fun treat for kids' parties, because you can use any flavor of cake mix, any color of coating, and any decorations you'd like in order to fit the occasion.

I've made these Halloween-themed "eyeballs" for years and they always make me laugh.

A big platter of eyeballs is always hilarious.

One 18-ounce box red velvet cake mix

½ teaspoon salt

One 18-ounce container vanilla or cream cheese frosting

2 cups each orange, green, and purple melting candy wafers, melted in separate bowls and cooled slightly

1 cup white candy melting wafers (or 2 ounces almond bark)

1 tube each black and red gel icing

1. Bake the cake according to package directions in any size pan you'd like (I used 2 round pans, but any size will do).

2. Use your (very clean!) hands to completely crumble the cakes into a large bowl.

3. Use a fork to break up any clumps, then stir in the salt.

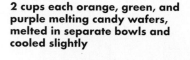

4. Add the frosting to the bowl . . .

5. And stir it around with a rubber spatula or wooden spoon . . .

6. Until the frosting "disappears" into the cake.

7. Retrieve a tablespoon of the mixture . . .

8. And roll it into a smooth ball.

9. Repeat with the rest of the cake mixture, placing the cake balls on a parchment paper–lined baking sheet. Place the balls into the freezer for 30 minutes, or until firm.

13. Use a toothpick to slide it gently off the fork, repeat with the rest of the cake balls and colors, and as the candy sets on the outside, score the bottom of the balls to separate them from the excess.

15. Then dot the top with a little black gel icing.

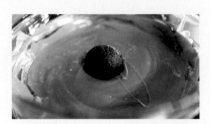

10. Then, one at a time, drop the cake balls into the candy color of your choice.

14. When the candy has set, use a toothpick to smear a little white candy on the top of each ball . . .

16. Finally, use red gel icing to create the "bloodshot" look. These cake balls should *not* have partied so hard last night.

17. Serve them in a big, black iron skillet.

NOTE: *Cake balls can be made the day before! The candy coating keeps them fresh.*

11. Use a fork to cover a ball with candy, then retrieve the ball from the candy with the fork, tapping the handle on the rim of the bowl to get the candy to sheet down the sides of the ball.

12. Place the ball on parchment or waxed paper.

Walter is thankful
for the kids.

THANKSGIVING

Ah, Thanksgiving! Where to begin?

How do you possibly sum up the one day each year when family gathers together and shares a beautiful, abundant meal while openly giving thanks for the innumerable blessings in their lives?

Oh. I think I just summed up Thanksgiving. I love it when that happens!

I love Thanksgiving. It's the day when I know the guys are going to keep their spurs off their boots and put all ranch work on hold. It's a day of relaxation and football. It's a total suspension of real world concerns and schedules. And even though the day usually means a huge amount of food preparation and planning for me, I cherish every minute of it.

(Especially if there's a *Godfather* marathon playing on TV.)

(*Gone With the Wind* is always nice, too. I've made many a pan of gravy while watching the South fall down around Scarlett O'Hara's knees!)

Thanksgiving. What a beautiful day. What a beautiful word. Over the years, I've begun to take the concept of Thanksgiving seriously and literally. And I don't mean I dress up my children as Pilgrims. At least I haven't in a couple of years.

What I mean is that I try—in the midst of the enormous meal preparation and busyness—to keep my mind fixed on the things in life that bring me joy, peace, contentment, and happiness. My husband. My children. My entire family. The health and well-being of the people I love. My own health. The land we live on. The beauty of the earth. The freedom we enjoy. It's enough to make me cry over my bowl of sweet potatoes as I mash them. And I've actually done this before.

But I also take it one step further. Thanksgiving, to me, isn't just an acknowledgment of the ways in which we're blessed. It's a recognition that there are others in the world who don't have the same peace . . . the same health . . . the same freedom. As I go about the busy work of Thanksgiving Day, I try to carry a sense of "There but by the grace of God go I" along with me, keeping in mind that there are fellow human beings who are struggling and suffering. Just as salt enhances the perception of sweet, this drives home the awareness of "blessing" even more.

I'm sorry. I didn't mean to get all serious on you. It happens when one turns forty. You vaguely remember a time when you were a teenager and all you could think about on Thanksgiving Day was what time you could start Christmas shopping the next morning. The next thing you know, you have a husband and four children, you're headed straight for middle age, and you're sobbing into the bowl of sweet potatoes you're mashing.

Thanksgiving is a day to give thanks. Enjoy and embrace it, friends!

THANKSGIVING FEAST

What to include in the Thanksgiving feast is always a personal/family decision, and tradition plays such a role. My menu is a mix of classics from my childhood—recipes I remember my grandmothers serving—and beloved new favorites that have cropped up through the years.

Here are all the beautiful and delicious dishes that define Thanksgiving for my family and me. I hope you find some new traditions for your crew!

DO-AHEAD GAME PLAN

ANYTIME THE WEEK OF THANKSGIVING

• Freeze the pumpkin pie filling for the Pumpkin Smoothie.

• Make the Cranberry Sauce.

• Make and freeze the pie crust for the Pecan Pie, Caramel Apple Pie, and Pumpkin Pie.

• Chop the pecans for the Pecan Pie.

THE DAY BEFORE

• Make My Favorite Turkey Brine.

• Make the Perfect Mashed Potatoes, but do not bake. Cover the casserole pan and store in the fridge. (Remove them from the fridge 45 minutes before baking so they won't be cold going into the oven.)

• Make the Skillet Cornbread for the dressing(s) you're making. Cut into cubes and let sit on a baking sheet to dry overnight.

• Cut all the bread into cubes for the dressing(s) you're making. Let sit on a baking sheet to dry overnight.

• Dice all the onions, carrots, and celery for the dressing(s) you're making.

• Roast the mushrooms for the Dressing with Sausage, Apples, and Mushrooms.

• Dice the onions for the Green Beans and Tomatoes.

• Dice the onions, carrots, and celery for the Broccoli Wild Rice Casserole.

• Blanch the broccoli for Broccoli–Wild Rice Casserole.

• Make the dough for the No-Knead Cloverleaf Rolls. Store in the fridge, covered, in the pot or in a large bowl. (Note: The dough will continue to rise, so you will need to punch it down 3 or 4 times to keep it from overflowing.)

• Brine the turkey!

• Lay out all your plates, flatware, napkins, serving dishes, serving spoons, and glassware.

• Make the pies. They can cool on the counter and sit at room temperature until serving.

EARLY THANKSGIVING DAY

• Get the turkey in the oven: Calculate the approximate cooking time, then count backward from your meal! Allow a good 45 minutes to 1 hour of cushion.

• Assemble the dressing(s) you're making (you'll need to do it early if you're stuffing the bird). Wait to bake the dressing(s) just before the meal.

• Make the Soul Sweet 'Taters. They can cool on the counter and be served warm or at room temperature.

• Make and assemble the Broccoli–Wild Rice Casserole, but wait to bake till just before the meal.

• Make the rest of the food!

PUMPKIN SMOOTHIE

MAKES 8 TO 12 SERVINGS

I started making these surprisingly delicious and addictive smoothies on Thanksgiving Day for the sole purpose of keeping my ravenous children away from the dang Thanksgiving food until it's time to eat! Sheesh! Give Mama some space, people.

On another note: These smoothies are pretty much the most delicious things you'll ever taste in your life. It's like sipping a cold, refreshing pumpkin pie . . . with a little bit of crunch on top. You'll absolutely inhale them, and they really are the perfect tide-me-over until the big feast is on the table.

One 15-ounce can pumpkin pie filling

3 cups milk (whole, 2%, 1% or skim—whatever your poison!)

½ cup vanilla yogurt

¼ teaspoon ground cinnamon

¼ cup cinnamon graham cracker crumbs

3. Then add the yogurt.

6. Next, add the cinnamon . . .

1. Anytime before Thanksgiving, spoon the pumpkin pie filling into muffin cups, then cover the pan with aluminum foil and place it in the freezer.

4. Pop 4 pieces of the frozen pumpkin pie filling out of the pan (save the rest for another time, or for a second batch of smoothies if one isn't enough to calm the hungry beasts) . . .

7. Then blend the mixture until totally smooth and pour it into individual glasses.

2. When you're ready to make the smoothies, add the milk to a blender . . .

5. And add them to the blender.

8. Sprinkle the tops with graham cracker crumbs before serving.

MY FAVORITE TURKEY BRINE

MAKES ENOUGH BRINE FOR ONE 16- TO 20-POUND TURKEY

I brine my Thanksgiving turkey every year because it's the right thing to do, and because the first time I ever roasted a brined turkey, my father-in-law's eyes rolled back in his head and he declared it the best turkey he'd ever eaten . . . and *boy* was he glad his son had married me so he could come to my house for Thanksgiving every year until the end of time!

Okay, so he didn't say that last part. But I like to imagine he did.

Brining involves soaking a turkey in a very salty solution for a certain length of time, long enough for the salt to infiltrate the turkey and actually alter the molecular structure of the meat. And contrary to what you might think, brine doesn't turn the turkey into an inedible, salty atrocity! Nosirree. What it does is give you a juicy, tender, fantastically delicious turkey that your father-in-law (or son-in-law, or girlfriend, or uncle, or mother, or friend, or boss's sister's cousin's boyfriend) will love.

A couple of important things to remember:

1. **YOU SHOULD BRINE ONLY FRESH (UNFROZEN) TURKEYS.** Most frozen turkeys are injected with a sodium solution as a preservative, so if you brine on top of that, the turkey will be too salty. Now, there are some organic frozen turkeys that have a much lower concentration of the sodium solution. Generally speaking, though, you'll want to brine fresh—not frozen—turkeys. Ask your butcher to direct you.

2. **GRAVY MADE FROM BRINED TURKEYS CAN BE ON THE SALTY SIDE.** I'll show you how to avoid that, though, so don't leave me yet!

Okay. I'm finished being bossy now. Let's go brine a turkey together!

3 cups apple juice or apple cider

2 gallons water

1½ cups kosher salt

2 cups packed brown sugar

4 fresh rosemary sprigs

3 oranges

5 garlic cloves, minced

3 tablespoons tri-color peppercorns

5 bay leaves

1. Into a very large pot, add the apple juice or cider . . .

2. The water . . .

3. The salt . . .

4. And the brown sugar.

5. Strip the leaves off the rosemary sprigs.

6. Then, with a vegetable peeler, strip the peel from the oranges in large strips.

7. Add the orange peel to the pot . . .

8. Along with the rosemary leaves . . .

9. The minced garlic . . .

10. And the peppercorns and bay leaves.

11. Bring the brine to a boil, then turn off the heat and allow it to cool. Chill completely.

12. When you're ready to brine the turkey, remove the bag of giblets from the turkey and refrigerate them. Place the bird in a large pot or brining bag . . .

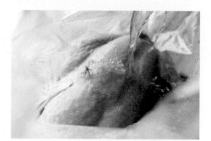

13. Then pour the chilled brine solution right over the turkey.

I'm thankful for my sweet niece!

14. If the turkey needs more liquid in order to be submerged, add up to another 4 to 6 cups of cold water to bring up the liquid level . . .

15. Then seal the bag (or cover the pot) tightly and refrigerate it for 16 to 18 hours. If the turkey is not fully submerged when it sits, make it a point to flip the turkey halfway through the brining process so that all the meat has a chance to be soaked.

16. (Pssst. I place the brining bag into a large stainless bowl just to keep it in place!)

17. After it has brined, place the turkey in the sink and discard the brine solution. Thoroughly rinse the turkey in cold water inside and out, then fill the sink with clean, cold water and allow the turkey to soak for 15 minutes to help remove the excess salt. This will make sure the turkey gravy isn't too salty.

18. Next, pat the turkey dry and move on with the roasting process (page 248).

ROASTED THANKSGIVING TURKEY

MAKES 16 TO 20 SERVINGS

It's beautiful! It's stunning! It's the centerpiece of the whole meal!

And here's the great news: *It's not hard to make at all.* Promise.

The secret to roasting the perfect Thanksgiving turkey is planning: First, you have to get the turkey in the brine the day before the big feast. Done. Second, you have to make yourself get up early enough on Thanksgiving morning to get the bird in the oven for a noontime feast. I've had many a year when I've pushed the snooze button a few too many times and we've had to eat an hour or two late.

Third, don't be like me.

One 18- to 20-pound turkey, brined, rinsed, soaked, and patted dry (see My Favorite Turkey Brine, page 245)

Peel of 1 orange

½ cup (1 stick) butter, softened

2 fresh rosemary sprigs, leaves stripped and finely minced

1 teaspoon salt

1 teaspoon black pepper

1. Be sure the oven rack is on its lowest level and preheat the oven to 275°F.

2. Place the turkey breast-side up in a roasting pan with a rack. Cross the legs and tie them with kitchen string to secure them.

3. Tuck the wings under the body . . .

4. Then cover the turkey completely in heavy-duty aluminum foil, making sure the foil tucks under the pan. For the first stage, roast the turkey for about 10 minutes per pound (so for a 20-pound turkey, it would roast at this temperature for 3 to 3½ hours).

5. While the turkey's in the oven, make a rosemary-citrus butter. Use a vegetable peeler to slice off the peel of 1 orange. With a very sharp knife, slice the orange peel into thin strips . . .

6. And throw them into a bowl with the butter and rosemary. Sprinkle in some salt and pepper, and stir until combined.

7. After the turkey has roasted for the first stage, remove the foil and smear the butter mixture all over the skin of the turkey (the skin won't be brown at all). Insert an oven-proof meat thermometer into the thigh of the turkey, and raise the oven temperature to 350°F. Return the turkey to the oven, uncovered, basting it with the juices in the bottom of the pan every 30 minutes.

8. Roast until the interior temperature registers 165°F and the skin is a deep golden brown. For a 20-pound turkey, this should take an additional 1½ to 2½ hours. (This turkey has about 30 minutes left on the second stage.)

9. Remove the turkey from the oven, cover it lightly with foil, and let it rest for 15 to 20 minutes before serving.

10. Serve the turkey on a big, pretty platter with orange slices and greenery if you wanna be fancy. Carve the turkey using the instructions on page 250.

NOTE: *Follow the meat thermometer! Don't remove the turkey from the oven until the thigh registers 165°F.*

Variation

Use plain butter unadorned with herbs or citrus. Still totally delicious!

HOW TO CARVE A TURKEY

1. Start with a slice on either side of the breastbone . . .

2. Then slice on either side to loosen all the breast meat.

3. Next, just cut neat slices . . .

4. And lift 'em right out!

5. Then cut the drumsticks at the base . . .

6. And lift the leg to slice it off at the joint.

7. After that, just make your way around the turkey, grabbing as much of the white and dark meat as you can find. Arrange all the meat on a platter or just serve it straight off the bird. (My family usually can't wait for the whole platter nonsense.)

"I get one of the drumsticks!"

GIBLET GRAVY

MAKES 6 CUPS

I have to say, I find it a little ironic that for all the prepping and chopping and planning and getting up early and cooking and organizing and coordinating that goes into a Thanksgiving meal, when it's all said and done, it all comes down to the gravy.

Really, it's true. Good gravy—really good gravy—absolutely makes (or breaks) the Thanksgiving Day meal.

No pressure or anything!

Giblets and neck saved from the turkey

Drippings from Roasted Thanksgiving Turkey (page 248)

½ cup all-purpose flour, more if needed

4 cups no-sodium chicken or turkey broth, more if needed

Salt and pepper (gravy won't need much salt)

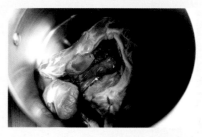

1. First, take the giblets and neck from the raw turkey and cover them with water by 2 inches in a small saucepan. Bring to a gentle boil over medium heat, then reduce the heat to low and simmer it for 1 hour to both cook the meat and make a giblet broth for the gravy.

2. Remove the cooked giblets and neck from the water (don't worry; they're supposed to look really grody) and set them aside. Keep the giblet broth in the saucepan for later.

3. When you're ready to make the gravy, pour all the drippings from the turkey roasting pan into a pitcher or bowl. Set the pan back onto the stove.

4. Let the drippings sit and separate naturally, then use a ladle to carefully separate the fat from the liquid drippings (the clear fat will be on top, while the cloudy drippings will settle at the bottom) and put them in a separate bowl.

5. Turn the heat to medium and add about 1 cup of the fat back into the roasting pan.

6. Sprinkle the flour all over the fat . . .

7. And immediately begin whisking it around to make a paste. Add more flour or fat as needed to create the right consistency: You want the mixture to be a stirrable paste and not overly greasy. If it looks a little greasy, whisk in a little more flour.

8. Once the paste/roux is the right consistency, whisk it slowly for a few minutes, allowing it to cook to a deep golden brown color. A nice brown roux is the secret to good gravy, baby!

Sorry I called you baby.

9. Once the roux is ready, pour in the chicken or turkey broth, along with 1 cup of the drippings (the stuff that separated from the fat), whisking constantly.

10. Then just let the gravy cook and thicken, whisking constantly for 5 to 8 minutes.

11. Meanwhile, use your fingers to remove as much of the neck meat as you can . . .

12. And chop up the giblets into fine pieces.

13. Add as much of the meat to the gravy as you'd like. Add it all if you like a really chunky giblet gravy, add a little less if you like the gravy more smooth.

15. Finally, season the gravy with a little bit of salt and plenty of black pepper! (Be sure to taste it and make sure the seasoning is perfect.)

14. If the gravy seems too thick, add a little of the reserved giblet broth (the water used to cook the giblets).

16. Serve the gravy piping hot at the table.

I'm Pioneer Woman, and I love gravy.

Amen.

I'm thankful for my awesome nephew!

PERFECT MASHED POTATOES

MAKES 12 TO 16 SERVINGS

These mashed potatoes are so perfect, they'll be remembered in history books.

These mashed potatoes are so perfect, they're served daily in Heaven.

These mashed potatoes are so perfect, they make grown men weep.

These mashed potatoes are so perfect, Shakespeare wrote sonnets about them.

These mashed potatoes are . . . well, perfect. I can't muster up any better word to describe them!

Aside from the luscious texture and the beautimous flavor, another thing that makes these mashed potatoes just right for Thanksgiving is that they can be made the day before. Gone are the days of last-minute mashing, stirring, and seasoning. This recipe completely eliminates the whole potato mess from the big day, which will leave you so much extra time, you'll be able to give yourself a pedicure before guests arrive.

Just be sure to wash your hands afterward.

5 pounds russet or Yukon gold potatoes

1 cup (2 sticks) butter, cut into pieces, more for the dish and topping

One 8-ounce package cream cheese, softened

½ cup half-and-half

½ cup heavy cream

½ teaspoon seasoned salt, more to taste

½ teaspoon salt, more to taste

1 teaspoon black pepper, more to taste

1. Peel all the potatoes . . .

2. Placing them in a bowl of cold water as you go to prevent browning.

3. Cut the potatoes into large cubes . . .

4. Then place them in a large pot. Cover them with water and boil over high heat for 20 to 25 minutes, until fork-tender.

5. Drain the potatoes, then place them back into the pot.

6. With the heat on low, mash the potatoes for 2 to 3 minutes, allowing the steam and excess moisture to escape.

7. Stop mashing when the potatoes are mostly smooth.

8. Place all the butter into the pot . . .

9. Then add the cream cheese . . .

10. The half-and-half and cream . . .

11. And the seasoned salt, salt, and pepper.

12. Use the masher to combine all the ingredients until totally smooth . . .

13. Then spread them in a large buttered casserole dish, smoothing out the surface of the potatoes. Cover and refrigerate for up to 2 days.

14. When you're ready to bake the potatoes, preheat the oven to 350°F. Dot the top of the potatoes with a little more butter.

15. Bake for 25 to 30 minutes, or until the potatoes are piping hot and golden brown on top.

16. Serve 'em with your turkey, gravy, and fixins!

CRANBERRY SAUCE

MAKES ABOUT 3 CUPS

You know what? I consider myself a pretty open-minded, nonjudgmental person.

Except when it comes to cranberry sauce.

You make the wrong kind of cranberry sauce on Thanksgiving Day and we're over!

But we can still be friends.

Here's the cranberry sauce I have to have on Thanksgiving Day, and it could not be any simpler. It's tart and sweet and thick and flavorful, unlike cranberry "relish," which is just a bunch of bitter, raw stuff thrown into a food processor and pulverized into chunks.

Ew! Yuck! Blech!

But other than that, I'm a pretty open-minded, nonjudgmental person.

| **One 12-ounce bag fresh cranberries** | **2 large oranges** | **1 cup pure maple syrup** |

1. Rinse the cranberries under cold water . . .

2. Then zest the oranges.

3. Place the cranberries and the zest in a medium saucepan . . .

4. Then squeeze in the juice of both oranges.

5. Pour in the maple syrup . . .

6. And bring the mixture to a gentle boil over medium heat. Reduce the heat to low and simmer for 10 to 15 minutes, until it's nice and thick.

7. If it still seems a little thin, just keep simmering away until it's the right consistency.

8. Transfer the sauce to a dish, then cover with plastic wrap and refrigerate it for at least 2 hours.

9. Spoon it over your turkey. Yum!

NOTE: *Cranberry sauce can be made up to 2 days before Thanksgiving and stored in the fridge.*

Variation

Add 1 teaspoon minced fresh rosemary to the sauce before cooking.

I'm thankful for our calves. They're cutie pies.

BASIC THANKSGIVING DRESSING

MAKES 16 TO 20 SERVINGS

Thanksgiving dressing is *such* a wildly personal thing. Some versions are light and airy, and can almost be tossed around with a spoon. Other dressings bake up firm and solid, and can almost be cut into uniform squares. Some people stuff their bird with dressing, in which case the dressing is called stuffing. Others are dead set against stuffing the bird and opt for baking their stuffing in a baking dish, which means it's called dressing. Some do a combination of both. Some dressing is basic: a combination of dried bread, aromatics, broth, and herbs. Other, more loaded, versions can contain oysters, mushrooms, and even dried fruit and nuts.

I grew up loving my mom's dressing. She never stuffed the bird, and her dressing fell into the slightly firm–very flavorful category. To serve it, we scooped out helpings with a spoon and for the most part, the stuffing stayed together in one homogenized piece. I still love it today.

A few years ago, however, I tried my *mother-in-law's* dressing/stuffing for the first time and everything became clear and beautiful. The larger chunks of dried bread break apart to some degree when mixing the dish together, but large chunks remain throughout—and that's what I love about this dressing. It isn't soggy at all; even after baking, it remains light and crumbly and beautifully textural. A real feast for the senses!

1 batch Skillet Cornbread (page 268)

1 loaf French or Italian bread

1 loaf ciabatta or other crusty artisan bread

1 large onion

5 celery stalks

½ bunch fresh parsley

½ cup (1 stick) butter

6 cups low-sodium chicken broth, more if needed for moisture

½ teaspoon dried basil

½ teaspoon ground thyme

1 tablespoon finely minced fresh rosemary

Salt and pepper

1. The day before Thanksgiving, cut the cornbread into 1-inch cubes.

2. Then do the same with the French bread . . .

3. And the ciabatta.

4. Lay all the bread on large baking sheets and leave it on the counter to completely dry out. You want the cubes to be crispy!

5. When you're ready to make the dressing, chop up the onion . . .

6. The celery . . .

7. And the parsley.

8. Melt the butter in a large skillet over medium-high heat . . .

9. Then throw in the onions and celery . . .

10. And stir it around for 4 to 5 minutes, until the vegetables are soft.

I'm thankful for our tradition of working calves the day after Thanksgiving. (Whatever happened to Christmas shopping?)

11. Pour in the chicken broth . . .

12. Then add the basil, thyme, rosemary, salt, pepper, and parsley. Stir it around and let it cook for another couple of minutes, then turn off the heat.

13. In a huge bowl or your bathtub (just kidding on the bathtub thing), combine all the dried bread cubes.

14. Then, using a ladle . . .

15. Spoon the broth mixture over the top. Keep adding the broth mixture, tossing as you go, until it's all mixed in.

16. Add a little more salt and pepper, then toss it around and taste it to check the seasonings. If you like the dressing a little more moist, splash in a little more broth until it reaches the consistency you like.

17. Pile the dressing into a large casserole pan . . .

18. And bake it, uncovered, at 375°F for 20 to 25 minutes, or until golden. Serve piping hot with the roasted turkey and gravy.

NOTE: *Some of the dressing can be used to stuff the cavity of the turkey before roasting; just check the temperature of the stuffing and make sure it reaches 165°F before you remove the turkey from the oven.*

Variations

- *Add 3 peeled, finely diced carrots to the skillet with the onions and celery.*
- *Add ½ teaspoon ground sage with the other herbs.*
- *Add ¼ teaspoon ground turmeric to add a slight golden color to the dressing.*
- *Add chopped cooked bacon to the bowl with the bread chunks and herb mixture.*

DRESSING WITH SAUSAGE, APPLES, AND MUSHROOMS

MAKES 16 TO 20 SERVINGS

While I love the simple perfection of good ol' basic dressing, loading it full of sausage, mushrooms, and apples (cooked in wine, no less!) is definitely my idea of a good time. A teeny bit of turmeric gives the dressing a gorgeous golden tint.

32 ounces white button or crimini mushrooms, washed and quartered

¼ cup olive oil

Salt and pepper

½ pound Italian sausage

2 tablespoons butter

5 Granny Smith apples, cored and cut into large dice

1 medium onion, cut into large dice

¼ cup packed brown sugar

1 teaspoon kosher salt

½ cup dry white wine

6 cups low-sodium chicken broth

1 teaspoon ground thyme

½ teaspoon ground turmeric

1 tablespoon minced fresh rosemary

¼ cup minced fresh parsley

1 batch Skillet Cornbread (page 268), cut into 1-inch cubes and dried

1 loaf French or Italian bread, cut into 1-inch cubes and dried

1 loaf ciabatta or other crusty artisan bread, cut into 1-inch cubes and dried

1. Preheat the oven to 475°F.

2. Drizzle the mushrooms with olive oil, then sprinkle them with salt and pepper. Toss them to coat, then roast them in the oven for 20 minutes, stirring once halfway through roasting. Remove them from the oven and set them aside.

3. Brown the sausage in a large skillet over medium heat . . .

4. Then remove it to a plate.

5. Add the butter to the same skillet over high heat . . .

6. And add the apples, onion, brown sugar, and kosher salt.

7. Stir the mixture around and cook the apples for 3 to 5 minutes, or until they start to brown.

8. Add the wine to the skillet . . .

9. Then let it cook until the liquid is thick and reduced, about 3 more minutes.

10. Transfer the apples to a large bowl . . .

11. Then add the broth, thyme, turmeric, rosemary, and parsley to the skillet. Stir and heat it completely.

12. Throw the bread cubes on top of the apples in the bowl.

13. Toss the mixture a bit, then use a ladle to begin adding the broth mixture.

14. Toss constantly until all the broth is added . . .

15. Then add the cooked sausage and roasted mushrooms . . .

16. And toss to combine. Add salt and pepper, making sure to taste to confirm the dressing is seasoned adequately. (The sugar in the apples might require a little more salt to be added to the dressing.) Splash in more broth if you'd like the dressing to be more moist.

17. Transfer the dressing to a large baking dish . . .

18. And bake, uncovered, at 375°F for 20 to 25 minutes, until golden brown.

Variation

Use a mix of apple colors for a pretty change.

I'm thankful for beautiful mornings on the ranch. Except when the alarm first goes off.

DRESSING WITH DRIED FRUIT AND NUTS

MAKES 16 TO 20 SERVINGS

Years ago, my mother-in-law and I made a dressing packed with dried fruit and nuts, and it's always been a favorite food memory of ours. It's got all the bready, savory wonderfulness of regular dressing, but with the occasional surprise of sweet, slightly chewy dried fruit. (And it's pretty, too, of course!)

½ pound thick-cut bacon, cut into 1-inch pieces

1 large onion, diced

5 celery stalks, diced

6 cups low-sodium chicken broth

½ teaspoon dried basil

½ teaspoon ground thyme

1 tablespoon minced fresh rosemary

1 cup prunes, halved

2 cups dried apricots, halved

1 cup dried cherries

1 batch Skillet Cornbread (page 268), cut into 1-inch cubes and dried

1 loaf French or Italian bread, cut into 1-inch cubes and dried

½ cup chopped walnuts

Salt and pepper

1. In a large skillet, fry the bacon over medium-high heat until it just begins to crisp. Remove the bacon to a plate and pour off the excess fat. Reduce the heat to medium.

2. In the same skillet, add the onion and celery . . .

3. And stir it around, cooking it for 3 to 4 minutes.

4. Pour in the broth, then add the basil, thyme, rosemary . . .

5. And the dried fruit. Stir the mixture and cook over medium heat for 5 minutes, or until the fruit slightly softens.

6. Combine the bread cubes and the fruit/broth mixture in a large bowl . . .

7. Along with the bacon . . .

8. And the walnuts.

9. Toss the mixture around, then add a little salt and pepper and continue tossing until it's all combined. Taste and adjust the seasonings as needed.

10. Pile the dressing in a large baking dish.

11. Bake it, uncovered, at 375°F for 20 to 25 minutes, or until golden brown.

Variations

- *Use any combination of dried fruit you'd like. (Psst: Cranberries are yummy!)*
- *Substitute pecans or pine nuts for the walnuts.*

OYSTER DRESSING

MAKES 16 TO 20 SERVINGS

It's salty! It's fishy! It's a classic dressing alternative that most definitely inserts an edge to your turkey dinner. Oyster dressing fans will love this delightfully salty-fishy masterpiece!

(Note: If you have fresh oysters available, you may substitute.)

½ **pound thick-cut bacon, sliced into small pieces**

2 **tablespoons butter**

4 **carrots, peeled and diced**

6 **celery stalks, diced**

1 **large onion, diced**

6 **cups low-sodium turkey or chicken broth**

½ **teaspoon ground sage**

Salt and pepper

Three 8-ounce cans oysters, drained, liquid reserved

1 **batch Skillet Cornbread (page 268), cut into 1-inch cubes and dried**

2 **loaves ciabatta or other crusty artisan bread, cut into 1-inch cubes and dried**

1 **tablespoon minced fresh rosemary**

1. Add the bacon to a large skillet over medium-high heat.

2. And fry it till it's chewy.

3. Remove it to a plate. Pour off and discard all the bacon grease but do not clean the skillet.

4. Return the skillet to medium-high heat and melt the butter. Add the carrots, celery, and onion . . .

5. And cook until the veggies just start to get tender, 3 to 4 minutes.

6. Pour in the broth . . .

7. Add the sage, salt, and pepper . . .

8. Then add the salty, fishy drained oysters! (If you like a stronger flavor, add in some of the reserved oyster liquid.)

9. Cook the mixture until the broth and oysters are hot.

10. Then combine all the bread and all the contents of the skillet in a large bowl . . .

11. And toss it around until it's totally combined.

12. Finally, add the bacon and the rosemary . . .

13. And stir until it's all combined. Check the seasonings, adding more salt and pepper if needed.

14. Pile the dressing into a large baking dish and bake, uncovered, at 375°F for 20 to 25 minutes, until golden brown.

SKILLET CORNBREAD

MAKES 1 PAN

This is the same cornbread my mom has made since the beginning of time, and it's as perfect smeared with softened butter as it is cubed and dried for Thanksgiving dressing. This is an absolute staple!

1 cup yellow cornmeal

½ cup all-purpose flour

1 teaspoon salt

1 tablespoon baking powder

1 cup buttermilk (if you don't have any, see page 21)

½ cup milk

1 egg

½ teaspoon baking soda

¼ cup plus 2 tablespoons shortening

1. Preheat the oven to 450°F.

2. In a bowl, combine the cornmeal, flour, salt, and baking powder and stir together.

3. Measure the buttermilk and milk in a measuring cup.

4. Add the egg. Stir together with a fork.

5. Add the baking soda and stir.

6. Pour the milk mixture into the dry ingredients.

7. Stir with a fork until just combined. Do not overmix.

8. In a small bowl, melt ¼ cup of the shortening in the microwave.

9. Slowly add the melted shortening to the batter, stirring constantly until just combined.

10. In an iron skillet over high heat, melt the remaining 2 tablespoons shortening.

11. Pour the batter into the hot skillet.

12. Spread to even out the surface. Cook on the stovetop for 1 minute, then bake for 20 to 25 minutes, until golden brown. The edges should be crispy.

13. Dice into cubes for your favorite Thanksgiving dressing!

I'm thankful for my sister, Betsy, and my nephew Elliot. Cute little turkeys!

GREEN BEANS AND TOMATOES

MAKES 12 SERVINGS

This is by far one of the most nostalgic, beloved, colorful, and delightful dishes I put on my Thanksgiving table. Both my grandmothers (my mom, too) made it every year both on Thanksgiving and Christmas, and I couldn't imagine a Thanksgiving feast without it. It's an absolutely gorgeous dish; the verdant green (is that redundant?) beans and bright red tomatoes provide a beautiful splash on a Thanksgiving plate otherwise laden with subtle earth tones.

Aside from that, however, the tangy tomatoes and green beans really lend a flavorful punch that's amazingly complementary to the rest of the Thanksgiving grub. I made this the first Thanksgiving Ladd and I were married, and my mother-in-law fell instantly in love.

You must try these to believe them!

8 slices thick-cut bacon, cut into 1-inch pieces

1 large onion, diced

2 pounds fresh green beans, ends trimmed

Two 14.5-ounce cans whole tomatoes

Salt and pepper

¼ to ½ teaspoon cayenne pepper

1. Place the bacon pieces in a large pot over medium heat and cook them for a couple of minutes, until the fat starts to render.

2. Add the onion . . .

3. And stir it around. Let the onion cook with the bacon for another 3 minutes, then drain off most of the fat.

4. Add the green beans . . .

5. And pour in the tomatoes (juice and all).

6. Add the salt and pepper . . .

7. And the cayenne pepper. Stir it around gently to combine . . .

8. Then place the lid on the pot, reduce the heat to low, and simmer for 45 minutes to 1 hour, or until the beans are tender, stirring occasionally.

9. Serve them right in the middle of your Thanksgiving table!

Oh, do I love these things.

I'm thankful for this fella. Like, totally.

SOUL SWEET 'TATERS

MAKES 12 SERVINGS

Soul Sweet 'Taters . . . ahhh, it just rolls off the tongue. Both my mom and my aunt used to make this every Thanksgiving, depending on whose household was hosting the feast, and I love it every bit as much now as I did then. It's technically a side dish . . . but if the world were a logical, sane place (which it is not, thank goodness), Soul Sweet 'Taters would most definitely fall under the category of dessert. It's sweet, crunchy, and beautiful . . . but has that lovely sweet potato flavor that's unmistakable. And it's every bit as decadent as Aunt Bessie's pecan pie.

Wait. Who's Aunt Bessie again?

4 medium sweet potatoes

1 cup milk

1 cup sugar

2 whole eggs

1 teaspoon vanilla extract

1 teaspoon salt

1 cup packed brown sugar

½ cup all-purpose flour

6 tablespoons (¾ stick) cold butter, cut into pieces

1 cup chopped pecans

1. Preheat the oven to 375°F.

2. Wash the sweet potatoes, then prick them a few times with a fork. Bake them for 35 to 40 minutes, until fork-tender.

3. Slice them in half and let them cool slightly. Raise the oven temperature to 400°F.

4. Scoop out the innards, place the potatoes in a bowl, and give them a good mash. Leave some texture to the sweet potatoes; no need to mash completely.

5. Add the milk, sugar, eggs, vanilla, and salt. Stir and mash the mixture around until everything is combined but not perfectly smooth.

6. Butter a 2-quart baking dish . . .

7. Then pour in the 'taters . . .

8. And smooth out the top.

9. To make the topping, combine the brown sugar and flour in a medium bowl . . .

10. And mix them together.

11. Throw in the butter and use a pastry blender to cut it all together.

12. Add the pecans . . .

13. And combine until the topping is nice and crumbly.

14. Sprinkle the crumb mixture on top of the sweet potatoes . . .

15. And bake for 30 minutes, or until golden brown.

16. Serve it in big spoonfuls . . .

And give thanks for glorious side dishes such as this!

Cowboy Josh is a combination uncle, big brother, and friend to my kids. I'm thankful for him.

BROCCOLI–WILD RICE CASSEROLE

MAKES 12 SERVINGS

Beware: This heavenly side dish takes everything you ever knew about broccoli-rice casserole and turns it upside down, shakes it up, messes with it, rearranges it, and totally changes things forever. The wild rice adds a nice chewiness and color, and my homemade approach to cream of mushroom soup might keep you from ever cracking open another can of the stuff as long as you live.

This is utterly luscious!

2 cups wild rice

8 cups low-sodium chicken broth

3 broccoli heads, cut into small florets

½ cup (1 stick) butter

1 medium onion, finely diced

1 pound white button or cremini mushrooms, finely chopped

2 carrots, peeled and finely diced

2 celery stalks, finely diced

¼ cup all-purpose flour

½ cup heavy cream

2 teaspoons salt

1 teaspoon black pepper

1 cup panko breadcrumbs

2 tablespoons minced fresh parsley

1. Preheat the oven to 375°F.

2. Add the wild rice into a medium saucepan with 5 cups of the chicken broth. Bring it to a boil over medium-high heat, then reduce the heat to low and cover the pan.

3. Cook the rice until it has just started to break open and is slightly tender, 35 to 40 minutes. Set it aside.

4. Meanwhile, blanch the broccoli by throwing the florets into boiling water for 1½ to 2 minutes, until bright green and still slightly crisp.

5. Immediately drain the broccoli and plunge it into a bowl of ice water to stop the cooking process. Remove it from the ice water and set it aside.

6. Heat a large pot over medium-high heat, then melt 6 tablespoons of the butter. Add the onions and the mushrooms . . .

7. And cook them, stirring occasionally, for 3 to 4 minutes, until the liquid begins to evaporate.

8. Add the carrots and celery . . .

9. And cook for 3 to 4 minutes, until the vegetables are soft and the mixture begins to turn darker.

10. Sprinkle the flour on the vegetables and stir to incorporate it . . .

11. Then pour in the remaining 3 cups of broth . . .

12. And stir to combine. Bring the mixture to a gentle boil and allow it to thicken, 3 to 4 minutes.

13. Pour in the heavy cream, stirring to combine.

14. Let the mixture cook until it is nice and thick. Season with the salt and pepper, then taste and adjust the seasonings as needed.

15. To assemble, add half the cooked rice to the bottom of a 2-quart baking dish . . .

16. Then lay on half the broccoli. Repeat with another layer of both.

17. Using a ladle, scoop out the vegetable-broth mixture . . .

18. And spoon it evenly all over the top.

19. Continue with the rest of the sauce, totally covering the surface with vegetables.

20. Melt the remaining 2 tablespoons of butter, then pour it into a separate bowl with the panko breadcrumbs.

21. Toss the mixture together to coat the breadcrumbs in butter . . .

22. Then sprinkle the breadcrumbs all over the top.

23. Cover the foil and bake the casserole for 20 minutes, then remove the foil and continue baking for 15 minutes or until golden brown on top. Sprinkle on the parsley after you remove it from the oven.

Then dig in!

NO-KNEAD CLOVERLEAF ROLLS

MAKES ABOUT 3 DOZEN ROLLS

The dough I use for my dinner rolls is the same glorious dough I use for cinnamon rolls, raisin bread, or anything in my life that calls for yeast-based dough. It is awesome.

½ cup (1 stick) butter, melted
1 batch Basic Dough (page 89)

1. Drizzle a small amount of butter into muffin cups (you'll get about 36 rolls out of the dough).

2. Pinch off a small amount of dough . . .

3. And roll it into a neat ball. Continue with the rest of the dough.

4. As you roll them, place them in groups of 3 in each muffin cup.

5. Set the pans in a draft-free, slightly warm place, cover with a lightweight dish towel . . .

6. And allow the rolls to rise for 1 to 1½ hours, until they're light and puffy.

7. Preheat the oven to 400°F.

8. Bake the rolls for 18 to 20 minutes, until deep golden brown.

9. Serve the rolls piping hot at the table.

They pull apart perfectly!

NOTE: *Time the rolls backward so that they're ready to put in the oven about 20 minutes before the feast. You want them to be nice and warm!*

CARAMEL APPLE PIE

MAKES 8 TO 12 SERVINGS

Dessert is a very important component of Thanksgiving, and this apple pie will make you cry. But in a good, cleanse-your-soul way. It's just so simple, so naturally beautiful, so intelligent, so altruistic, talented, and charming. And it can juggle and dance the tango like there's no tomorrow. It's the coolest apple pie on earth!

My father-in-law likes pie. He likes pie *a lot*. And when I served this for the first time at 1:23 P.M. on Thanksgiving Day approximately 15.9 years ago, he devoured his first piece within 1.2 minutes. Then he decided his slice was crooked, so he kept evening out the pan until he'd pretty much polished off half of the thing. Then he went back for more.

I decided there was no need to branch out from there. I'd made the apple pie of a lifetime. It was so profound, I even remember the time and place.

Give or take 700 years.

1 unbaked Perfect Pie Crust (page 286)

7 to 8 cups peeled and sliced Granny Smith apples

½ cup sugar

¼ cup all-purpose flour

¼ teaspoon salt

Juice of ½ lemon

TOPPING

¾ cup (1½ sticks) butter

½ cup flour

1 cup packed brown sugar

¼ teaspoon salt

½ cup quick oats

½ cup finely chopped pecans

½ cup jarred caramel topping

1. Preheat the oven to 375°F.

2. Remove the pie crust from the freezer and allow it to sit on the counter for 30 minutes.

3. Roll it out on a lightly floured surface so that it's about 1 inch larger in diameter than the top of your pie pan.

4. Carefully fold it in half in order to transfer it to the pan, then unfold it so that it covers the whole pan.

5. Carefully tear off the excess dough so that it just hangs below the lip of the pan . . .

6. Then tuck the edges underneath so that there's a neat dough rim.

7. Now, you can leave the crust just like this if you like a more rustic look. I like this option because I'm lazy.

8. Or you can use your fingers to create a little bit of a decorative edge.

9. Keep going until it's all frilly and fancy.

10. Throw the apples into a large bowl with the sugar, flour, salt, and lemon juice . . .

11. Then stir them around to combine. Let them sit for a few minutes while you make the crumb topping.

12. In a separate bowl, combine the butter, flour, brown sugar, and salt with a pastry blender . . .

13. Until the mixture is crumbly and lumpy.

14. Add the oats . . .

15. And the pecans, then stir it to combine completely.

16. Mound the apples into the pie crust . . .

17. Then sprinkle on all the topping.

18. Lightly cover the crust edges with aluminum foil and bake the pie for 25 minutes, then remove the foil and continue baking for another 25 to 30 minutes, until the top is golden brown. Watch the top as it bakes, and if it seems like it's browning too quickly, cover the pie with aluminum foil.

19. Remove it from the oven, drizzle the caramel sauce all over the top of the pie . . .

20. And serve big ol' wedges.

Variations

- *Serve with a dollop of Sweetened Whipped Cream (page 369).*
- *Serve with a scoop of Cinnamon Ice Cream (page 152).*

I'm thankful that I get to be their mama.

PECAN PIE

MAKES 8 TO 12 SERVINGS

Not to play favorites . . . but pecan pie is definitely my favorite. So I guess saying "not to play favorites" is really my way of saying "I'm about to play favorites." It's so weird how we humans skate around things.

Pecan pie. Let me say it once again in case you didn't hear me: Pecan pie. There's nothing in the entire universe like it. It's dark and gooey and sinful and crunchy to the extent that it's literally impossible to take a bite without closing your eyes and giving thanks to God for all things on the earth that made a pie like this possible. The wheat that made the flour that went into the crust. The corn responsible for the sticky sweet syrup. The sugarcane that gave birth to the molasses and brown sugar. And the Pecan Fairy, who faithfully sprinkles pecans over the earth every fall.

Wait. I'm confusing theologies here. Pecan Fairy? I meant pecan tree!

I'm going to be quiet now.

1 cup light corn syrup

1 cup sugar

¼ cup packed brown sugar

3 eggs, beaten

⅓ cup (⅔ stick) butter, melted and slightly cooled

½ teaspoon salt

¾ teaspoon vanilla extract

1 heaping cup finely chopped pecans

1 unbaked Perfect Pie Crust (page 286), rolled out and prepared in a pie pan as on page 280

1. Preheat the oven to 350°F.

2. In a large bowl, combine the corn syrup . . .

3. The sugar . . .

4. The brown sugar . . .

5. The eggs . . .

6. The butter, salt, and vanilla. Whisk the mixture until it's totally combined.

7. Place the chopped pecans in the bottom of the pie crust . . .

8. Then pour the sticky mixture right over the top.

9. Cover the pie in foil and place it on a baking sheet. Bake the pie for 35 minutes. Remove the foil, then bake for 25 to 30 minutes more, being careful not to burn the crust or pecans. (If it seems to be browning too quickly, cover it with foil again.)

10. The pie should not be overly jiggly when you remove it from the oven. If it is, just continue baking it in 5-minute intervals until it's done.

11. Let the pie cool before slicing it into wedges . . .

And absolutely devouring it!

Variations

- Serve with Sweetened Whipped Cream (page 369).
- Serve with Cinnamon Ice Cream (page 152).

PUMPKIN PIE

MAKES 8 TO 12 SERVINGS

As traditional and quintessentially "Thanksgiving" as pumpkin pie is, I have to admit that it doesn't generally compel me to eat it. Next to the tart fruitiness of apple pie and the heavenly goodness of pecan pie, it's easy for me to walk right past the pumpkin version and never think twice. So when I force myself to make a pumpkin pie, it had better be gosh darn good—good enough to compel me to take a walk on the pumpkin side of life.

This beautiful baby is smooth, sweet, and definitely something special!

2 cups pumpkin puree (not pumpkin pie filling), canned or fresh

One 14-ounce can sweetened condensed milk

2 eggs

1 tablespoon vanilla extract

¼ teaspoon ground cloves

½ teaspoon ground cinnamon

¼ teaspoon ground ginger

½ cup packed brown sugar

1 unbaked Perfect Pie Crust (page 286), rolled out and prepared in a pie pan as on page 280

1. Preheat the oven to 425°F.

2. Add the pumpkin puree to a large bowl.

3. Pour in the sweetened condensed milk.

4. Add the eggs . . .

5. The vanilla . . .

6. The spices . . .

7. And the brown sugar.

8. Whisk until the mixture is perfectly smooth . . .

9. Then pour it into the pie crust.

10. Bake the pie for 15 minutes, then reduce the oven temperature to 350°F and bake for 40 minutes more. Watch the crust and make sure it doesn't brown; lightly cover the pie with foil if it browns too quickly.

11. Remove the pie from the oven when it's no longer jiggly, then let it cool before serving.

12. Serve on its own (delicious!) or with Sweetened Whipped Cream (page 369) (even more delicious!).

PERFECT PIE CRUST

MAKES TWO 9-INCH PIE CRUSTS

This pie crust—shared with me years ago by my friend Sylvia—really is perfect, whether you're making pie, pot pie, or tarts. Get a head start and make several in advance—they keep perfectly in the freezer!

3 cups all-purpose flour

1 teaspoon salt

¾ cup vegetable shortening, cut into pieces

¾ cup (1½ sticks) butter, cut into pieces

1 egg

1 tablespoon distilled white vinegar

5 tablespoons cold water

1. Combine the flour, salt, shortening, and butter in a large bowl.

4. Beat the egg with a fork and add it to the mixture . . .

7. Stir it all together until it comes together, adding another tablespoon or two of cold water if it needs the moisture.

2. Using a pastry cutter, gradually work it all together . . .

5. Along with the vinegar . . .

8. Form the mixture into two balls . . .

3. Until the mixture resembles coarse crumbs.

6. And the cold water.

9. And wrap them in individual plastic bags. Seal the bags and place them in the freezer. Remove them from the freezer 30 minutes before you need them.

I'm thankful for
cowboys and cowgirls!

TURKEY DAY LEFTOVERS

The great thing about the big Thanksgiving feast is that you don't have to worry too much about whether you're going to make too much food. Because if you do, there are so many glorious dishes you can make with all the leftovers!

Here's a scrumptious handful of my very favorite ways to use all good stuff we don't polish off on Thanksgiving Day. They're so good, I'm always tempted to roast a *second* turkey just to make sure I'll have enough!

TURKEY POT PIE

MAKES 12 SERVINGS

It doesn't get much better than pot pie. It just doesn't. It's that thick brothy gravy . . . that golden, crisp crust . . . those tender, flavorful vegetables. Gosh, gosh, gosh. Times a million!

Using leftover Thanksgiving turkey to make a pot pie is one of the best ways to enjoy one. And if you happen to have an unused, unbaked pie crust after the Thanksgiving meal is said and done, even better!

This makes you feel comforted, frugal . . . and fantastically *full* all at the same time!

4 tablespoons (½ stick) butter

½ cup finely diced onion

½ cup finely diced carrot

½ cup finely diced celery

2 cups leftover turkey, shredded or chopped (a mix of light and dark meat is fine)

¼ cup all-purpose flour

3 cups low-sodium chicken broth, more if needed

¼ teaspoon turmeric

Salt and pepper

1 tablespoon chopped fresh thyme

¼ cup heavy cream, more to taste

1 unbaked Perfect Pie Crust, page 286

1 egg

1. Preheat the oven to 400°F.

2. Melt the butter in a large pot over medium-high heat, then add the onion, carrot, and celery.

3. Stir them around until the onions start to turn translucent, about 3 minutes.

4. Mix in the leftover turkey . . .

5. Then sprinkle the flour over the top and stir it until it's all combined with the turkey and vegetables. Cook for 1 to 2 minutes.

6. Pour in the chicken broth . . .

7. And stir it around.

8. Add the turmeric . . .

9. The salt and pepper . . .

10. And the thyme.

11. Pour in the cream . . .

12. Then stir the mixture and let it bubble up and thicken, about 3 minutes. (If it seems overly thick, splash in a little more broth.) Turn off the heat.

13. Pour the filling into a 2-quart baking dish.

14. Roll out the pie crust on a floured surface . . .

15. And lay it over the top of the dish, pressing it lightly into the surface of the filling.

16. Press the dough so that the edges stick to the outside of the pan.

17. Use a knife to cut little vents here and there in the surface of the dough.

18. Mix together the egg with 2 tablespoons water . . .

19. And brush it all over the surface of the crust. (You will have some egg wash left over.)

20. Place the pie on a rimmed baking sheet and bake for 25 to 30 minutes, until the crust is deep golden brown (this pie got about as "deep golden brown" as you want to go!) and the filling is bubbly.

21. Serve it up by the (big ol') spoonful!

Variations

• *To save time, use a store-bought pie crust.*

• *If you do not have leftover turkey, any shredded cooked chicken is just fine.*

"I'm thankful for leftover turkey."

LEFTOVER THANKSGIVING PANINI

MAKES 1 SANDWICH, WHICH SERVES 2!

If Thanksgiving ever disappeared from the planet, and I don't expect it to, but just in case it ever did, I would still prepare the entire turkey feast just so I could make this sandwich the next day. It is, without question, one of the most delicious things I've ever eaten.

It's also one of the most filling! One sandwich easily feeds two hungry souls.

2 tablespoons Dijon mustard

2 slices sourdough sandwich bread

2 slices Swiss cheese

⅓ cup shredded leftover Roasted Thanksgiving Turkey (page 248)

3 tablespoons leftover Cranberry Sauce (page 256)

⅓ cup leftover dressing (any variety)

2 tablespoons leftover Giblet Gravy (page 251)

2 tablespoons butter, softened

1. Spread the mustard on both slices of bread . . .

2. Then lay a slice of cheese on each piece.

3. On one slice, arrange the turkey . . .

4. And the cranberry sauce.

5. On the other slice, lay on the dressing . . .

6. And spoon the gravy over the top.

7. Carefully unite the two halves into one sandwich, then spread the top side of the bread with 1 tablespoon of the butter.

8. Invert the sandwich, butter-side down, onto a hot panini maker (or a grill pan or skillet over medium-low heat). Spread the top with the remaining 1 tablespoon of butter.

9. Close the panini maker and grill the sandwich until the bread is crusty and golden, the fillings are hot, and the cheese is melted. Note: If you use a grill pan or skillet, place a second heavy pan or skillet on top of the sandwich to press it. Flip the sandwich halfway through to grill the other side.

10. Pull it off the heat and slice it in half!

This sandwich is *to die for.*

I'm thankful for my dear sister-in-law, Missy.

TURKEY SPRING ROLLS

MAKES 8 SPRING ROLLS

These easy-to-make spring rolls are light and crisp and crunchy and green. Perfect for post-Thanksgiving bloat!

   Did I just say bloat? Not a very appetizing word. Sorry.

TURKEY SPRING ROLLS

2 cups shredded leftover Roasted Thanksgiving Turkey (page 248)

3 tablespoons soy sauce

1 teaspoon rice vinegar

1 teaspoon sesame oil

½ teaspoon hot chili oil

1 package cellophane noodles

Eight 8½-inch rice paper wrappers

3 leaves green leaf lettuce, torn into pieces

½ cup alfalfa sprouts

1 carrot, cut into julienne

1 cucumber, cut into julienne

3 tablespoons finely chopped cilantro

DIPPING SAUCE

1 cup leftover Cranberry Sauce (page 256)

2 tablespoons soy sauce

1. Place the turkey in a bowl and drizzle in the soy sauce . . .

2. The rice vinegar . . .

3. The sesame oil and the hot chili oil.

4. Stir to combine and give it a taste. If you'd like a stronger flavor, add a little more of any of the ingredients.

5. Next, place the cellophane noodles in a large bowl.

6. Cover them with boiling water and let them sit according to the package directions.

7. When they are tender but still have a nice bite, drain them and set them aside.

8. Soften the rice paper wrappers by placing them one by one into a bowl of warm water . . .

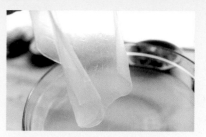

9. And taking them out when they're soft but still hold together.

10. To assemble each spring roll, lay a wrapper on a plate. Lay a small line of noodles in the center.

11. Add a small amount of lettuce . . .

12. A small amount of the turkey . . .

13. A small amount of the alfalfa sprouts . . .

14. A few carrot and cucumber strips . . .

15. And a sprinkling of cilantro.

16. Fold in the sides of the wrappers . . .

I'm thankful for every drop of rain.

17. And roll it into a tight roll. Repeat to make the rest of the rolls.

18. To make the dipping sauce, combine the cranberry sauce and soy sauce.

19. Then dip away!

So fresh and delicious!

NOTES

- *Best if made within 1 hour of eating.*
- *Let kids have fun making different combinations!*
- *You will have leftover noodles; make a noodle salad with more spring roll ingredients! Toss in a little of the dipping sauce as a dressing.*

Variations

- *Use shredded cooked chicken instead of turkey.*
- *Add slices of avocado along with the other ingredients.*
- *Spring rolls can be dipped in regular soy sauce instead of the cranberry-soy dipping sauce.*

TURKEY TETRAZZINI

MAKES 12 SERVINGS

Tetrazzini is a triumph. Nothing short of a triumph.

It's the best use of leftover Thanksgiving turkey there is! Creamy, dreamy, flavorful, rich, comforting, beautiful, decadent . . . and doggone delicious! This serves a big ol' crowd.

4 tablespoons (½ stick) butter

4 garlic cloves, minced

1 pound white mushrooms, quartered

½ teaspoon salt, more to taste

½ teaspoon black pepper, more to taste

1 cup dry white wine

¼ cup all-purpose flour

4 cups turkey or chicken broth, more if needed for thinning

One 8-ounce package cream cheese

3 cups shredded or diced Roasted Thanksgiving Turkey (page 248)

1 cup finely chopped black olives

1½ cups frozen green peas

4 bacon slices, fried and chopped

1 cup grated Monterey Jack cheese

½ cup grated Parmesan cheese

12 ounces thin spaghetti, broken in half and cooked

1 cup panko breadcrumbs

1. Preheat the oven to 350°F.

2. Melt the butter in a large pot over medium heat and add the garlic.

3. Throw in the mushrooms, salt, and pepper . . .

4. Then stir the mushrooms and cook for 2 to 3 minutes to brown slightly.

5. Pour in the wine . . .

6. And cook them, stirring occasionally, for 3 to 4 minutes, or until the liquid is reduced by half.

7. Sprinkle the flour all over the mushrooms . . .

8. Then stir to combine.

9. Pour in the broth.

10. Stir and continue to cook . . .

11. Until the sauce is nice and thick, 3 to 4 minutes.

12. Add the cream cheese and stir until it mixes in. (Don't worry if it seems a little lumpy at first. That will go away!)

13. Add the turkey . . .

14. The olives . . .

15. The peas . . .

16. The bacon . . .

17. And the Monterey Jack and Parmesan.

18. Stir it until everything is well combined, then add salt and pepper to taste.

19. Add the spaghetti . . .

20. And stir to combine. If the mixture is too thick, splash in ½ cup of broth.

21. Pour the whole shebang into a large casserole dish . . .

22. And even out the surface.

23. Sprinkle on the panko breadcrumbs . . .

24. And bake it for 20 to 25 minutes, or until the crumbs are golden brown and the casserole is bubbly.

25. Serve it to hearty appetites!

Variations

• *Use shredded cooked chicken instead of turkey.*

• *Substitute low-sodium chicken broth for the wine, if you prefer.*

• *Substitute cooked elbow macaroni for the spaghetti.*

Horses enjoying
their Christmas feast.

CHRISTMAS

Christmas is, without question, my very favorite holiday, in no small part because of the following:

The smell of fir trees. *It's a Wonderful Life.* Johnny Mathis. Christmas shopping. Decorating Christmas cookies. Bing Crosby. Memories of my grandmother's house. Trimming the tree. Advent calendars. Christmas cards. Delivering cinnamon rolls. The scent of simmering cider. My mom's nativity set. Anticipation. Family togetherness. Wrapping presents. Andy Williams. *How the Grinch Stole Christmas.* Hanging the stockings. Tinsel. Christmas sweaters. Candy canes. Carolers. Mistletoe. *The Nutcracker.* The smell of new perfume. The sound of jingle bells. Eating Christmas cookies. Eating cinnamon rolls. Christmas Eve. "O Holy Night." "Have Yourself a Merry Little Christmas." Placing bets with my husband to see how close we can get to 7:00 A.M. on Christmas morning before the kids run downstairs and shriek "SANTA CAME!" at the top of their lungs.

I mean, c'mon. How could any other holiday possibly compete?

There are the memories from my childhood. Tuning into that old *Rudolph the Red-Nosed Reindeer* special back when there were only four TV channels. Watching my brother Mike unwrap the single baby sock our Aunt Nancy always wrapped up for him as a Christmas gag. Playing with my Barbie dream house for hours on end while also trying to keep my baby sister from eating Ken's head.

But there are also the new memories from Christmases with my own children. Years ago, for the very first Christmas card I ever sent out on behalf of my new family, I took our baby daughter to get her picture taken at a mall kiosk that dressed up children as angels. Fortunately for my new husband, I sent that card to everyone either of us had ever known, including all his college friends and every agriculture purveyor with whom he'd ever done business. A couple of years later, after our second daughter was born, I did the exact same thing again. What a lucky, lucky man my husband was!

Christmas is about Christ's birth. It's about memories. It's about celebration and togetherness and love and family.

And it's about food—pure and simple. Here are all the recipes that define Christmastime for me.

CHRISTMAS DELIGHTS AND DELIVERIES

From a scrumptiously colorful cookie platter to sinfully delicious sweet rolls, these treats are perfect to deliver to friends and neighbors . . . or to enjoy at home while you're decorating the tree!

OTHER RECIPES TO CONSIDER: Candy-Dipped S'mores (decorate with Christmas colors) (page 71); Homemade Chocolate Truffles (decorate with Christmas colors) (page 60); Krispy Eggs (roll into balls and decorate with Christmas sprinkles) (page 96); Caramel Apples (page 230); Eyeball Cake Balls (decorate with Christmas-colored melting candies and sprinkles) (page 238)

BRANDY SNAPS 🦋

MAKES 12

Before you break into your best Peter Clemenza impersonation, take note: These beautiful babies are *not* cannoli. They just play them on TV.

I realize that made absolutely no sense. Or, as Yoda would say, "Little sense I realize that absolutely made. Hmmmm?"

I love movies. Can you tell?

What these *are* are brandy snaps, which do resemble cannoli in the sense that they're crispy, crunchy shells with a creamy, dreamy filling. But the crispy shells in this case are made with a butter, sugar, and molasses mixture spiked with (you guessed it) brandy, which makes them oh-so-perfect for holiday time. And if the shells alone weren't enough to sell ya, the totally tubular wonders are filled with glorious booze-spiked whipped cream. Every time I bite into one, I wonder what in the world I could have done to deserve something so marvelous.

These do take a little finesse, as it's important to bake the shells long enough that they start to harden soon after you take them out of the oven (but hopefully not before you get a chance to roll them up). If they still seem a little soft and pitiful after baking, just throw 'em back into the oven for a couple of minutes and try again.

SHELLS

1 stick (½ cup) butter

½ cup regular/unsulphured molasses

¼ cup packed brown sugar

¼ cup sugar

¾ cup all-purpose flour

⅛ teaspoon salt

¼ teaspoon ground ginger

1 tablespoon brandy

FILLING

2 cups heavy cream

⅓ cup sugar

2 tablespoons brandy, more to taste

1. Preheat the oven to 325°F. Line a baking sheet with a baking mat or parchment paper.

2. Begin by melting the butter in a skillet over medium heat.

3. Add the molasses . . .

4. The brown sugar . . .

5. And the sugar.

6. Stir to combine and let the mixture cook until it starts to bubble. Let it bubble up for about a minute, then turn off the heat.

7. Stir in the flour and the salt until it's all combined.

8. Then add the ground ginger . . .

9. And a generous tablespoon of brandy! Give or take a gallon.

10. Use a tablespoon to spoon the marvelous mixture onto the prepared baking sheets. Plan on only 6 or 7 cookies per sheet, as they will spread like crazy in the oven.

11. Bake 'em for 13 to 14 minutes, or until they're really bubbling away. Remove the baking sheet from the oven and let the cookies cool on the pan for 3 to 5 minutes.

12. Using a small spatula or knife, carefully lift up the edges of the circles one at a time and drape them over a cannoli mold (or, if you're me, the large metal handle of a whisk or potato masher!). The cookies will naturally drape over the mold; help them along by pressing the seal. (They should be pretty firm by the time you've rolled them; if they're still very soft, return the remaining cookies to the oven.)

13. Slide the cookies off the mold . . .

14. And set them on a cold plate. Be prepared to slightly reshape the cookies as they cool; they often need a little reminder of what they should look like.

15. When the shells are cooled, combine the cream (make sure it's very cold!), sugar, and brandy in the bowl of a mixer fitted with a whisk attachment.

16. Mix on high until the cream is very stiff (it might take a couple of minutes because of the booze). Consider adding all of this to your next cup of coffee.

17. Come to your senses, then place the cream into a pastry bag fitted with a large tip . . .

18. And carefully fill the cooled brandy snaps until the cream is bulging out of the sides. That's when you know you've done it right.

IMPORTANT NOTE: *Serve brandy snaps within a couple of hours of filling, as the shells will begin to soften. If you include these on your cookie platter, just let the guests know they need to inhale these first.*

Gotta love those photography kiosks at the mall around Christmastime.

CHOCOLATE CANDY CANE COOKIES

MAKES 32 COOKIES

When I make these delicious delights at Christmastime, I commit the cardinal sin of gluttony. Repeatedly. Until they're all gone and I'm staring at an empty platter.

But wait! Before you condemn me to whatever wretched place people who commit one of the deadly sins at Christmastime go (that made no grammatical sense), please hear me out. I have a really good excuse!

They are really, really yummy.

I mean it. There's something about the slightly soft chocolate cookie, coated with white chocolate and dipped in crushed mints. One is never enough. Ten is never enough. How many does this recipe make again? Thirty-two? Well okay, then. Thirty-two isn't enough either!

But then again, I might have issues.

1 cup (2 sticks) butter, softened

1 cup powdered sugar

1 egg

2 teaspoons vanilla extract

½ cup unsweetened cocoa powder

2½ cups all-purpose flour

1 teaspoon salt

Large handfuls of both red and green peppermints

4 ounces (4 squares) almond bark or white baking chocolate

2. Beat them together until the mixture is nice and smooth.

3. Mix in the egg and vanilla.

5. And mix just until the dough comes together. Press a piece of plastic wrap on the surface of the dough and refrigerate it for a couple of hours.

1. Add the butter and powdered sugar to the bowl of an electric mixer fitted with the paddle attachment.

4. Add the cocoa powder, flour, and salt . . .

6. While the dough is chillin' away, unwrap the candies and place them in separate plastic bags.

7. Grab a rolling pin and release your rage upon the mints. You want to crush them! You want to obliterate them! Just think of all the ways they've wronged you!

8. Throw the crushed mints into separate bowls and set 'em aside.

9. When the dough is finished chilling, preheat the oven to 375°F. Roll the dough into balls . . .

10. Throw the balls onto baking sheets lined with parchment paper or baking mats . . .

11. And flatten them slightly with the bottom of a coffee mug or glass. Bake the cookies for 7 to 9 minutes, or until just set. Remove 'em from the oven and let 'em cool completely.

12. While the cookies cool, melt the almond bark in a double boiler or a microwave-safe bowl. Stir until smooth.

13. One at a time, dip the cookies halfway into the melted almond bark . . .

14. And sprinkle the top side generously with crushed mints, holding the cookies over the bowls to catch the excess. You can mix red and green on the same cookie, or you can do some cookies with just red and some with just green. No one can make that decision but you.

15. Lay the cookies, sprinkled side up, on parchment paper or a baking mat and allow them to set completely.

16. Serve them with a few whole mints on the side. You'll absolutely love these.

NOTE: *Store in an airtight container at room temperature for up to 3 days before delivering, or in the freezer in storage bags for up to 3 months.*

Variations

- *Dip in Christmas-colored sprinkles instead of peppermints.*

- *Use different colors of candy melts (red, green, etc.) instead of white.*

- *Roll out the cookies and cut candy cane-shaped cookies. Dip half the cookies and coat in candy.*

CHRISTMAS CHERRY COOKIES

MAKES 32 COOKIES

These precious little red-and-green cutie pies (I mean cutie *cookies*. Mixed up my sweets. Sorry, man) add lots of pretty color to your Christmas cookie plates. They have a pleasant sweetness and a lovely citrus edge, plus I think they sort of look like outie belly buttons. *Red and green* outie belly buttons at that.

I'm sorry if that statement disturbs you.

It actually disturbs me, too.

1 cup (2 sticks) butter, softened

½ cup sugar

2 egg yolks

1 lemon, zested and juiced

Zest of 1 orange

1 teaspoon vanilla extract

2 cups all-purpose flour

Candied green and red cherries (available at holiday time)

1. Add the butter to the bowl of an electric mixer fitted with the paddle attachment. (Or you can just use a bowl and a wooden spoon if you're feeling feisty.)

2. Toss in the sugar, egg yolks, lemon juice and zest, orange zest . . .

3. And vanilla. Cream the mixture together until it's nice and smooth and lickable. And likable!

4. If you have the patience, sift the flour twice into a separate bowl. Or, if you're like me, sift the flour once into a separate bowl. Who has the time to sift flour *twice* these days? Not me, that's who! I mean whom. I mean who. I mean . . . I have no idea what I mean.

5. Add the sifted flour to the bowl . . .

6. And mix it gently until the dough is just combined. Consider eating half of the dough right out of the bowl. Conquer your fleshly desires. Proceed to the next step.

7. Place the dough into a plastic bag and refrigerate it for at least 1 hour, or until firm. Consider eating half the dough again. Conquer again. Then consider and conquer at least once more during the hour it's chilling. Feel really good about yourself, then go eat a bite of ice cream straight out of the freezer. Proceed to the next step.

8. When you're ready to make the cookies, preheat the oven to 300°F and grab those wacky red candied cherries, along with those even wackier green cherries. (Green cherries? I'll never understand.)

9. Slice them in half and set them aside.

10. Roll the dough into small balls and set them on a baking sheet lined with a baking mat or parchment paper.

11. Gently press the cherry halves, cut side down, into each ball . . .

12. And bake the cookies for 20 minutes.

13. Keep an eye on them and remove them from the oven before they start to brown. They should be just barely golden around the edges.

14. Let them cool slightly, then serve 'em up! Cutest outie belly button cookies on earth!

(Sorry.)

Variations

- *Instead of adding cherries, make thumbprint cookies. Before baking, use your thumb to make an impression in the cookies. Fill the wells with your choice of jam and bake as directed.*

- *Instead of cherries, press a pecan half into each cookie.*

MARSHMALLOW POPS

MAKES 24 POPS

These are an easy-to-make treat for any holiday, and they add a special touch of fun and whimsy to a Christmas cookie platter. And everyone knows that a Christmas cookie platter without whimsy is no Christmas cookie platter at all.

These are really great treats for kiddos to make because no baking is involved and very little can go wrong. The bonus is that no two marshmallow pops are ever the same!

Lollipop sticks (found at craft stores)

24 regular marshmallows

8 ounces white almond bark, melted and cooled slightly

8 ounces chocolate almond bark, melted and cooled slightly

Various sprinkles, nonpareils, chopped nuts, crushed candy— anything you want!

1. Have your sticks, marshmallows, melted chocolate, and sprinkles at the ready.

2. One at a time, dip the sticks into the melted white or chocolate almond bark so that about 1 inch of the stick is covered.

3. Gently insert one into a marshmallow so that it goes three quarters of the way through.

4. Repeat with the rest of the marshmallows so that half the pops are white and half are chocolate. Allow the sticks to set for about 20 minutes.

5. To coat the marshmallows, gently roll the marshmallows on the surface of the melted almond bark until it's totally covered.

6. Lightly tap the stick on the side of the bowl, allowing the excess to drip off. Get some on your finger. Lick it off. Repeat as needed.

7. Sprinkle decorations all over the surface.

8. Then do the same with the chocolate!

9. Poke holes in the bottom of a cardboard box: Instant Marshmallow Pop Holder! This'll give you a place to keep them while they set. (A Styrofoam block works, too.)

How cute are these?

Variations

S'MORES: *Dip marshmallows in chocolate, then coat with crushed graham crackers.*

ROCKY ROAD: *Dip marshmallows in chocolate, then coat with chopped pecans.*

COOKIES & CREAM: *Dip marshmallows in white almond bark, then sprinkle with crushed Oreos.*

OTHER HOLIDAYS: *Use colored meltable wafers and different sprinkles to create pops for Valentine's Day, St. Patrick's Day, Easter, Fourth of July, and Halloween!*

SPREADS

MAKES ABOUT 50 SMALL SQUARE COOKIES

These small, yummy bars are called Spreads for three reasons. First, the cookie dough base is *spread* all over the baking sheet. Second, the melted chocolate chips are *spread* all over the top of the baked cookie. Third, and most important, one's bottom *spreads* after eating too many of these.

But it's Christmas. Calories don't count!

This is my older brother Doug's absolute favorite cookie recipe ever, and he used to command either my younger sister Betsy or me to make them for him at least weekly. I have no idea why my mother tolerated this hierarchical behavior, but I'm definitely teaching my boys to make cookies for their sisters, and to make them with a smile!

So in a way, I'm both ending and perpetuating destructive family patterns at the same time.

I'm so glad we had this talk.

1 cup (2 sticks) butter

1 cup packed brown sugar

1 egg

1 teaspoon vanilla extract

2 cups all-purpose flour

½ teaspoon salt

6 to 8 ounces semisweet chocolate chips

1. Preheat the oven to 350°F.

2. Add the butter and brown sugar to the bowl of a mixer fitted with the paddle attachment.

3. Mix together until it's all smooth and wonderful.

4. Add the egg and vanilla . . .

5. And the flour and salt . . .

6. And mix again, scraping the sides to make sure everything mixes and mingles.

7. Throw the dough onto a baking sheet and use a dinner knife to spread it into a rough rectangular shape about ⅓ inch thick. Bake for 15 to 17 minutes, or until light golden brown.

9. Use a knife or spatula to spread the chocolate all over the surface of the cookie.

11. When you're ready to serve 'em up, use a pizza cutter or sharp knife to slice them into uniform squares.

8. Sprinkle the chocolate chips all over the top, then return it to the oven for about a minute. When you take it back out, the chocolate chips will have softened.

10. Then set it aside for a while, long enough for the chocolate to set!

Variations

• Mix ½ cup chopped pecans into the dough before spreading on the baking sheet.

• Sprinkle chopped pecans, crushed pretzels, or crushed toffee bars over the chocolate before it sets.

MY FAVORITE CHRISTMAS COOKIES

MAKES 36 COOKIES

These are my very favorite Christmas cookies from my childhood, and even way before that. That made no sense. Let me start over.

These are my very favorite Christmas cookies from my childhood! My mom has made them since the day I was born (Oh, how fondly I remember that day! Just kidding) and they're charming, vintage, and so much fun to make. Whip up as many colors of the simple egg glaze as you want and paint to your heart's content. I've always very proudly used little plastic-handled paintbrushes like the ones you'd find in a child's watercolor kit. Heck, I think I've probably used little plastic-handled paintbrushes from *my* child's watercolor kit!

They're nontoxic paints. We're cool!

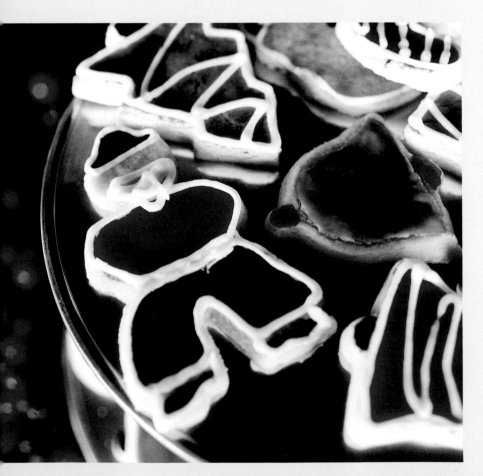

MY FAVORITE SUGAR COOKIE DOUGH

1⅓ cups shortening
(or softened butter)

1½ cups sugar

1 teaspoon grated orange zest

2 eggs

1 teaspoon vanilla extract

4 cups all-purpose flour

3 teaspoons baking powder

½ teaspoon salt

2 tablespoons plus 2 teaspoons whole milk

EGG YOLK GLAZE

(for each color of glaze; make as many different colors as you wish)

1 egg yolk

2 to 3 drops food coloring

ROYAL ICING

2 pounds powdered sugar, sifted

⅓ cup whole milk

2 egg whites

1. Add the shortening, sugar, and orange zest to the bowl of an electric mixer fitted with the paddle attachment.

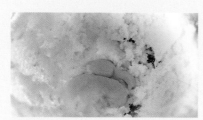

2. Beat until smooth, then add the eggs . . .

3. And vanilla. Beat again, scraping the sides of the bowl halfway through.

4. Sift together the flour, baking powder, and salt, then add it to the bowl and mix until just combined.

5. Pour in the milk and mix until the dough is combined.

6. Divide the dough in half, then flatten both halves into discs and place them in plastic bags. Chill the dough for at least 1 hour.

7. After the dough is chilled, preheat the oven to 375°F. Roll out both halves of the dough to ⅓ inch thick and cut out as many cookies as you can.

8. To make the colored glazes, place the egg yolks in separate small dishes.

9. Add 1 tablespoon of water to each dish . . .

10. And 2 or 3 drops of food coloring.

11. Whisk it around with a fork . . .

12. And repeat with the other colors.

13. Carefully transfer the cookies to a baking sheet lined with parchment or a baking mat and use small paintbrushes to paint the cookies with the glaze. Use a dabbing motion to apply it as thick as possible, getting as far out to the edge as you can.

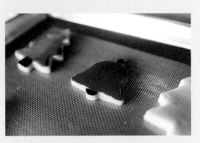

14. On a side note, when I was a little girl, I had to mix together every color of food coloring in order to make the black glaze. Now, guess what? They actually make *black food coloring*. It's a world gone mad.

15. Bake the cookies for 7 to 8 minutes, or until the cookies and glaze are just set. Don't let 'em get brown!

16. While they're cooling, beat together the royal icing ingredients until the mixture is very smooth.

17. Place it in a piping bag fitted with a very small round tip (or you can fill a plastic storage bag and snip a tiny bit off the corner) and outline/accent the cookies however you'd like.

18. If you've got the guts, adorn the suckers with sprinkles and balls and bells and whistles! Just do it before the royal icing sets, which happens really fast.

Santa was a cowboy, by the way.

It's one of those things they never tell you in school.

Variation

Instead of glazing, decorate cookies with Buttercream Frosting (page 93) and Christmas-colored sprinkles after baking.

Christmas card
photo, 2007.
Oh, my heart.

GINGERBREAD HOUSE . . . COOKIES!

MAKES 8 (VERY LARGE!) COOKIES

I have a confession to make. A *Christmas* confession. But I'm not going to tell you what it is unless you promise to love me no matter what. Do you promise? Okay. Here goes:

I am not the sort of mother who constructs three-dimensional gingerbread houses with her children.

Are you still there? Oh, whew. Good! I feel so much better having finally come clean. (And I love you, too, by the way.)

Don't get me wrong. I love the *idea* of gingerbread houses. I love the tradition of it all. The bricks-and-mortar perseverance it takes to make one structurally sound enough not to fall over two hours after you make it.

But you know what? I'm thoroughly convinced that my Christmas season will remain more peaceful and angst-free if I stick with this simpler 2-D version. The real fun is the decorating . . . use candies and other store-bought treats to make whatever kind of house you'd like!

6 cups all-purpose flour

1 teaspoon salt

½ teaspoon allspice

½ teaspoon ground cloves

½ teaspoon ground ginger

½ teaspoon ground nutmeg

½ teaspoon ground cinnamon

¾ cup (1½ sticks) margarine (or softened butter)

1½ cups packed dark brown sugar

1 cup dark molasses

2 eggs

1 tablespoon maple extract

1 batch Royal Icing (page 314), placed in a pastry bag fitted with a small round tip

Miscellaneous candies, sprinkles, and so on, for decorating

1. In a large bowl, combine the flour, salt, allspice, cloves, ginger, nutmeg, and cinnamon . . .

5. Drizzle in the molasses, mixing well, scraping the sides halfway through if necessary.

9. The dough will be pretty dense and slightly dry to the touch. That's the way you want it!

2. And whisk them together. Set the mixture aside for a minute.

6. Add the eggs, one at a time, beating well after each addition.

10. Wrap the dough in plastic wrap and refrigerate it for at least 2 hours.

3. In an electric mixer fitted with the paddle attachment, add the margarine (or butter) and the brown sugar . . .

7. Add the maple extract and mix well.

11. Remove the dough from the fridge and preheat the oven to 350°F. Divide the dough in half and roll out one half to about ⅓ inch thick. (Rolling it out between 2 sheets of plastic wrap keeps the rolling pin from sticking.)

4. And cream them together until fluffy.

8. Add the flour mixture in three batches, beating until just combined after each addition.

12. Use a large cookie cutter to cut houses out of the dough. If you don't have a cutter, just freehand it using a regular dinner knife! They'll look more rustic that way. Repeat with the other half of the dough.

13. Transfer the houses onto baking sheets lined with a baking mat or parchment . . .

14. And bake for 16 to 18 minutes, or until the cookies are baked through but still soft. (Don't worry if you get little bubbles here and there. That just means you're awesome.) Allow the cookies to cool completely.

15. Use the royal icing to outline the shape of the house . . .

16. And as a glue . . .

17. To help attach whatever candies you like.

18. And whatever you do . . .

19. Have lots of fun!

20. And the most important thing: Don't make any two houses alike!

(There's no neighborhood association you have to worry about.)

Hey! Wrong holiday!

Variation

Use a double batch of chocolate cookie dough (page 306) to make chocolate cookie houses.

CARAMEL APPLE SWEET ROLLS

MAKES ABOUT 30 ROLLS

My mom's cinnamon rolls are legendary, and while nothing beats the original recipe, I always have fun coming up with new and decadent variations on the theme. These caramel apple beauties—glazed with a heavenly icing—are just about as good as you can get.

Deliver these to family and friends around Christmastime. They make an unforgettable gift!

½ batch Basic Dough (page 89)

FILLING

4 Granny Smith apples

1 stick butter, plus more for greasing the pans

1 cup packed brown sugar

½ cup heavy cream

1 teaspoon ground cinnamon

CARAMEL ICING

½ cup (1 stick) butter

1 cup packed brown sugar

½ cup heavy cream

2 cups powdered sugar

¼ teaspoon salt

1. First, make the caramel apple filling: Dice up the apples pretty finely,

2. Then throw them in a skillet over medium-high heat and stir them around to cook.

3. After 3 to 4 minutes, when they've gotten nice and golden brown, remove them to a plate.

4. Throw a stick of butter and the brown sugar into the same skillet over medium heat . . .

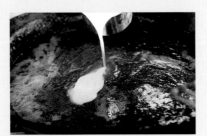

5. And stir it around until the butter is melted and the sugar is dissolved.

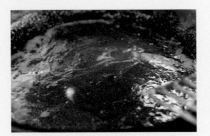

6. Pour in the cream.

7. Then stir it around and let it bubble up and thicken for about a minute.

8. Turn the heat down to low, then add the apples back to the skillet and sprinkle on the cinnamon.

9. Stir the mixture and let it thicken for another 1 to 2 minutes.

10. Then spoon it into a bowl to cool.

11. When you're ready to make the rolls, preheat the oven to 375°F and roll out the dough in a rectangle about 10 x 30 inches.

12. Spoon the caramel apples over the dough and use your fingers to spread them evenly over the surface.

13. Roll the dough toward you into a nice, tight roll . . .

14. And pinch the seam when you get to the end. Turn the seam over so that it's facedown against the countertop.

15. Slice the dough into rolls ½ to ¾ inch thick.

16. Grease 3 round, disposable foil cake pans with butter. Place 7 to 8 rolls in each pan, being careful not to crowd them. Set aside to rise in a warm place for 20 to 25 minutes.

17. Bake for 15 to 18 minutes, or until they're nice and golden brown.

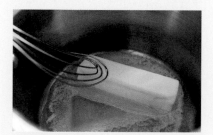

18. While the rolls are baking, make the caramel icing: Melt a stick of butter in a saucepan over medium heat . . .

19. And add the brown sugar.

20. Let it melt, then whisk in the cream. Cook for 2 minutes, whisking constantly, then remove from the heat.

21. Sift in the powdered sugar and salt and stir until you have a smooth icing.

22. Remove the rolls from the oven and immediately spoon a good amount of icing over the top. Use a knife to spread it evenly . . .

23. And watch it slowly seep into the cracks and crevices.

NOTE: *These are incredibly rich! A little goes a long, long way.*

Variations

CINNAMON ROLLS: *Drizzle 1 stick melted butter all over the dough, then sprinkle on a good amount of cinnamon and sugar. Roll and bake as directed. Top with a maple icing made with 3 cups powdered sugar, ½ cup milk, ¼ cup coffee, 1 tablespoon maple extract, 2 tablespoons melted butter, and a dash of salt whisked together.*

ORANGE ROLLS: *After rolling out the dough, drizzle on 1 stick melted butter, then spread on ½ cup orange marmalade and sprinkle on ½ cup brown sugar. Follow the rolling/slicing/baking instructions. Top with an orange glaze made with 3 cups powdered sugar, ½ cup milk, ½ cup orange juice, zest from 1 orange, 2 tablespoons melted butter, and a dash of salt whisked together.*

RASPBERRY CREAM CHEESE ROLLS: *After rolling out the dough, drizzle on 1 stick melted butter, then spread on ½ cup raspberry preserves. Follow the rolling/slicing/baking instructions. Top with a frosting made with 3 cups powdered sugar, ½ cup milk, 4 ounces softened cream cheese, ¼ teaspoon vanilla extract, and a dash of salt whisked together.*

CHRISTMAS RUM PUDDING CAKE

MAKES 1 BUNDT CAKE

My mother-in-law, Nan, always makes this luscious, booze-soaked cake around holiday time, and I always stand in her kitchen and eat it, piece by piece, as if my life depends on it. It starts as a humble, unadulterated, unapologetic, simple, sweet, and somewhat timid box cake mix . . . which is very quickly *adulterated* by a sinful, syrupy, rummy glaze. It's absolutely to die for.

Nan makes this to keep around the house and serve to wayward redheaded daughters-in-law who might drop by for a visit eight times a day during Christmastime . . . but it also makes a beautiful Christmas delivery to that special person on your list.

CAKE

½ cup lightly packed brown sugar

½ cup finely chopped pecans

1 box yellow cake mix

One 3.4-ounce package vanilla cook-and-serve pudding mix

4 eggs

½ cup canola oil

½ cup dark rum

GLAZE

¾ cup (1½ sticks) butter

1½ cups sugar

¾ cup dark rum

2. Throw the cake mix and the pudding mix into the bowl of an electric mixer.

5. The canola oil . . .

6. And plenty o' rum. *Hiccup!*

3. Crack in the eggs,

1. Preheat the oven to 325°F and thoroughly grease a Bundt pan. Sprinkle the brown sugar and chopped pecans in the bottom of the pan. This will serve as the topping of the cake when the cake is eventually turned out of the pan.

4. Then add ½ cup water . . .

7. Mix the batter together until it's smooth and totally combined.

8. Pour the batter into the prepared pan, then bake the cake for 50 to 60 minutes, or until a skewer or long toothpick comes out clean.

11. Remove the cake from the oven and let it cool in the pan for 5 minutes.

14. Carefully invert the cake onto a serving platter and very slowly drizzle the rest of the glaze all over the top, giving the cake a chance to absorb as much as possible.

9. When the cake has about 10 minutes to go, make the naughty (in a good way) glaze! Melt the butter and sugar in a medium saucepan over medium heat . . .

12. Use a skewer or long toothpick to poke approximately 27.3 holes all over the surface of the cake. If you go too far and poke 27.8 holes, the cake will be totally ruined. (Not really.)

15. Let it sit for a couple of hours to make sure it's really moist and rummy.

10. Then add ¼ cup water and bring the mixture to a boil for 4 to 5 minutes, or until thick. Add the rum (be careful if you're cooking with an open flame!) and cook for 1 minute more.

13. Drizzle half the glaze over the surface of the cake, then let the cake sit for a good 10 to 15 minutes to give the glaze a chance to soak in. Make sure you pour it around the edges so it drips down the sides.

Variations

• *Use coconut rum instead of dark rum for a yummy tropical flavor.*

• *Use spice or pumpkin cake mix instead of yellow.*

16. Serve individual slices or deliver the whole cake to a friend!

MULLED APPLE CIDER

MAKES ABOUT 1¼ GALLONS

Warm, mulled apple cider makes life worth living on freezing cold winter days. Warm apple cider spiked with brandy? Ditto. Times a thousand. *Mmmmm.*

Serve this in a nice mug with a piece of rum cake, then curl up by the fire wrapped in a fuzzy blanket and work on your Christmas list.

    And that's an order!

1 gallon apple cider	**1 tablespoon allspice berries**	**½ cup sugar**
3 Granny Smith apples	**5 to 7 cinnamon sticks**	**1 cup apple brandy or regular brandy (optional)**
1 orange	**½ cup fresh cranberries**	

1. Pour the apple cider into a large pot over medium-high heat.

2. Dice up the apples . . .

3. And toss them into the cider.

4. Then peel the rind off the orange in large pieces . . .

5. And toss that in, too.

6. Add the allspice berries . . .

7. The cinnamon sticks . . .

8. And the cranberries.

9. Add the sugar and stir it around to dissolve.

10. Bring the mixture to a low boil, then reduce the heat to low and simmer for 45 minutes to 1 hour. Add the brandy if using, then simmer for another 10 to 15 minutes. Serve warm.

"Baby, it's cold outside."

CHRISTMAS EVE DINNER

Every family's approach to the Christmas meal is different. Our big, elegant feast is always on Christmas Eve, just before we head to the candlelight service at church. Since we had our obligatory turkey and dressing on Thanksgiving a few weeks earlier, the Christmas Eve meal is always, always about the beef. I look forward to this luscious, flavor-packed menu every single year!

DO-AHEAD GAME PLAN

EARLY IN THE DAY

- Crush the peppercorns for the Prime Rib.

- Make the batter for the Yorkshire Pudding (be sure to refrigerate it until you bake them).

- Mince the garlic and rosemary for the Prime Rib and Rosemary-Garlic Roasted Potatoes. Make the sauce.

- Make the balsamic reduction for the Brussels Sprouts with Cranberries.

- Start the Burgundy Mushrooms! They take lots of time and you can keep them warm until serving.

- Make and assemble the Boozy Bread Pudding, but do not bake or pour on the sauce. Store in the fridge and bake that night!

OTHER RECIPES TO CONSIDER: Roasted Thanksgiving Turkey (page 248); Bacon-Wrapped Filet (page 76); Glazed Easter Ham (page 100); Asparagus with Dill Hollandaise (page 104); Roasted Garlic Mashed Potatoes (page 78); Perfect Mashed Potatoes (page 254); Green Beans and Tomatoes (page 270); Caesar Salad (page 187); No-Knead Cloverleaf Rolls (page 278); Pecan Pie (page 282); Caramel Apple Pie (page 279)

PRIME RIB ✦

MAKES 12 TO 18 SERVINGS

What cut of beef we decide to roast on Christmas Eve depends entirely on our mood, our astrological chart, the results of several rock/paper/scissors rounds, and what side of the coin is faceup after the big flip, but it generally toggles between tenderloin and prime rib. And while tenderloin in all its tender (get it?) lusciousness is pretty hard to pass up, I've never seen a roomful of Drummond men grunt louder—or proclaim their affection more ardently—than when they see big, thick slices of juicy prime rib on the table. Prime rib is the most impressive, seductive hunk of beef there is, and I associate it with Christmas Eve more than any other cut.

Despite its somewhat intimidating elegance, making prime rib really is a cinch; it just involves seasoning the heck out of the outside of the beef and being patient enough to roast it to medium-rare perfection. The only way you can mess up prime rib is to overcook it. And if that happens, hoo *boy*. You best git yourself out of town before the sheriff finds you.

Don't let this happen to you! Use a meat thermometer. I tell you this out of love.

(Psst. The drippings from prime rib are used to make the Yorkshire Pudding (page 332) just before the meal, so don't get all hasty and wash that prime rib pan four seconds after the meat is done! Not that I would ever do this. I'm one of those weirdos who puts off her Christmas Eve dishes until July.)

4 tablespoons tricolor peppercorns (or any peppercorns)	**3 thyme sprigs**	**1 rib-eye roast (bone-in or boneless), 10 to 14 pounds**
3 rosemary sprigs	**⅓ cup kosher salt**	**4 tablespoons olive oil**
	8 garlic cloves, minced	

1. Move the oven rack to the bottom and preheat the oven to 500°F, then start with the seasoning! Grab the peppercorns. I love these tricolor ones.

2. Throw them in a big plastic bag and pound them with a rolling pin to break them open.

3. Pull the leaves off the rosemary and thyme sprigs.

4. Throw the crushed peppercorns into a bowl with the kosher salt and the herb leaves and add the minced garlic. Flavor galore! Use your fingers to toss it all together, then set it aside.

5. Place the beef, fat side up, onto a rack in a roasting pan. Drizzle the olive oil all over the surface and rub it in with your hands.

6. Sprinkle the peppercorn/herb/salt mixture all over the surface of the beef, pressing it lightly with your hands.

7. Roast the beef for 45 minutes for the first stage.

8. Reduce the oven temperature to 300°F and insert the meat thermometer sideways into the roast. Roast the beef for an additional 1 hour and 15 minutes to 1 hour and 30 minutes, or until the meat thermometer registers 120°F to 125°F in the center for medium rare. (The meat will continue to cook for a bit after you remove it from the oven.)

9. Remove the beef from the rack and let it rest for about 15 minutes. This is an important step because it allows the juices to redistribute throughout the meat. (And this is a perfect time to get the Yorkshire Pudding in the oven!)

10. When you're ready to serve, carve it into slices in between the bones (if boneless, cut it into slices of your preferred width).

Geez Louise. That's all I can say.

You know what? I've never known who Louise is. But I sure utter her name a lot when I see that first slice of prime rib.

Heaven. Pure heaven.

YORKSHIRE PUDDING

MAKES 12 SERVINGS

The first time I ever ate Yorkshire pudding was at my very first boyfriend's parents' house. His name was Kev, and he played golf and the guitar equally well. Kev was a good Irish Catholic lad and I remember him fondly. But part of me wonders if part of that fondness is due to his dear mother, Mary, who was well read and well traveled and was always so sweet to me. It was Kev's mom, Mary, who introduced me to bona fide Yorkshire pudding one cold winter evening at their house, just after Kev's sister Eileen and I won a round of Pictionary by successfully sketching (and guessing) "surveyor." Don't ask me how either of us even knew what a surveyor was. To this day I believe it was divinely inspired.

Anyway, Yorkshire pudding was one of Mary's specialties, and even though I was only sixteen—and even though I was probably wearing acid wash jeans that tapered and zipped at the ankles—as soon as I took my first bite I knew I'd just experienced something special.

Yorkshire pudding isn't actually pudding at all but a popover. A popover that sizzles and poufs and bakes in a delicate bath of drippings from roast beef, which is almost always a precursor for Yorkshire pudding. Because of this, it really is a relatively rare treat—one that must be appreciated and savored. And devoured.

Make the batter before you remove the prime rib from the oven; that way, it'll be all ready to go!

5 eggs

1 cup half-and-half

1 cup all-purpose flour

2 teaspoons salt

Drippings from Prime Rib (page 330)

1. To make the batter, combine the eggs and half-and-half in a bowl.

2. Whisk until they're totally combined . . .

3. Then throw the flour and salt into a sifter . . .

4. And sift them straight into the bowl.

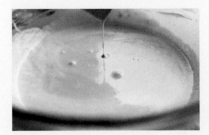

5. Whisk until it's nice and smooth, then refrigerate until the prime rib is ready.

6. After the beef is removed from the pan, increase the oven temperature to 450°F.

7. Use a slotted spoon to remove the peppercorns, herbs, and excess salt from the drippings.

8. Pour the remaining drippings into a separate container. They should be speckled and lovely!

9. Pour a small amount (about ½ teaspoon or so) of the drippings into each cup of a standard muffin pan and place the pan in the hot oven for a couple of minutes, or until just before the drippings begin to smoke.

10. Carefully remove the pan from the oven and immediately fill the muffin cups about ½ to ⅔ full.

11. Bake for 13 to 14 minutes, or until they've "popped" about as much as they can pop.

12. Serve them in a basket with a pretty napkin right next to the prime rib.

ROSEMARY-GARLIC ROASTED POTATOES

MAKES 12 TO 18 SERVINGS

For this simple and oh-so-flavorful side dish, you can use any little ol' potatoes you can get your little ol' hands on. I love to use packages of mixed fingerling potatoes, then separate them according to color for a neato bandito presentation.

This is one of the simplest side dishes there is!

6 garlic cloves

2 rosemary sprigs

½ cup (1 stick) butter

2 pounds brown fingerling potatoes

2 pounds small purple potatoes

2 pounds small red potatoes

Salt and pepper

2 tablespoons minced fresh parsley

1. Preheat the oven to 400°F.

2. Mince the garlic really finely . . .

3. Then strip the leaves off the rosemary sprigs and mince them finely, too.

4. Melt the butter in a small skillet over medium heat, then throw in the rosemary and garlic.

5. Reduce the heat to low and simmer for 10 minutes, or until the butter is totally infused.

6. Arrange all the potatoes on baking sheets . . .

7. And toss them with the butter mixture.

8. Roast them for 35 to 45 minutes, or until the potatoes are tender and nice and golden brown.

9. Arrange them on a large platter, add salt and pepper to taste, and sprinkle the parsley over the top!

Variations

• *Substitute 1 cup olive oil for the butter.*

• *Use sage, thyme, chives, or any mix of herb you'd like.*

• *Cut larger potatoes into quarters for a different texture and presentation.*

• *Sprinkle the top with freshly grated Parmesan cheese.*

Christmas card photo, 2005. They were so wittle.

BRUSSELS SPROUTS WITH CRANBERRIES

MAKES 12 TO 18 SERVINGS

I have no idea when, where, why, and how Brussels sprouts were given such a bad rap, but I consider it one of the real injustices of the vegetable world. In fact, I've developed a theory that anyone who criticizes Brussels sprouts has either never tried Brussels sprouts or they just want to jump on the bandwagon with all the other people who say they hate Brussels sprouts. In other words, they have serious father issues!

This is one of my favorite ways to enjoy beautiful Brussels sprouts, and while it's tempting to make them for Thanksgiving, I usually save them for Christmas because of the glorious red and green going on.

Try them. Just once. You'll be a believer for life.

1 cup balsamic vinegar
½ cup sugar

6 pounds Brussels sprouts
½ cup olive oil

Salt and pepper
1 cup dried cranberries

1. First, make the balsamic glaze: Pour the balsamic vinegar into a small saucepan.

2. Add the sugar and stir to combine.

3. Bring the mixture to a boil over medium-high heat, then reduce the heat to medium-low and cook for 15 to 20 minutes, or until the sauce is nice and thick and your kitchen smells like balsamic has taken over the planet. Remove it from the heat and set aside.

4. Preheat the oven to 400°F.

7. Drizzle them with the olive oil . . .

11. And sprinkle the dried cranberries all over the top.

8. And sprinkle on salt and pepper to taste. Use your hands to toss them so they're all evenly coated and seasoned.

12. Finally, slowly pour the balsamic glaze all over the top, allowing it to trickle to the layers below.

5. Rinse the sprouts and tear off any outer leaves that are dried or bruised. Slice them in half . . .

9. Roast them for about 25 minutes, or until they're nice and brown with some crisp leaves.

These are seriously a Christmas miracle.

Variations

- Use dried cherries instead of cranberries.

- Sprinkle chopped walnuts or pecans over the top after pouring on the glaze.

- Add a rosemary sprig to the balsamic mixture before boiling and reducing. Remove and discard the sprig after the glaze is thick.

6. And spread them in a single layer on 2 baking sheets.

10. Pile the sprouts onto a large platter . . .

BURGUNDY MUSHROOMS

MAKES 12 SERVINGS

This nothing-short-of-sublime recipe for slow-cooked burgundy mushrooms appeared in my first cookbook, and it's back for an encore here for two very important reasons:

1. I can't imagine a Christmas Eve dinner without them.

2. They're pretty much the best things you'll ever put in your mouth. Thus, they deserve to be in two cookbooks. Amen.

My mother-in-law has made these since I joined the family, and they're as much a part of my holiday experience as running out of tape before all the presents are wrapped and forgetting all about the stockings until 11:37 on Christmas Eve.

(Psst. Be sure to start these early in the day. They cook for nine hours! This has been a public service announcement.)

4 pounds white button mushrooms

1 cup (2 sticks) butter

4 chicken bouillon cubes

4 beef bouillon cubes

1 teaspoon freshly ground black pepper

1 teaspoon dill seed

5 garlic cloves, peeled

1 liter burgundy wine (or any red wine, such as cabernet or merlot)

1½ teaspoons Worcestershire sauce

2 cups boiling water

2 teaspoons salt

1. Throw the mushrooms in a large pot with the butter, bouillon cubes, pepper, dill seed, and garlic.

2. Add the wine . . .

3. The Worcestershire . . .

4. And the boiling water.

5. Bring the mixture to a boil over medium-high heat . . .

6. Then reduce the heat to low, cover the pot, and let it simmer for 6 hours. (Yes, I said 6 hours!)

7. After 6 hours, remove the lid and continue simmering for another 3 hours. (Yes, I said 3 hours!)

8. After the 9-hour cooking time, stir in the salt. The mushrooms will be very dark in color and exceedingly luscious.

9. Ladle them into a serving dish and get ready for the best mushroom experience of your life.

NOTE: *The mushrooms keep for days in the fridge if you want to make them ahead of time. Just reheat them on the stovetop before serving.*

Christmas card photo, 2004. Time, please stop moving!

BOOZY BREAD PUDDING

MAKES 12 SERVINGS

I adapted this sinfully scrumptious bread pudding from a Tom Perini recipe my mother-in-law shared with me years ago. It's simple and divine and has ruined me forever on all other bread puddings in the universe. The kids can eat the bread pudding on its own, as it's perfectly wonderful . . . but since you've been so good all year long, you get to drizzle yours with a naughty, boozy rum sauce!

BREAD PUDDING

1 loaf crusty Italian bread or other artisanal loaf

3 eggs

2 cups milk

1 cup half-and-half

1 tablespoon vanilla extract

2 cups sugar

¼ cup (½ stick) butter, melted, plus more for the pan

½ cup pecans

BOOZY SAUCE

½ cup (1 stick) butter

½ cup sugar

¾ cup heavy (whipping) cream

¼ cup dark rum

1. Preheat the oven to 325°F.

2. Cut the bread into 1-inch slices.

3. Then cut the slices into 1-inch strips and cut the strips into cubes.

4. In all, you should have 8 to 10 cups of bread cubes.

5. To make the custard mixture, whisk together the eggs, milk, and half-and-half . . .

6. Then add the vanilla . . .

7. And sugar.

8. Stir it around to combine.

9. Melt the butter in the microwave and whisk it into the mixture.

10. Generously butter a baking dish and add all the bread cubes to the pan.

11. Pour the egg mixture all over the bread cubes.

12. Then chop the pecans pretty finely . . .

13. And sprinkle the pecans all over the top. Pop it in the oven for 1 hour.

14. While the bread pudding is baking, make the boozy sauce: Combine the butter, sugar, cream, and rum in a medium saucepan over medium heat.

15. Bring the mixture to a boil, whisking constantly. Reduce the heat to low and simmer for 10 to 15 minutes, then remove the pan from the heat and set aside.

16. To serve, pour the rum sauce into a small pitcher or gravy boat . . .

17. And drizzle a little bit over the bread pudding right when it comes out of the oven.

(Drizzle it over individual portions, too!)

This is truly delicious stuff. The perfect thing to finish off the very best night of the year.

Variations

- *Sprinkle raisins on top of the bread pudding with the pecans before baking.*
- *Use whiskey or brandy instead of dark rum.*

Merry Christmas, Kitty Kitty!

CHRISTMAS MORNING BRUNCH

While Christmas Eve is all about busy anticipation, our Christmas Day is all about relaxation. We roll out of bed whenever the kids start to wake up, leisurely open presents, belt out Bing Crosby songs (oh, wait. That's just me), and eventually get around to a midmorning brunch. The menu is a tradition in my husband's family, but there's nothing fussy about it. It's just good ol' Christmastime comfort food.

OTHER RECIPES TO CONSIDER: Resolution Smoothies (page 3); Bagel and Cream Cheese Baked French Toast (page 12); Glazed Easter Ham (page 100); Eggs in Hash Brown Nests (page 102); Maple-Bacon Scones (page 171); Perfect Cream Scones (page 166); Salmon Scrambled Eggs (page 172); Caramel Apple Sweet Rolls (page 321)

FRIED QUAIL

MAKES 12 SERVINGS

Fried quail is as integral to our family's Christmas morning as playing Johnny Mathis songs and searching in vain for AAA batteries for our kids' Christmas presents. My husband grew up enjoying fried quail at his grandfather's house every Christmas morning; today, my father-in-law is usually the one manning the skillet. Back in those days, it was 100 percent certain that the quail had come from a recent hunt. These days, quail hunts on the ranch aren't as common, so we aren't averse to hunting down (get it?) the game birds from local markets if we have to. Saves time for more important things.

Like remembering to buy AAA batteries for our kids' Christmas presents.

Fried quail, in case you've never tried them, are just delicious. The only downside is that they're tiny little things and can take a little time to eat. But that just makes them more special!

12 whole quail, cleaned (available frozen at good meat counters)

3 cups buttermilk

3 cups all-purpose flour

2 tablespoons seasoned salt (such as Lawry's)

1 tablespoon ground black pepper

4 cups peanut or vegetable oil, for frying

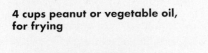

1. Grab a bunch of quail—as many as you have appetites for!

3. Seal and place the quail in the fridge for at least 1 hour.

5. Dredge each quail in the flour mixture, pressing to make sure it coats the quail thoroughly.

2. Throw them into a large plastic bag or bowl and pour the buttermilk over the top.

4. Meanwhile, mix together the flour, seasoned salt, and pepper.

6. Lightly shake off the excess flour, then place it on a baking sheet and repeat with the rest of the quail.

7. Heat the oil in a large, heavy skillet over medium-high heat. Preheat the oven to 350°F.

8. Fry the quail, 4 or 5 at a time, turning halfway through, until golden brown . . .

9. About 2 to 3 minutes per side.

10. Remove the quail to a paper towel–lined baking sheet and repeat with the rest of the quail.

11. After all the quail have been fried, remove the paper towel and set the baking sheet in the oven for 6 to 8 minutes, or until the quail are cooked through.

12. Serve the quail in a bowl next to Drop Biscuits (page 346) and Quail Gravy (page 348).

This is as dreamy a Christmas morning brunch as you can get.

Variations

- *Instead of quail, simply fry patties of breakfast sausage and continue with the gravy recipe.*

- *Instead of quail, do fried chicken. Buy chicken pieces to make it super easy (note that chicken pieces will take longer to cook through). Use the same gravy procedure as on page 348.*

DROP BISCUITS

MAKES 24 BISCUITS

I love drop biscuits. My grandma Helen used to make them for me, and anything my grandma Helen used to do is pure gold in my book. Drop biscuits are delicious and textured, and you don't have to mess with rolling out dough, cutting neat circles, and transferring the circles to a baking sheet. It's as simple as mixing the dough, dropping it in big plops onto the pan, throwing them in the oven, and then counting the seconds until you get to scarf them down.

Whether you spread them with softened butter or douse them with cream gravy, they'll become a permanent part of your biscuit world.

6 cups all-purpose flour

4 tablespoons baking powder

1 teaspoon salt

3 sticks cold butter, cut into small pieces

2½ cups buttermilk (if you don't have any, see page 21)

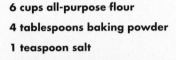

1. Preheat the oven to 425°F.

2. Add the flour, baking powder, and salt to the bowl of a (large!) food processor.

3. Throw in all the butter pieces . . .

4. Then pulse until the mixture is completely worked together. (You can also just cut the dry ingredients with the butter in a large bowl with a pastry cutter!)

5. Drizzle in the buttermilk while pulsing (or stirring) the butter/flour mixture . . .

6. And stop just when the dough all comes together.

7. Using a spoon, drop 2- to 3-inch balls of dough onto a baking sheet lined with a baking mat or parchment paper.

8. Bake them for 12 to 15 minutes, or until golden brown.

9. Serve with gravy . . . or jelly . . . or just a nice ol' pat of butter.

Variation

- Add 1 tablespoon coarse black pepper to the dry ingredients for black pepper biscuits.

Sisters yesterday, today, and tomorrow.

QUAIL GRAVY

MAKES 12 SERVINGS

Gravy is a crazy thing, isn't it? Bizarre, even! Nutso! But spooned over fresh-from-the-oven biscuits? Oh, dear heavenly goodness. It's a creation I'm sure glad was . . . well, created.

You can make gravy with any grease left in a skillet after frying meat, whether it be quail, bacon, sausage, or chicken. So you have no excuse not to make it!

Unless, of course, your excuse is that you eat neither quail, bacon, sausage, nor chicken.

And then I'm not sure I can help you, my friend.

Drippings from Fried Quail (page 344) pan oil, from frying

6 to 8 tablespoons all-purpose flour

4 to 5 cups milk

Black pepper

1. First, pour all the grease out of the skillet after frying the quail. Don't clean the skillet or you'll regret it every day for the rest of your life!

2. Set the skillet over medium heat, then pour ½ cup of the grease back into the skillet.

3. Slowly sprinkle in 6 tablespoons of the flour, whisking as you go. Continue adding the flour until you have a smooth, nongreasy paste. If it's still greasy looking, whisk in more flour. If it's too dry and clumpy, whisk in a little more grease.

6. Add plenty of black pepper, which makes gravy even more magical.

7. Cook the gravy, whisking constantly, until it's nice and thick. If it gets too thick, just splash in a little more milk. Gravy is very forgiving.

8. Spoon the gravy over warm Drop Biscuits (page 346) and serve with Fried Quail (page 344).

Merry Christmas, everyone!

NOTE: *The gravy will continue to thicken as it sits, so make it at the last minute. Thin it with a splash of milk as needed.*

4. Cook the paste, whisking constantly, until it's nice and dark golden brown. Be sure to scrape the bottom of the pan with the whisk in order to loosen all the flavorful bits. You just made a roux, baby!

5. Pour in 4 cups of milk, whisking constantly.

"Look! It's that Santa dude!"

"Let's get this party started!"

NEW YEAR'S EVE

I have a New Year's Eve tale to tell. I was in my mid-twenties and was home from California visiting my parents. I decided to attend the annual New Year's Eve party at the country club, and I wore a very sleek, very spiffy one-piece black pantsuit with spaghetti straps. I know that sounds terribly dated and dorky, but I promise you it was cute. It had somewhat wide pant legs that swung as I walked, and my then-thin arms, which are no longer thin, looked toned and taut. I wore long, dangly earrings that almost reached my shoulders, along with spiked black patent pumps that made me nearly six feet tall, and my then-thick auburn hair, which is no longer thick, bounced and behaved as it never had before.

I hadn't been home for awhile, and I hadn't seen the country club crowd in ages, so I got really excited about making a statement. When I entered the club, I made a beeline for the bathroom so I could do some last-minute touching up of my bright red lipstick and heavy black mascara. Oh, and do the things most normal people do in bathrooms: I went to the bathroom.

I won't take you through every step of what happened next; I'll just sketch some broad strokes. I finished my bathroom business, headed out to the party, and spent the next twenty minutes mingling from one acquaintance to another, covering the room with more speed, style, and grace than anyone surely had before.

Then I glanced down at my feet and saw the foot-long stream of toilet paper I'd been dragging around with me the whole time.

Moving on . . .

New Year's Eve is exactly one week after Christmas Eve, and the pace of the two holiday evenings couldn't be more different. While Christmas Eve is bustling with anticipation, gift wrapping, church services, Christmas carols, and snowy travel, New Year's Eve is much more chilled out. Even if you're hosting or attending a New Year's Eve celebration, the pressure has definitely been turned down a few notches. While Christmas Eve is a type A go-getter, New Year's Eve is a laid back surfer dude.

Now, there *is* anticipation relating to New Year's Eve, but it's mostly just abstract and reflective. Where did this year go? What will my resolutions be? Will I be able to stay awake to watch the ball drop? How will I remember to write a brand-new year on my checks? But it's a nice, relaxing brand of anticipation. My very favorite kind!

RING IN THE NEW YEAR COCKTAIL PARTY

I remember a good handful of elegant-but-casual New Year's Eve gatherings my parents used to host at our house. It was in the late seventies, era of large pointed collars and sideburns, and my parents' friends must have wondered why Gerre and Bill's redheaded, freckled daughter sat on the stairs and stared at the party through the banister the whole time.

Turns out, it wasn't because I was fascinated by my parents' friends' large pointed collars and sideburns (though I still think they were just groovy). And it wasn't because I was eavesdropping on their conversations about Jimmy Carter and test tube babies. It was because I was waiting for an opportunity to make a mad dash for the hors d'oeuvre table, scoop up as many treats as I could, and hightail it up to my room without being detected.

When I host my own New Year's Eve celebrations, I choose food that will make my own children want to do the same.

Happy New Year, friends! Here's to a wonderful, happy night of celebration.

OTHER RECIPES TO CONSIDER: Grilled Corn Dip (page 34); Potato Skins (page 36); Deviled Eggs (page 114); Homemade Chocolate Truffles (page 60); Brandy Snaps (page 303)

DO-AHEAD GAME PLAN

THE DAY BEFORE

- Chill the Champagne and liqueur/juice for the Champagne Cocktails.

- Make the marinade for the Skewers of Glory.

- Make the Salted Pita Wedges.

- Make the peanut sauce for the Grilled Chicken Skewers. (Refrigerate, then bring to room temperature before serving.)

- Make the Sweet and Savory Bacon Crackers. (Cool and refrigerate, then bake them in a warm oven for 10 minutes just before serving to freshen them up.)

- Make the lemon curd for the Lemon Crème Pie Shooters.

- Make the Chocolate Mint Shooters. (Don't top with whipped cream until the next day.)

- Make the cherry and cheesecake mixtures for the Cherry Cheesecake Shooters.

EARLIER THE DAY OF

- Soak the wooden skewers for the Skewers of Glory and Grilled Chicken Skewers.

- Make the Spinach-Artichoke Dip. (Cover and refrigerate, then bake just before serving.)

- Make the Cocktail Wieners! (Warm them up right before serving.)

CHAMPAGNE COCKTAILS

MAKES AS MANY AS YOU LIKE!

You know what? Champagne makes me happy.

Don't take that the wrong way. I don't have to have Champagne to be happy. It's just that I don't drink Champagne very often, and when I do, it's either New Year's Eve or some other exciting celebratory occasion. Like my kid's graduation from kindergarten.

I kid.

Back to my original point: Champagne makes me happy, and it really is a nice treat. And while it's fine straight up and bubbly, I actually prefer to up the "treat" factor by adding a tiny bit of fruit juice or—even better—fruit liqueur.

Champagne cocktails are the prettiest and bubbliest way to ring in the new year!

5 parts cold Champagne

1 part cold fruit liqueur (such as Chambord, crème de cassis, or crème de framboise), or fruit juice (such as pomegranate or cranberry)

Small berries (raspberries, cranberries, and so on), for garnish

2. Then grab the liqueur . . .

4. Drop a piece of fruit into each glass.

1. Fill champagne glasses with the Champagne . . .

3. And pour it in.

5. And serve them immediately!

6. For the fruit juice version, splash in fruit juice . . .

7. Followed by the Champagne!

8. And the fruit. Enjoy!

My father-in-law isn't exactly the Champagne type. But that's okay— I'll take his share!

SKEWERS OF GLORY

MAKES ABOUT 30 SKEWERS

Addictive and divine. That's how I'd describe these juicy, flavorful skewers of glory.

In fact, I think that's what I'll call these heavenly objects from now on. Skewers of Glory. The most fitting name for any skewer recipe throughout the history of time!

½ cup teriyaki sauce

3 garlic cloves, minced

1 tablespoon minced fresh ginger

1 tablespoon sugar

½ teaspoon red pepper flakes

Juice of ½ lemon

Dash of kosher salt

2 whole green onions, sliced

1 fresh pineapple

2 pounds jumbo shrimp, peeled and deveined

1 pound bacon, cut in half crosswise

1. Soak about 30 wooden skewers in water for 30 minutes to 2 hours.

2. Preheat the oven to 400°F.

3. To make the marinade, pour the teriyaki sauce into a bowl . . .

5. Next, cut the pineapple into chunks by lopping off the top . . .

4. Then throw in the garlic, ginger, sugar, red pepper flakes, lemon juice, salt, and green onions. Stir it around and set it aside.

6. Slicing off the rind . . .

7. Cutting the pineapple into wedges . . .

8. Slicing off the hard inner core, then cutting the wedges into chunks. Store half the chunks in the fridge for snacking.

9. Place a chunk of pineapple on top of a shrimp . . .

10. Then wrap the whole thing in one of the half-slices of bacon.

11. Stick a skewer through the whole thing so that it holds the pineapple, shrimp, and bacon securely.

12. Then lay them all on a baking pan with a cooling rack.

13. Brush each skewer generously with the marinade . . .

14. Then roast the skewers for 10 minutes. Remove them from the oven . . .

15. Then brush them with a second coat of marinade. Return them to the oven and bake them until the bacon is sizzling and the shrimp are cooked, 5 to 7 minutes.

16. Serve them hot or at room temperature. Divine!

Variations

- *Cook several pineapple shrimp together on a metal skewer.*

- *Substitute large sea scallops for the shrimp.*

- *Grill the skewers instead of placing them into the oven. Just be sure to adequately soak the skewers in water so they won't burn, or use metal skewers.*

GRILLED CHICKEN SKEWERS

MAKES 20 TO 25 SKEWERS

Chicken skewers (called chicken satay by dem fancy folks) are a cocktail party classic, and a creamy, spicy peanut sauce is such a perfect accompaniment.

These are super easy to throw together and so versatile, and while the peanut sauce is darn delicious, you can dip them in whatever your heart desires!

½ cup smooth peanut butter

¼ cup soy sauce

¼ cup honey

½ teaspoon hot chili oil

Juice of 2 limes

1 teaspoon crushed red pepper flakes

1 tablespoon minced ginger

2 pounds chicken tenders

½ cup minced cilantro

Barbecue sauce, for serving

1. Soak 20 to 25 wooden skewers in water for at least 2 hours.

2. Preheat the grill to medium heat.

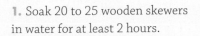

3. Make the peanut sauce by placing the peanut butter in the blender . . .

4. With the soy sauce . . .

5. The honey . . .

6. The hot chili oil . . .

7. The lime juice . . .

8. The red pepper flakes . . .

9. And the ginger.

10. Add ¼ cup very hot water as you blend the mixture.

11. Check the consistency and add a little more hot water if needed to make it very smooth. Transfer the sauce to a small dish, cover it with plastic wrap, and set it aside.

12. Thread the chicken with the skewers . . .

13. And grill them on both sides until the chicken is done in the middle, 2 to 3 minutes per side.

14. Remove them to a serving platter . . .

15. And sprinkle on the cilantro.

16. Serve them with dishes of peanut sauce and barbecue sauce for dipping.

I could eat a dozen of these!

I think I have, actually.

Variations

- Mix ½ cup honey with ¾ cup Dijon mustard for a honey mustard dipping sauce.

- Blend 1 cup mayonnaise with 2 chipotle peppers for a spicy dipping sauce.

SPINACH-ARTICHOKE DIP

MAKES 18 SERVINGS

I remember helping my mom host one of her New Year's Eve parties. I know I was a teenager, because I can vividly recall my mom turning up her eyebrows at me when I poured myself a glass of Champagne (which I then pronounced as "Shayum-pipple," thanks to *Sanford and Son*. I watched too much TV) when the clock was getting close to midnight.

Anyway, other than my mother's eyebrow-raises, the thing I remember most about that New Year's Eve party was the artichoke dip my mom and I made. It was delicious, and it was gone within the first hour of the party. And okay, I'm responsible for approximately 75 percent of its disappearance. But still.

This scrumptious version is a bit of a variation on the theme, incorporating spinach and lots of different cheeses. It's absolutely to die for.

6 tablespoons (¾ stick) butter

4 tablespoons minced garlic

One 12-ounce bag baby spinach

Two 14.5 cans artichoke hearts, drained, rinsed, and halved (or roughly chopped)

3 tablespoons all-purpose flour

1½ cups whole milk

One 8-ounce package cream cheese, softened

½ cup crumbled feta cheese

½ cup grated Parmesan cheese

1 cup shredded pepper Jack cheese

Chicken broth, as needed for thinning

¼ teaspoon salt

½ teaspoon black pepper

¼ teaspoon cayenne pepper

Salted Pita Wedges (page 363), for serving

1. Preheat the oven to 375°F.

2. Melt 3 tablespoons of the butter in a large skillet over medium heat and stir in the garlic. Cook for 1 minute.

3. Add the spinach . . .

4. And cook it around until it's wilted. This takes less than a minute!

5. Remove the spinach to a plate and set it aside . . .

6. Then throw in the artichoke hearts and stir them around to cook for 2 minutes.

7. Remove the artichokes and set them aside.

8. Melt the remaining 5 tablespoons of butter in the skillet, then sprinkle in the flour.

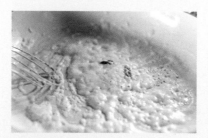

9. Whisk it around until it forms a paste. Cook the paste for 1 minute, whisking constantly.

10. Pour in the milk . . .

11. And whisk the sauce until it's nice and smooth.

12. Add the cream cheese . . .

13. Along with the feta, Parmesan, and ½ cup of the pepper Jack.

14. Stir the mixture until all the cheese is melted. It will be slightly lumpy because of the feta. If it seems overly thick, splash in a little chicken broth.

15. Add the salt and black pepper . . .

16. The cayenne pepper . . .

17. And the spinach and artichokes. Make sure to get all the juices from the plate into the mixture!

18. Stir it until it's all combined . . .

19. Then pour it into a small baking dish.

20. Top with the remaining ½ cup pepper Jack cheese . . .

21. And bake till the cheese is melted and golden and the dip is bubbly, 15 to 20 minutes.

22. Serve hot with pita wedges!

SALTED PITA WEDGES

MAKES 18 WEDGES

These yummy little snack wedges are the perfect vessel for any dip . . . and they're also slightly addictive on their own. I love 'em!

6 pieces pita bread   **½ cup olive oil**   **2 to 3 tablespoons kosher salt**

1. Preheat the oven to 375°F.

2. Cut each piece of pita bread into sixths using a knife or pizza cutter.

4. Then brush both sides of the wedges with olive oil.

3. Arrange them all on a baking sheet lined with aluminum foil . . .

5. Sprinkle both sides generously with the salt . . .

6. Then bake them for 15 to 18 minutes, until they're golden brown and crisp.

H-h-h-happy N-n-n-new Y-y-y-year! (It's c-c-c-cold!)

Variation

Make a spice blend of salt, garlic powder, cayenne pepper, and freshly ground black pepper to sprinkle over the pita wedges before they bake.

SWEET AND SAVORY BACON CRACKERS

MAKES 36 CRACKERS

These totally retro munchies are a staple in our house throughout the holiday season. My mom used to make them for her New Year's shindigs, and I don't remember ever seeing one left over. Not once. And believe me, I searched. These glorious little beauties disappear almost instantly no matter how many you make, and even though their ingredients are beyond simple, they taste like something much more profound has gone into their preparation.

They're one of the most addictive treats in the history of anyone's mom's cocktail parties.

I'm crossing my fingers that made sense.

36 country club–style crackers
¾ cup grated Parmesan cheese
¾ cup brown sugar
1 pound bacon (not thick-sliced)

1. Preheat the oven to 250°F.

2. Lay the crackers on a rack set on a rimmed baking sheet.

3. Place a tablespoon of Parmesan cheese on half the crackers . . .

4. And a tablespoon of brown sugar on the other half.

5. Slice the bacon in half . . .

6. And wrap each cracker with a half-piece of bacon, tucking the end of the piece underneath the cracker.

7. Bake them for about 2 hours. The bacon will cook slowly and start to wrap tightly around the crackers, and the excess grease will drip off.

8. Serve them warm on a platter!

NOTE: *You may serve the savory and sweet versions on different platters if you'd like your guests to have a choice . . . or just throw them all together and let it be a surprise!*

I love winter. None of those pesky bathing suits to worry about.

COCKTAIL WIENERS!

MAKES ABOUT 80 WIENERS

My BFF Hyacinth and I have a running chuckle over her husband, John's, unbridled love for cocktail wieners in barbecue sauce. Anytime they attend any kind of party or festive gathering, Hy says she crosses her fingers that the host has found it in his/her heart to serve a chafing dish of the crazy little sausages.

While I would love to say this easy little appetizer is an uninventive culinary sacrilege, I'm way too busy wolfing them down to speak.

There's something deliciously approachable about them.

SPICY COCKTAIL WIENERS

One 12-ounce bottle chili sauce (sold in the ketchup aisle)

2 tablespoons prepared horseradish

2 tablespoons hot sauce (Tabasco, Louisiana, and so on)

1 tablespoon Worcestershire sauce

Two 14-ounce packages cocktail sausages

BBQ COCKTAIL WIENERS

One 12-ounce bottle BBQ sauce

Two 14-ounce packages cocktail sausages

1. To make the spicy version, pour the chili sauce into a small saucepan.

2. Add the horseradish . . .

3. The hot sauce . . .

4. And the Worcestershire.

5. Stir the sauce over medium heat until it's thoroughly warmed . . .

6. Then add the cocktail wieners.

7. Stir them into the sauce, then cover the pan and reduce the heat to low.

8. Simmer for 15 to 20 minutes, until the sausages are warmed through.

9. Serve them in a small chafing dish or iron skillet with toothpicks.

10. To make the classic version, pour the barbecue sauce into a medium saucepan over medium heat. Heat the sauce until it's warm . . .

11. Then pour in the sausages.

12. Stir them around, then cover the pan and reduce the heat to low. Simmer for 15 to 20 minutes, until they're heated through.

13. Serve them in a small chafing dish or iron skillet with toothpicks.

Yum. I love you, cocktail wieners!

(And so does Hy's husband!)

LEMON CRÈME PIE SHOOTERS

MAKES 18 SHOOTERS

I once ate at a restaurant in Orlando, Florida. The end.

Interesting story, yes?

Oh . . . wait. I didn't finish the story. No wonder it had no point!

Okay, I'll start over: I once ate at a restaurant in Orlando, Florida, and they offered an irresistible assortment of shooter-style sweets on their dessert menu. One of the options, if one couldn't narrow down the choice to one or two, was to order a *sampler* platter, which included a couple of choices of each.

It goes without saying that I selected that option.

It also goes without saying that there wasn't a bite left of that option.

These little three-or-four-bite desserts are perfect for a cocktail party and always add a little extra whimsy and elegance to your spread. So many different flavor combinations are possible, but I'm partial to these bright yellow lemon numbers, which include a super-easy-to-make whole egg lemon curd.

Miniature desserts are one of my favorite things on earth.

EASY LEMON CURD

½ cup fresh lemon juice

1 cup sugar

5 eggs

½ cup (1 stick) butter, cut into pieces

6 store-bought soft lemon cookies, crushed

Lemon wedges, for garnish

SWEETENED WHIPPED CREAM

2 cups heavy cream

¼ cup powdered sugar

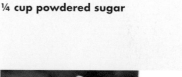
5. Then add the butter . . .

3. And whisk to combine.

6. And whisk the mixture gently over medium-low heat until the butter melts.

1. Into a medium saucepan, add the lemon juice . . .

2. And the sugar . . .

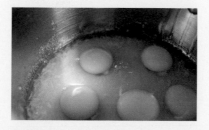
4. Crack in the eggs . . .

7. Continue cooking the mixture slowly, stirring constantly, until it is very thick.

8. Pour it into a bowl, then cover the bowl and chill the curd for at least 2 hours.

9. After the curd has chilled, make the whipped cream: Add the heavy cream to the bowl of an electric mixer fitted with the whisk attachment . . .

10. Then add the powdered sugar . . .

11. And whip it until stiff. Place the whipped cream into a pastry bag with a medium hole snipped off the end.

12. Grab scoops of the cold curd and place it into a separate pastry bag with a medium hole snipped off the end.

13. Grab the cookies . . .

14. And use your clean hands to crumble them into fine crumbs.

15. Into small shot glasses, place a small amount of curd.

16. Pipe in a small amount of whipped cream . . .

17. Then sprinkle in a small amount of cookie crumbs.

18. Repeat with another layer of curd and whipped cream . . .

19. And a final sprinkling of crumbs.

20. A teeny wedge of lemon is good, too!

21. Repeat with the rest of the curd, cream, and crumbs (alliteration alert!) and chill the shooters for at least 2 hours before serving.

22. Line them up on a pretty platter with a few lime and lemon wedges scattered around.

23. Serve with demitasse spoons.

Dangerously delightful!

NOTES

- *Shooters can be made up to 12 hours ahead of time and chilled in the fridge.*

- *Miniature glasses and demitasse spoons can be found at restaurant supply stores or good kitchen or department stores.*

Variations

- *Substitute lime juice and sugar cookies for the lemon juice and lemon cookies.*

- *Substitute chilled chocolate pudding and chocolate cookie crumbs! (Yum.)*

CHERRY CHEESECAKE SHOOTERS

MAKES 18 SHOOTERS

This is such an easy way to get a cheesecake fix without worrying about that big, annoying Grand Canyon–size crack that forms when a whole cheesecake is baking.

(That happens to you . . . right?)

Anyway, these are a delicious and charming cinch. The crumbs and cheesecake base can be topped with absolutely anything you'd top a regular cheesecake with, and they're just adorable—especially if you serve 'em in miniature wineglasses.

Two 12-ounce bags frozen pitted sweet cherries

¼ cup honey

¼ cup whiskey

4 tablespoons (½ stick) butter

1 teaspoon cornstarch

Juice of ½ lemon

Two 8-ounce packages cream cheese, softened

One 14-ounce can sweetened condensed milk

12 graham crackers

¼ cup sliced almonds

1. Combine the cherries and honey in a medium saucepan.

4. Add the butter . . .

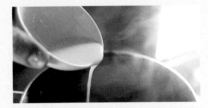

7. And add the mixture to the cherries.

2. Add the whiskey . . .

5. And continue cooking until the cherries are hot and bubbly.

8. Stir and continue cooking the cherries until they're nice and thick, about 2 minutes.

3. Then turn the stove to medium heat and mix to combine.

6. Whisk together the cornstarch and the lemon juice . . .

9. Pour the cherries into a bowl . . .

10. And refrigerate them until they're totally chilled and thick.

11. Combine the cream cheese and condensed milk in the bowl of an electric mixer fitted with the whisk attachment . . .

12. And whip until fluffy. Place the mixture into a pastry bag or a plastic storage bag with a medium hole snipped off the end.

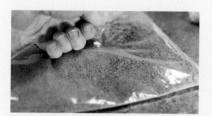

13. Finally, place the graham crackers in a large plastic storage bag and crush them into fine crumbs.

14. To assemble, spoon a large helping of crumbs into the bottom of a miniature wineglass or shot glass.

15. Squeeze in 2 to 3 tablespoons of the cream cheese mixture . . .

16. Then spoon in 1 to 2 tablespoons of the cherry mixture.

17. Add a few slivered almonds. Repeat with the rest!

18. Serve with demitasse spoons.

Variations

- For more of a shortcut, use canned pie filling instead of the cooked cherry mixture: Cherry, blueberry, apple—any variety will do!

- Stir 4 tablespoons melted butter into the graham cracker crumbs to make them a little more moist.

CHOCOLATE MINT SHOOTERS

MAKES 24 SHOOTERS

These diminutive little darlings are chock full of chocolate richness, with just a teeny hint of mint to make them extra delightful. I use my classic *pots de crème* recipe for the chocolate mixture, and trust me, chocoholics: You'll never find anything more smooth or satisfying.

12 ounces semisweet chocolate chips

Very small dash of mint or peppermint extract

4 eggs, room temperature

1 cup strong hot coffee

1 cup heavy cream

¼ cup powdered sugar

Small mint leaves

1. Place the chocolate chips and mint extract in a blender . . .

2. Crack in the eggs . . .

3. And blend for 15 or 20 seconds, until the chocolate chips are largely pulverized.

4. With the blender on medium speed, slowly pour in the hot coffee until it's totally mixed in.

5. The mixture will be nice and thick!

6. Pour the mixture into a squirt bottle or other vessel with a small pouring spout and fill 24 shot glasses two-thirds full.

7. Continue until the glasses are all filled up . . .

8. Then chill them for at least 2 hours, until they're totally firm.

9. Whip the heavy cream with the powdered sugar until stiff, then place the whipped cream into a pastry bag with a large star tip. Pipe pretty dollops on the top of each glass . . .

10. Then place a small mint leaf on the top of each one.

11. Keep them in the fridge until you need them!

And make no mistake: *You need them.* Serve with demitasse spoons.

Happy New Year!

ACKNOWLEDGMENTS

To my precious friend and inspiration, Pam Anderson, who sat in my kitchen sipping coffee (or was it wine?) a few years ago and said, "Hey, you should do a holiday cookbook . . ." Thank you, dear Pam. I've said it before and I'll say it forever: I want to be you when I grow up. You're a beautiful woman, a fantastic wife and mother, a shining example, and a forever friend. Thank you.

To the tremendous Tiffany Poe, the marvelous Meseidy Rivera, and the talented Trey Wilson. You're amazing and inexhaustible. Thank you for keeping me going, for wiping food off my camera, for blasting eighties tunes louder and louder toward the end . . . and for your precious friendship. Love you guys! And special thanks to Andy Fusco and Laron Chapman, for being, like, totally awesome.

To Journey, the Eagles, REO Speedwagon, Bon Jovi, Cyndi Lauper, Guns N' Roses, Duran Duran, Billy Idol, Rick Springfield, Foreigner, and Pat Benatar. You've been with me every step of the way and I'll never forget you.

To my beautiful and unflappable editor, Cassie Jones Morgan. Thank you for always believing in me. You're the best editor in the whole wide world, and you're stuck with me.

To the amazing Kris Tobiassen, Kara Zauberman, Liate Stehlik, Lynn Grady, Sharyn Rosenblum, and Susanna Einstein, for your unending help and support.

To the incredibly kind and generous readers of my website, The Pioneer Woman. You have expanded my world, my experiences, and my perspective. I love and appreciate each and every one of you.

To the circle of blogging friends I'm beyond blessed to know: Donna Booshay, Erika Piñeda, Maggy Keet, Alice Currah, Diane Lang, Katherine Stone, Britt Reints, Joy Wilson, Angie Dudley, Amanda Rettke, Maria Lichty, Amy Johnson, Bridget Edwards, Sandy Coughlin, Wendy Hondroulis, Rebecca Lindamood, Robyn Stone, Gaby Dalkin, Catherine McCord, Sheila Johnson, Cecily Kellogg, Dresden Shumaker, Anissa Mayhew, Lori Lange, Jenny Flake, Amanda Bottoms . . . and so many others. You inspire me daily.

To my great friend Adam Lang. High five, Adam!

To Sophie Hudson and Melanie Shankle, my soulmates in TV, movies . . . and a few other things, too.

To Elise Bauer and Jaden Hair, for being my sisters.

To Hyacinth, Beccus, Connell, Jenn, Jules, Mitch, Sarah, Ang, Kash, Shelley, Kristie, Susan, Shane, and Katy, for being my lifelong friends.

To Nan, Chuck, Tim, Missy, Caleb, Halle, Patsy, Matt, Reagan, Elliot, Nicholas, Stuart, Carol Sue, Nancy, and Jeff, for being my family.

To Mom, Dad, Doug, Mike, and Bets, for the memories.

To Ladd, Alex, Paige, Bryce, and Todd, for being my entire life.

And to you. Thank you. xoxo

RECIPES BY CATEGORY

INDEX

The End